VAGUENESS AND CONTRADICTION

Vagueness
and
Contradiction

Roy Sorensen

CLARENDON PRESS · OXFORD

OXFORD
UNIVERSITY PRESS

Great Clarendon Street, Oxford OX2 6DP

Oxford University Press is a department of the University of Oxford.
It furthers the University's objective of excellence in research, scholarship,
and education by publishing worldwide in

Oxford New York

Athens Auckland Bangkok Bogotá Buenos Aires Cape Town
Chennai Dar es Salaam Delhi Florence Hong Kong Istanbul Karachi
Kolkata Kuala Lumpur Madrid Melbourne Mexico City Mumbai Nairobi
Paris São Paulo Shanghai Singapore Taipei Tokyo Toronto Warsaw
with associated companies in Berlin Ibadan

Oxford is a registered trade mark of Oxford University Press
in the UK and in certain other countries

Published in the United States
By Oxford University Press Inc., New York

British Library Cataloguing in Publication Data

Sorensen, Roy A.
Vagueness and contradiction / by Roy Sorensen.
p. cm.
Includes bibliographical references and index.
1. Vagueness (Philosophy)   2. Contradiction.   I. Title.
B105.V33 S67 2001   165—dc21   2001033957
ISBN 0-19-924130-9 (alk. paper)

Library of Congress Cataloging in Publication Data

10 9 8 7 6 5 4 3 2 1

Typeset by Graphicraft Limited, Hong Kong
Printed in Great Britain by Biddles Ltd., Guildford & Kings Lynn

This book is dedicated to my son
Maxwell Sorensen

Acknowledgments

Key ideas in *Vagueness and Contradiction* occurred to me while upside down—in Australia (at the University of Queensland in Graham Priest's anarchical office). These thoughts were in the back of my head when I flew back to New York University. They seeped forward at meetings of the New York Vagueness Group. Ancestors of chapters were presented to lively audiences at the University of Notre Dame, Oxford, Princeton, St Andrews University, Stockholm University, and the University of Glasgow. Drafts of the book were discussed in seminars at New York University, the University of Edinburgh, and by a reading group at Dartmouth College. I thank all who participated in these instructive events. I especially thank J. C. Beall, Alexander Bird, and Timothy Williamson.

Parts of *Vagueness and Contradiction* have been published elsewhere in article form. Chapter 1 uses some sections of 'The Epistemic Conception of Vagueness: Comments on Wright', *The Southern Journal of Philosophy*, 33 supplement, 1995: 161–70. Chapter 2 adapts a section from 'Direct Reference and Vague Identity', *Philosophical Topics*, 29/1 (spring 2001). Chapter 7 is adapted from 'Modal Bloopers: Why Believable Impossibilities are Necessary', *American Philosophical Quarterly*, 33/1 (July 1996): 247–61. Chapters 9 and 10 draw heavily on 'Reason Demands Belief in Infinitely Many Contradictions', *American Philosophical Quarterly*, 36/1 (Jan. 1999): 21–33.

I thank the respective editors of these journals for permission to publish these writings in book form.

RS

Contents

List of figures

Introduction

My strangest belief is that vague words have hidden boundaries. I think that the subtraction of a single grain of sand might turn a heap into a non-heap. I think I was, briefly, the youngest man on earth (having just previously been the oldest boy on earth).

Oddly, these unusual opinions do not issue from scientistic zeal or deep-sea metaphysics. They are imposed by boring beliefs, in particular, allegiance to lightweight common sense and textbook logic. (Logicians marvel at how small a dose of each is sufficient.) Given this modest degree of intellectual conservatism, the ancient sorites paradox corners me into the belief that all vague terms are sensitive to arbitrarily small differences:

> Base step: a collection of one million grains of sand is a heap.
> Induction step: if a collection of n grains of sand is a heap, then so is a collection of $n - 1$ grains.
> Conclusion: a collection of one grain of sand is a heap.

The argument is valid by mathematical induction. (If that is too fancy for you, just do *modus ponens* 999,999 times.) The first premise is obviously true. The conclusion is obviously false. Therefore, my only recourse is to reject the induction step.

At first blush, the induction step seems ripe for rejection. After all, we can see that it encapsulates a conditional slippery slope. That is, in addition to implying highly compelling conditionals such as 'If a collection of 999,999 grains of sand is a heap, then so is a collection of 999,998 grains of sand', the induction step also entails absurd conditionals such as 'If a collection of 999,999 grains of sand is heap, then so is a collection of two grains of sand' (Boolos 1991). What entails an absurdity is itself absurd. Thumbs down on induction step!

But the matter is not so painless. If I reject the induction step, I thereby accept its negation. The negation is true only if there is a value for n such that n grains of sand is a heap and $n - 1$ grains is not a heap. In other words, there must be a sharp threshold at which an eroding heap turns into a non-heap. Ouch!

The threshold will vary from heap to heap and from mode of decomposition to mode of decomposition. Context counts! But under any relativization of 'heap', there will always be some point at which the removal of a single grain was enough to transform the heap into an ex-heap. Soothing talk of context should not anesthetize our sense of predicament.

What works for 'heap', works for any vague predicate that applies to some things without applying to all things. Therefore, amazingly, all vague predicates have sharp boundaries. I call this 'the basic argument for sharp boundaries' and defend it throughout this book. My adversaries all believe that there is some subtle flaw to the basic argument. They do not agree on a diagnosis. Some offer no diagnosis. Some simply confess to being stumped.

Everybody admits that there are surprising boundaries. Prior to Albert Einstein, most physicists accepted the following argument:

1. Any object can move at least 1 meter per second.
2. If an object can move at least n meters per second, then it can move at least $n + 1$ meters per second.
3. Therefore, there is no upper bound on how fast an object can move.

The second premise is intuitive. If an object is moving at a certain rate, you can also give it a further push and make it move faster. By repeated pushes, you can accelerate it to any speed whatsoever.

Einstein showed that the second premise fails when $n = 299{,}792{,}458$ (the speed of light in a vacuum). He established the counterexample by embedding a speed limit in the best theory of acceleration.

Few philosophers expect a similar refutation of the second premise in the paradox of the heap. I side with the majority of philosophers who believe that it is analytically impossible to discover a specific counterexample. This absolute unknowability is part of the meaning of 'vague'. I react to reports that a threshold has been discovered by concluding that either the reporter is conceptually confused or that I am conceptually confused. For instance, W. D. Hart (1991–2) argues the smallest heap consists of four objects: three on the bottom, one on top. To the extent that I find this charming quota plausible, I suspect that I am mistaken in viewing 'heap' as vague. If I were to learn that extra-terrestrials know the threshold of all our ordinary vague predicates, I would conclude that vagueness does not exist. After all, if they knew the size of the smallest heap, they could resolve the 'vagueness' by transmitting the answer by radio. Indeed, just the metaphysical possibility of such

an extra-terrestrial intelligence would show that there is no vagueness. Thresholds for vague predicates are not just unknown; they are
unknowable.

Well, perhaps the extra-terrestrials would radio but their answer
would be beyond our ken. Recall Gary Larson's cartoon contrasting
what we say to dogs ('Okay, Ginger! I've had it! You stay out of the
garbage! Understand, Ginger? Stay out of the garbage, or else!') with
what dogs hear ('blah blah GINGER blah blah blah blah blah blah blah
blah GINGER blah blah blah blah blah . . .'). A number of linguists,
philosophers, and biologists have revived John Locke's idea that human
beings have species-wide cognitive defects. They conjecture that some
philosophical problems are not intrinsically difficult; the questions are
unanswerable by human beings because *Homo Sapiens* lacks the conceptual prerequisites (McGinn 1993).

Locke's idea is reinforced by developmental psychology. Children
believe that each grain of rice weighs nothing even though a heap of rice
weighs something. If you do not believe them, they will hand you a
grain of rice so that you can feel its weightlessness for yourself. You
will insist that appearances are misleading; the grain *must* have weight
because a heap of grains is heavy. But you will have little chance of
rationally persuading them. The children are in a cognitive phase that
makes it difficult for them to absorb the principle that weight is a dissect-
ive property. Speculative psychologists extrapolate to healthy adults:
maybe we all end up in final stage that has its own limitations and quirks.

Steven Pinker lovingly catalogs progress that evolutionary psychologists have made in *How the Mind Works*. But he concludes with a
dismal contrast:

Sentience and will are different. Far from being too complicated, they are
maddeningly simple—consciousness and choice inhere in a special dimension or coloring that is somehow pasted onto neural events without meshing
with their causal machinery. The challenge is not to discover the correct
explanation of how that happens, but to imagine a theory that *could* explain
how it happens, a theory that would place the phenomenon as an effect of
some cause, in any case. (Pinker 1997: 562)

We do not know what could make it the case that 15 minutes after noon
is the last noonish minute. Indeed, any theory that implies that 15 minutes after noon is the last noonish minute is made unacceptable by that
very implication. The theory could only be acceptable if it were taken to
be about a different concept that was related to noonish—an explication

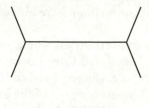

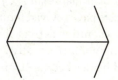

FIG. 0.1 Müeller–Lyer

FIG. 0.2 Whiter than white boundary

or a precisification of noonishness. The unspecifiability of the boundaries is a deep feature of vague concepts.

Part of the depth is psychological. Consider the classic Müeller–Lyer
illusion (Fig. 0.1). One line continues to look longer than the other
even after we prove their equality with a ruler. You can continue to
'see' the inequality because homunculi underlying visual judgment are
dogmatic.

Or consider the 'whiter than white' boundary between the rows of
bars (Fig. 0.2). If you cover one of the rows, you can see that the 'whiter
than white' boundary is not any whiter than the rest of the page. But
when you uncover the row again, the illusory boundary appears again.
The visual judgment of a boundary is cognitively impenetrable. We
continue to 'see' a boundary.

The bands of colour in a colour spectrum do not correspond to objective discontinuities in light wavelengths. These apparently external
bands arise from our biology rather than simple physics. The empirical

demonstration that there are no objective bands will not affect your perception of the spectrum. Similarly, the logical proof that there must be a boundary between green and yellow does not make any headway against linguistic homunculi who 'see' there is no boundary.

Our penchant for inserting and deleting boundaries is old news to color scientists. Our arboreal ancestors developed color vision to discern fruit in dappled backgrounds. This discriminative capacity is enhanced by accentuating some differences while suppressing others—rather like the processes astronomers exploit with imaging technology. As some bits of information are nurtured while others are weeded down, the perceiver achieves focus. This process needs to be fast. Thus the perceiver has little control over what he sees and has little ability to 'learn to see'. A physician learning how to read X-rays can sensitize himself to some initially overlooked boundaries. But most of the information present in an X-ray photograph cannot be exploited by even a trained eye.

In vision, there are errors of omission and errors of commission. We are not merely missing the boundary between yellow and green when looking at a spectrum. We are seeing the absence of a boundary. Other creatures may have less opinionated visual systems and so need not succumb to the illusion of boundarylessness. They would be free of an obstacle that stands in our way of accepting the simple solution to the sorites paradox.

The illusion of boundarylessness is not like the illusions of probability. When I learn probability theory, I overwrite a powerful system of heuristics that previously guided my judgment. This suppressed system reasserts itself when I am not cued to apply my expertise. So I tend to lapse back into primitive thinking. Unlike probability theory, the belief in sharp boundaries for vague predicates is not a body of expert knowledge that is written over a more rudimentary theory. Even when cued, I 'see' the boundarylessness. At the theoretical level, I do not believe what my linguistic homunculi report. But I am still in a state of dissonance. My homunculi may have lost temporary control of my mouth but they will often make me look and feel like I believe in boundarylessness.

Layers of our linguistic system are built on a platform of more rudimentary linguistic reflexes. Instead of compensating for certain kinds of illusions, a cognitive system can exploit the illusions for the sake of greater representational power and efficiency. Gestalt principles of continuity help us see motion when there is only a rapid sequence of still pictures. Perhaps mental imagery is a similar elaboration on perceptual illusions. In any case, my hypothesis is that natural languages exploit rudimentary judgments of boundarylessness. The illusion of boundarylessness prevents speakers from wasting time searching for a boundary. Since speakers ought to draw distinctions only where they can perceive differences, the perception of boundarylessness becomes a platform for a norm.

Suppose a baby is born with a mutation that enables it to learn one of those logically possible languages that the rest of us cannot learn. Since the child now has a larger search space, he learns language more slowly than his narrower-minded competitors—er, playmates. The mutation is a genetic disorder. His healthy playmates may owe their rapid language acquisition to their ancestors' race to dumb down.

Few people fight the appearance of boundarylessness. The appearance embeds itself in our communicative practices. It becomes tempting to infer that boundarylessness is part of the meaning of vague words.

But I have conclusive, indirect proof that there must be a threshold for each vague predicate that applies to some things but not others. In a way, I owe it to my father. He encouraged a sense of proportion by ruling out extremes: 'There is always a bigger fish', 'No matter how much you earn, there will always be someone richer', 'Nobody is perfect'. I began to echo these anti-superlative generalizations. My wise sayings eventually provoked an irreverent friend into refuting me with *The Guinness Book of Records*. This encyclopedia of extremes had fascinating pictures of the tallest man, the heaviest man, and so forth. Not satisfied with mere counterexamples, my friend went on to sternly observe that I should have been able to figure out that extremes exist just from the fact that there were only so many things in the universe. 'No matter who you are, there is always someone taller' can be true only if the population is infinite. I was thunderstruck by the rebuttal. 'Well', I concluded, 'no matter how smart you are, there is always someone smarter.'

Slowly, my friend's extremist moral took root. Superlative generalizations are a priori truths—at least relative to the background knowledge that the property in question is possessed by just a finite number of things. There must be an oldest man. There must be a smallest heap.

We utter false anti-superlative generalizations with surprising frequency. Happily, their falsehood is compatible with their utility. Ancient fishermen inferred that some fish are bigger than any man from a wide sample of marine life that mistakenly included whales as fish. But the error did not undermine their conclusion that some fish are bigger than any man. False premises do not always prevent the reasoner from extracting knowledge of the conclusion from the unsound argument.

Counterexamples to some generalizations never arise in ordinary circumstances. Kit Fine's favorite example is 'If you cut butter in half, both halves are themselves butter'. When applied in the kitchen, this false generalization must yield truths. Counterexamples can only be obtained in the laboratory. Scientific people may come to regard the generalization as false. But even they employ the generalization in circumstances in which this falsehood functions as a reliable source of truths.

Although the induction step of the sorites is a priori false, it can still be a source of knowledge in the way other anti-superlative falsehoods are sources of knowledge. Economists employ anti-superlatives in their explanation of efficient markets. For instance, proponents of the random walk theory of the stock market explain that one cannot make profitable predictions of stock prices because someone else always assimilates the new information before you. By the time you can complete your prediction, the price of the stock already reflects the new information. I accept the random walk theory. I invest accordingly: I follow a buy and hold strategy, never researching a single investment, merely aiming to match average stock performance through random purchases. My investment strategy is unoriginal; I am doing exactly what most academic economists advise. Nevertheless, the anti-superlative aspect of the economic reasoning is odd. The absurdity is epitomized by the joke about a business man and an economist walking down Wall Street. The business man says 'Look, there is a twenty dollar bill on the sidewalk!'. The economist replies 'No there is not; someone else would have picked it up already'.

Milton Friedman (1953) says he accepts economic axioms because of their true consequences, not their truth. There is a difference between the epistemic utility of a generalization and its truth-value. An evolutionist must reject 'Every chicken comes from a chicken'. But he may still use the principle to infer that *this* chicken came from another chicken. I am happy to use the induction steps of sorites arguments in the same instrumental fashion.

There is an art to reliably inferring truths from falsehoods. In the case of sorites' induction steps, the trick is to avoid using them too much. One can make this art into a sort of science by providing more detail as to how much is too much. Haim Gaifman pictures the induction step of the sorites in the way surveyors view their theodolites. A theodolite has limited accuracy, so repeated uses of the instrument accumulate error. The amount of error is calculable, so one can take precautions and make adjustments. But this enterprise does not constitute *verification* of the induction step.

In *Blindspots* I presented logical and methodological arguments for *epistemicism*. This is the view that vagueness is a purely epistemological phenomenon. Just as this ignorance theory of probability denies that there is objective chance, the ignorance theory of vagueness denies that there is any objective indeterminacy. Previous characterizations of vagueness as ignorance portrayed the ignorance as surmountable (Cargile 1969; Campbell 1974; Scheffler 1979). Indeed, one of Israel Scheffler's motives for propounding the ignorance theory was to rally support for imaginative inquiry. Normally, the point of declaring something to be a borderline *F* is to renounce any further effort to discover whether it is an *F*. For instance, some who weary of the abortion debate conclude that 'person' is too vague to permit a non-arbitrary answer to 'When does a fetus first become a person?' Derek Parfit maintains that many thought experiments concerning the relation 'x is the same person as y' are really raising 'empty questions'. He offers an analogy. Suppose a club is 'revived' after years of inactivity. Have the people reconvened the same club or have they merely started another club? Unless the original club had rules specifying how it can only be reconvened, there is no determinate answer to this question. 'Though there is no answer to our question, there may be nothing that we do not know' (Parfit 1984: 213).

This rationale conflicts with the law of bivalence: every proposition is either true or false. Deviant logicians suggest that this wise resignation can be rescued by changing logic. I have nothing against supplemental logics such as modal logic. These *add* new theorems or inference rules. A supplemental logic cannot undermine the validity of the sorites argument because it only increases the stock of validated arguments. The sorites can only have its validation revoked by a *deviant* logic. For only a deviant logic *subtracts* a classical theorem or inference rule.

Retreat is often wise. I have done my share! But we should not retreat from standard logic to rescue speculative hypotheses about how language operates. Change in the web of belief should be made at the most peripheral portion available. Beliefs about how language works are far more peripheral than beliefs about logic. After all, anti-boundary beliefs emanate from philosophy of language, not linguistics or some other scientific discipline. Instead of changing logic, we should change our opinions about how language works.

Every healthy human being above 5 is a linguistic genius. No one is a meta-linguistic genius. The ability to theorize about language is a separate ability. There has been intense evolutionary pressure to master language at an earlier and earlier age. The pressure to accurately comment upon the nature of language is much weaker. A hunter-gatherer profits from sensitivity to ambiguities in a promise but not nearly as much as he profits from being able to make a promise. Consequently, the meta-linguistic competence of a fluent speaker is spotty. The inferiority of our meta-linguistic ability is self-masking. Our weak grasp of the use/mention distinction impedes recognition of the difference between being able to speak competently and being able to articulate that competence. Consequently, we are incompetently opinionated about how language operates. One's meta-linguistic intuitions have some warrant but only as much as intuitions about, say, one's digestive system.

Until recently, linguistic immodesty has stupefied deaf people (Kyle and Woll, 1985). When deaf people live together in a community, they spontaneously develop sign language. However, until the 1960s, signing was regarded as pantomime—as a pictorial signal system. To the outsider, sign language appeared to lack a grammar and so was not regarded as a genuine language. Paradoxically, sign language also appeared this way to signers themselves. Only after William Stokoe published *Sign Language*, did linguists gradually begin to recognize the syntactic aspects of handshape, location, and movement. Now we know that sign language is a language in the same full sense that English is language. But in the nineteenth century, this was not known. Although sign language flourished at deaf schools, it was regarded as a mental crutch that impeded the acquisition of a genuine language. In 1880, reformers at the Milan conference banned sign language at deaf schools. This forced deaf students to waste most of their educational hours acquiring a marginal ability to speak orally.

Our opinions of vagueness are affected by meta-linguistic immodesty. Most are so confident in our generalizations about meaning that they will not brook correction by logic itself. They demand we change logic rather than our opinions of boundarylessness.

The history of deviant logics is without a single success. Bivalence has been denied at least since Aristotle, yet no anti-bivalent theory has ever left the philosophical nursery. Many-valued logic does have many applications in the sense that it has a mathematical structure that usefully models empirical phenomena. Some engineers, especially in Asia, prefer cautious circuitry that employ functions isomorphic to those at the heart of many-valued logic. In this (misleading) sense, Hitachi's subway in Sendai, Japan does owe its smooth stops and starts to fuzzy logic. Back when Japan was in economic ascent as America was in decline, a popular magazine article suggested that the Japanese prospered because of their use of fuzzy logic. While rigid Westerners languished in yes-no thinking, the flexible Japanese thought in terms of a continuum. (For book-length elaborations of this theme, see Bart Kosko's *Fuzzy Thinking* and *Fuzzy Logic* by Daniel McNeil and Paul Freiberger.) The author of the magazine article conceded that fuzzy logic was actually invented by the Western computer engineer Lotfi Asker Zadeh but took this to illustrate the Japanese genius for assimilating foreign thought—without paying royalties. (Actually, the core of many-valued logic was pioneered by the Polish logician, Jan Łukasiewicz, who hoped to solve the problem of determinism. Zadeh's innovation was the connection to vagueness—and coining the term 'fuzzy logic'.)

Zadeh promotes fuzzy logic as a genuine alternative to standard logic when he says 'Nature writes with a spray can, not a ball-point pen'. His critics counter that quantum mechanics shows that reality is crisp to a part in 10^{16}. They draw invidious comparisons between Japanese success with fuzzy elevators and American success at sending a man to the moon.

This patriotic debate rests on a shared misconception about logic. Logic is about the consequence relation. It is about what follows from what. Consequently, pure logic cannot have any contingent implications. Therefore, logic cannot be refuted or confirmed by a discovery that reality, as it happens, is continuous. Or chaotic. Or what have you. Logic can be applied to issues about what follows from what, as in assessing the validity of arguments. A structure that is useful in modeling the consequence relation might also be useful for modeling contingent relations such as the relation between input and output flows of an exotic liquid. Suppose we let 1 equal the fastest speed the liquid can travel and express liquid flows as a fraction of that maximal speed. We discover that when two pipes converge, their output equals the product of the speeds of the liquid in the slower pipe. This will raise the possibility of applying probability theory because it assigns the output flow a speed equal to the product of the two input flows. On the other hand, we will try fuzzy logic if their output equals that of the slowest moving pipe. (Perhaps the particles are like ships in a fleet; the fleet can only sail as fast as its slowest ship.) The success of fuzzy logic in modeling the exotic liquid would be irrelevant to its success in modeling the consequence relation. Australians may find that paraconsistent logic can be used to model cooking processes and use this discovery to construct a paraconsistent barbecue oven. The paraconsistent oven could occupy the same kitchen as the fuzzy washing-machine—and the supervaluational toaster. This pluralism is possible because the different systems are being used to model different relations. There is rivalry only when they are applied to the same phenomenon. And there is logical rivalry only when they are modeling the consequence relation.

In this book, I am concerned with standard logic (first order logic with identity) as applied to the consequence relation. I am a logical conservative in that I deny that vagueness provides any reason to reject any theorem or inference rule of standard logic. The phenomenon of higher order vagueness shows that the basic problem posed by vagueness (sharp boundaries for vague terms) is inescapable. Since nothing but gratuitous complexity is obtained by interposing a deviant logic, parsimony demands that the whole issue be treated directly and comprehensively within the domain of standard logic.

In the realm of science and mathematics, a conflict with standard logic is invariably fatal. Scientists and mathematicians have thought it deeply ad hoc to rescue a theory by altering logic. What theory cannot be rescued by such a revision?

Scientific proof is rationally compelling and difficult to improve upon. The weakest elements of such proofs are the empirical premises. So one of few ways to improve on a scientific proof is to delete superfluous empirical premises, that is, premises which are not needed to validly deduce the conclusion. The fewer the empirical assumptions, the better. The argument for sharp boundaries achieves this ideal to an admirable degree.

Parfit thinks that empty questions involve propositions that are neither true nor false. Scheffler traces this belief to an argument that rests on the analytic/synthetic distinction: True statements are made true by something, in particular, either by words or by the world. Borderline statements such as 'Pudding is a solid' are not supported by words because our linguistic framework does not necessitate its truth. The statement is not made true by the world because nothing would count as verifying that pudding is a solid. Therefore, 'Pudding is a solid' is neither true nor false. Invoking Quine, Scheffler complains that this argument overlooks the possibility that language and words grow together so that what counts as verifying 'Pudding is solid' develops out of empirical inquiry. I agree with Scheffler that the classic conception of a borderline cases rests on an analytic/synthetic distinction. But I do not have his enmity toward the analytic/synthetic distinction. Like the male/female distinction, there are puzzle cases and issues about the *nature* of the difference. But I am satisfied that the distinction exists and that it illuminates the incredulity (plus much else). A main theme of this book is that the sorites sufferer must rest on a bed of nails formed by analytic beliefs. The dilemmas posed by vagueness are of our own making. They spring from our representational system rather than the world.

I have always been a futilitarian about borderline cases. Parfit eloquently promotes this resignation in *Reasons and Persons*. We should not waste energy on issues that are 'void for vagueness'. Recall the wise resignation to which John Locke aspired:

I suppose it may be of use to prevail with the busy mind of man to be more cautious in meddling with things exceeding its comprehension; to stop when it is at the utmost extent of its tether; and to sit down in quiet ignorance of those things which, upon examination, are found to be beyond the reach of our capacities. (Locke 1690: i. 28)

Showing that a debated statement is borderline is a standard technique of dissolving problems (Sorensen 1993: 191–5). An account of inquiry should accommodate this fact, not campaign against it. One of the strengths of epistemicism is that it allows us to widen the scope of this technique of problem dissolution. If vagueness is ignorance, then *any* sufficiently stubborn obstacle to knowledge can generate the inquiry resistance associated with vagueness. As we shall see in Chapter 2's discussion of higher order vagueness, epistemicism implies a greater variety and quantity of borderline cases.

Scheffler and others resist this technique partly for the reason people bridle at impossibility claims. They say anything is possible. Such optimism is self-defeating. If anything is possible, then it is possible to prove that something is impossible. And if it is possible to prove that something is impossible, then necessarily, something is impossible.

With these Lockean thoughts in the background I sought a logically conservative, epistemological rationale for curbing inquiry. I pressed an analogy between threshold statements of the form 'n minutes after noon is the last noonish minute' and blindspots such as 'n is the successor of the largest integer that has ever been thought of'. A blindspot is a consistent but inaccessible proposition. Hence, my position was that the threshold statements have truth-values but are unknowable. This analysis put the sorites paradox at the flattering end of a continuum of increasingly sophisticated slippery-slope arguments.

Critics welcomed the preservation of defeatism but complained of explanatory gaps. In particular, the resemblance between threshold statements and blindspots is not a sufficient account of the necessary ignorance of the threshold. Timothy Williamson was one of these critics. Later, in *Identity and Discrimination* (1990, sect. 6.4), he speculated that the margin for error principle might fill the explanatory gap. This principle says that if I know that x is F, then anything insignificantly different from x must also be F. For if it were not F, then my belief that x is F was due to luck. Had my attention alighted on the non-F which is an indistinguishable neighbor of F, I would have also judged it to be F. The sorites monger arranges cases so closely together that I am not in a position to detect the last F because it is too close to the first non-F.

In 1994, Timothy Williamson's speculation matured into the centerpiece of his classic *Vagueness*. In this second book, Williamson abandons his earlier reservations about epistemicism and becomes its most forceful and methodical proponent. Perhaps because of his confidence in the explanatory prowess of his margin for error principle, Williamson comes close to agreeing with those who say that the epistemic view is *obliged* to explain the ignorance of boundaries.

My reservations about the potency of the margin for error principle turn on a distinction introduced in Chapter 1. Usually, 'borderline case' refers to a case that cannot be settled by a given process or method. I call this a 'relative borderline case' because the undecidability varies with the cognizer. Williamson 'characterizes vagueness in a concept as its indiscriminability from other possible concepts' (1994: 217). The indiscriminability is relative to members of the speech community—human beings. However, I contend that vagueness consists in the possession of *absolute* borderline cases. Since these do not require any relativization to a cognizer, I think Williamson is (brilliantly) explaining the wrong sort of borderline case.

Williamson relates ignorance to vagueness in the immediate way Pierre Simon de LaPlace links ignorance with probability. LaPlace denies that there is objective chance and takes probability to be relative to the cognizer's ignorance. Similarly, Williamson takes vagueness to arise directly from the indiscriminability relation. In contrast, I prefer an account in which vagueness arises from a semantic feature (such as truthmaker gaps) which precipitates ignorance as a necessary byproduct.

Given a coarse standard of explanation, any proof that *p* explains *p* in the sense of showing it to be so. In this heavy-handed fashion, the basic argument for sharp boundaries does explain the ignorance. But even mathematicians have a predilection for refined standards of explanation that allow them to complain that *reductio ad absurdum* proofs are inferior to direct proofs. Similarly, mathematicians complain that existence proofs fail to show *why* the thing exists. General criteria may show that an alleged prime number has two divisors without providing a clue as to which numbers are the divisors. It would be nice to know the identity of the divisors. But it would be silly to reject the existence proof on the grounds that it does not name names. In the context of proof, explanatory desiderata are supererogatory. No mathematician rejects a *reductio ad absurdum* or an existence proof on the grounds that they have not been supplemented with an account of *why* the conclusions hold. The basic argument for sharp boundaries is an existence proof. Yet philosophers do object to it on explanatory grounds. Williamson panders to this illogical aversion to inexplicable truths. Philosophers should follow the mathematicians who sharply distinguish the context of proof from the context of explanation. Proof is well understood. Explanation is a more psychological and epistemological enterprise.

I certainly hope and yearn for a nice explanation of the ignorance. This book cooperates with this project in two ways. The first chapter clarifies what is to be explained by introducing the distinction between absolute borderline cases and relative borderline cases. Absolute borderline cases involve a kind of ignorance that is not relative to any thinker. Consequently, an explanation of the ignorance associated with vagueness should not relativize to cognizers. Williamson's explanation of the ignorance does not even purport to account for absolute borderline cases. His margin for error merely aims to explain why *human beings* would be ignorant of thresholds for vague predicates if there were sharp thresholds: 'The cognitive capacities of creatures outside the speech community are simply not to the point' (Williamson 1994: 212). Williamson defines the whole problem in this provincial way: 'The datum is that we have no idea how to acquire knowledge in borderline cases; epistemicism can explain it' (Williamson 1996: 41).

My concern is that the margin for error principle is a solution looking for a problem, not a solution to an antecedent problem. Vagueness theorists have always had a broader concern. This is evident from the sweeping way they have tried to model the ignorance associated with vagueness. They try to ensure that even God could not know the proposition. Whether by truth-value gaps or gluts or degrees of truth or inferential restrictions, they try to design a proposition that is not in the category of things that can be known.

My concerns about the limits of the margin for error principle are compatible with hopes for its role in a larger explanation of absolute borderline cases. In Chapter 3 I propose an empathic principle that would de-relativize the results of the margin for error principle (or other such principles that appear to only enforce human ignorance). However, my quest for absolute borderline cases also generates an independent explanation—a derivation of absolute borderline cases from truthmaker gaps. This proposal requires some complications and digressions into the liar paradox. To avoid distractions, I have stationed this discussion at the end of the book. I hope at least one of these proposed explanations of the ignorance succeeds. But acceptance of the epistemic solution to the sorites should not be made contingent on furnishing such an explanation. Reality is insensitive to explanatory cravings.

In any case, this book's primary concern is *incredulity* rather than ignorance. The basic argument for boundaries is a simple, sound argument, that has been in wide circulation for many years. Yet less than 10 per cent of current experts are persuaded by it. Worse, most of the experts complain that they cannot make sense of the claim that 'heap' is sensitive to differences of a single grain. Epistemicism strikes these able philosophers as conceptually absurd. Let me put their objection in raw form: 'Sharp boundaries for vague predicates are inconceivable. What is inconceivable is impossible. Therefore, vague predicates cannot have sharp boundaries.' My goal is to furnish an account of vagueness that replies to this objection and to its refinements.

This account is intended to solve the sorites meta-paradox. In my opinion, the sorites paradox has a clear, exciting solution. The meta-paradox is that people, especially those with philosophical acumen, fail to accept the solution. Their reaction to the basic argument for sharp boundaries echoes Lady Brute's in John Vanbrugh's *The Provok'd Wife*: 'I think, sir, your sophistry has all the effect you can reasonably expect it should have: it puzzles, but don't convince'.

The situation has precedents. Mind-brain identity theorists were familiar with the old argument against contingent identity. (If $a = b$, then b has all the properties that a has. Individual a has the property of being necessarily identical to a. Therefore, if $a = b$, then it is a necessary truth that $a = b$.) They dismissed the argument as sophism. After all, were there not scientific demonstrations of contingent identities such as

'Lightning is electrical discharge in the atmosphere'? In *Naming and Necessity*, Saul Kripke defended the little 'sophism' as a decisive demonstration. He does not attempt to shore up the proof with extra premises. Kripke merely disinhibits our inferential mechanism by removing confusions and distractions.

Yesterday's fallacy can become tomorrow's textbook demonstration. Introductory discussions of infinity commonly feature Galileo's proof that the squares of natural numbers are as numerous as the natural numbers:

Natural numbers: 1, 2, 3, 4, . . .
Squares of natural numbers: 1, 4, 9, 16, . . .

Although Galileo followed the correct proof procedure (establishing a one to one correlation with the natural numbers), he was not persuaded by his argument. He boggled at the possibility that the part (the infinite collection of squares) could be as big as the whole (the infinite collection of natural numbers which properly contains the squares).

Noam Chomsky distinguishes between two epistemological problems. Plato's problem is to explain how we manage to know on the basis of so limited evidence. As Bertrand Russell (1948, p. v) put it, 'How comes that human beings, whose contacts with the world are brief and personal and limited, are nevertheless able to know as much as they do know?' Chomsky's hypothesis of an innate grammar is intended as a solution to this kind of problem. The opposite epistemological problem, named after the author of *1984*, George Orwell, is to explain how human beings fail to know in the face of overwhelming evidence:

Orwell was impressed with the ability of totalitarian systems to instill beliefs that are firmly held and widely accepted although they are completely without foundation and often plainly at variance with obvious facts about the world around us. The problem is far broader, as the story of religious dogma suffices to show. To solve Orwell's problem we must discover the institutional and other factors that block insight and understanding in crucial areas of our lives and ask why they are effective. (Chomsky 1986, p. xxvii)

Chomsky's own efforts at solving Orwell's problem are Marxist. According to Chomsky, the elites in democratic societies are, unsurprisingly, pursuing their own interests at the expense of other groups. The elites obfuscate their exploitation through ruses. They slant newspaper coverage, divide the opposition, and mystify the political process. Chomsky rains down counter-propaganda.

My Orwell problem is confined to arguments. It is also restricted by allegiance to the principle of charity. Thus narrowed, my task is to explain how rational people fail to be enlightened by a simple, cogent proof.

Orwell problems have attracted other philosophers. Daniel Dennett wrote *Darwin's Dangerous Idea* to explain why evolutionary arguments fail to produce as much knowledge as they ought. The evidence for evolutionary theory is staggering. Darwin's reasoning is interesting and accessible. Yet an enormous portion of his readership is unpersuaded—including highly educated academics. Dennett is a champion of the principle of charity. So he is reluctant to dismiss the naysayers as irrational. In the end he postulates a bias: evolutionary theory violates a cherished belief that there is a plan behind the universe and human existence. People cannot bear the implication that life is meaningless.

I think the evidence for sharp boundaries is even more overwhelming than the evidence for evolutionary theory. At least the alternatives to evolution are consistent! The evidence for sharp boundaries is also simpler and does not pose a distracting challenge to our place in the universe. Yet the shortfall in knowledge production is far greater. Virtually all professional biologists accept evolutionary theory. Virtually all professional philosophers reject epistemicism.

It gets worse. Even though I accept epistemicism, I have signs of also disbelieving it. Despite the new respectability of epistemicism, I continue to be embarrassed by its characteristic tenet. I cannot suppress a nervous smile when asserting that the entry of one more individual into an auditorium might make it crowded. Michael Tye finds this telling. He maintains that one should believe a theory only if one can present it with a straight face.

Tye's principle is too stern. Evolutionary explanations of the ferocious sexual practices of insects are systematically comical. The truth is sometimes incongruous. One would expect the humorous dissonance to subside as other beliefs are reshaped to fit the novel truth. Yesterday's heterodoxy is today's orthodoxy. Yet, I confess that a measure of misalignment has survived my seventeen-year subscription to epistemicism. This enduring embarrassment is a disturbing sign that I fail to believe in sharp boundaries. Even worse, it has the air of a lie.

Sometimes the appearance of a lie can be explained away. When I began teaching, I frequently felt that I was lying. My first lecture contained a carefully scripted account of how a valid argument can have false premises. I stated the standard definition of 'valid argument' but felt I was only mouthing the words. There was no inner glow of assent. I said yes but my autonomic nervous system said no. I eventually traced this feeling of insincerity to a correlation. The only previous circumstances in which I prepared what I said was when planning a deception. The association was fortified by my inexperience and the agnostic atmosphere students emit when taught by beginning instructors. As I became more experienced, the correlation with prevarication was diluted. I relaxed.

But I am still red-faced when lecturing about the sorites. Like polygraph operators, members of my audience frequently detect the physiology of duplicity. Some try to shame me out of my position: 'Come on! Do you *really* believe that the addition of one pound made Buddha fat?'.

I resemble a disbeliever in my attitude to instances of my core generalization. Normally, if a person finds each 'confirming' instance of an existential generalization absurd, he rejects the generalization as a whole. For instance, I find each report of psychokinesis incredible. My loyalty to physics makes each psychic spoon bending an absurdity. And indeed, I reject the existential generalization 'There is at least one instance of psychokinesis'. Similarly, each hypothesis of the form 'n seconds after noon is the last noonish second' strikes me as absurd. This is a sign that I also reject the existential generalization 'There is an n such that n is the last noonish second'. If absurdity is compositional, then I ought to regard the generalization as absurd. But I instead regard the *negation* of this generalization as absurd!

In *Blindspots* I reacted to this dissonance by maintaining that threshold statements such as 'Sixteen minutes after noon is the last noonish minute' are consistent but unknowable statements. Just as we are never in a position to assert 'The number of stars is even but no one knows it', we are never in a position to assert that the threshold is this or that particular value. If you assert something while realizing that you do not know it to be true, you are lying. So each threshold statement will resemble a lie in so far as we picture it as being asserted by someone.

Although I still think that true threshold statements are blindspots, I think the blindspot explanation does not fully explain the a priori unacceptability of threshold statements. All threshold statements look worse than unassertible; they look *contradictory*. I now think the correct explanation of this appearance is that almost all threshold statements are indeed contradictions. Instead of merely being blindspots, they owe their unbelievability to representational constraints which compel us to round off insignificant possibilities. In a typical sorites series, almost all of the hypotheses as to where the boundary might be have the same semantic status as 'Sixteen is a large number but seventeen is not a large number'. Moreover, the single true threshold statement in the sequence is such that competent speakers of English must construe it as a contradiction. Thus I believe 'There is a minimum number of sands needed to make a heap' is a tautology but each proposal for the minimum ought to be regarded as a contradiction.

How can these apparently inconsistent claims be reconciled? I am asserting that although English is free of inconsistency, competence in English compels one to regard infinitely many tautologies (the true threshold statements) as contradictions. The negations of these hidden tautologies are hidden contradictions. English compels its speakers to regard these contradictions (false anti-threshold statements) as tautologies. Therefore, there are infinitely many tautologies that we are required to construe as contradictions and infinitely many contradictions that we are required to believe to be tautologies.

These remarks hold even if 'tautology' is read narrowly to cover only statements that owe their truth to the meanings of their logical words. (More about that in Ch. 7.) From here we can quickly infer that there are valid arguments that we should judge invalid and invalid arguments that we should judge valid.

All of these analytical errors are irremediable. After reading this book, you (and I) will continue to believe them because it is impossible to precisely identify them. The modular psychology behind this recalcitrance is discussed in Chapter 5.

Epistemicism conflicts with many current beliefs about language. Philosophers are strongly attracted to conventionalism. In particular, they think words (with the possible exception of natural kind terms) can have sharp boundaries only if speakers stipulate them. But how would the words used in the speaker's fiat get *their* sharp boundaries? If all of your 'definiens' lacks sharp boundaries, you will not be able to get any sharply bounded words by definition. And if some of your undefined terms have enough sharp boundaries to be used in a definition of word that has sharp boundaries, then you must have antecedently had all the sharp boundaries you needed. Stipulation can never increase the number of concepts that have sharp boundaries.

Philosophers are also attracted to the view that meaning is mind-dependent. This semantic internalism has come under independent attack during the last twenty years. Epistemicists naturally ally with externalists who believe that meaning partly depends on aspects of one's environment and social circumstances. An internalist may be tempted to view epistemicist commitments to an infinite fleet of 'stealth contradictions' as a reductio. That is, they might picture my brand of epistemicism as an illustration of why extreme content externalism is absurd.

I counter this impression in Chapters 8, 9, and 10 by deriving similar conclusions about contradictions from premises acceptable to an internalist. Chapter 8 gets a foot in the door with a transcendental argument showing that it is possible for someone to believe an impossibility. The next chapter widens the opening with the more controversial thesis that reason demands that I actually believe a contradiction. The door is pushed wide open in Chapter 10 which presents a viral theory of inconsistency, which claims we are committed to infinitely many contradictions. I there also argue that infinitely many of these contradictions must be believed to be tautologies. These three Cartesian chapters deliberately make no mention of vagueness or the sorites. They are intended to forestall the impression that my cure to the sorites is worse than the disease: 'The good news is that the sorites paradox has been solved. The bad news is that the solution comes at the price of believing infinitely many contradictions.' The Cartesian chapters are intended to discount the bad news by showing how we were antecedently committed to contradictions on a massive scale.

The Cartesian interlude is followed by a final speculative chapter on truthmaker gaps. This draws me into deep waters: the nature of truth, the principle of sufficient reason, and so on. I offer the theory tentatively and partly as an instrument of clarification. The question 'How do absolute borderline cases arise?' is obscure. Those who ask obscure questions often clarify them by trying to answer them. Defects of the answers (which are hard to anticipate without specimens) lead to improvements in the question.

Unlike most paradoxes, the difficulty with the sorites paradox is not devising a subtle solution. The solution is straightforward: reject the induction step and adjust to the consequent commitment to sharp boundaries. The real problem is to explain why people have so much trouble accepting the simple solution. Including me.

1 Absolute Borderline Cases

The New York Vagueness Group has convened up and down Manhattan since 1997. The membership is infinite. Proof: there is at least one member. Me. And for each member, there is another member with a stranger solution to the sorites paradox.

Despite our numbers, we agree on particular borderline cases. This is noteworthy because the group's usage of 'borderline case' rarely matches the ordinary use. Our curious solidarity became evident in the course of some automated ordinary language philosophy.

1. Relative Borderline Cases

Log on to a search service such as Lexis Nexis. As your keyword, enter 'borderline case'. Less than 5 per cent of your hits will include the intractable borderline cases that philosophers talk about.

More than 10 per cent of your hits will include a usage that at first seems alien from philosophy. This is the geographic use. Territorial borders give rise to a rich variety of social phenomena: draft dodging, communication gaps, tax loopholes, and so on. Reporters illustrate these borderline phenomena with case studies. My favorite borderline case featured an elderly gentleman who made an enormous number of bicycle trips between Northern Ireland and the Irish Republic. Border guards knew he was smuggling. They searched his sack and even disassembled the bicycle but found nothing. Stumped, the guards finally called a truce and asked the elderly gentleman what he was smuggling. 'Bicycles' was his reply.

The geographic usage can be connected with the more common usage (accounting for over 75 per cent) that concerns sorting. Candidates for parole, job applicants, and test takers must all be distributed into categories. Since human beings think about problems spatially, they picture sorting problems as questions of placement. To the right are positive cases. To the left lie the negatives. The problem is to draw the line between the positive cases and the negative cases. It is natural for us to represent hard to classify items as falling between the two categories.

We may even make 'borderline' a separate category just as clerks make a separate folder for miscellaneous items. 'Miscellaneous' must be relativized to a set of other folders. That's why the introduction of a new folder sometimes necessitates the export of a document from the miscellaneous folder. 'Borderline' is similarly relative to ambient categories. But there is an instructive contrast. If a document is in the miscellaneous file, then it does not belong in any other file. But assignment as a borderline F is compatible with membership in the F category and compatible with membership in the non-F category. In the 1992 Kurdistan election, thousands of under-aged youngsters claimed to be 18 to vote. The Gulf War had plunged this rebellious region of Iraq into administrative chaos. Officials could decide some of the clear cases. But they had to defer to physicians to settle borderline cases. Even so, everybody took for granted that each borderline 18-year-old was either 18 or not 18.

The epistemicist draws unexpected sustenance from ordinary language: In the most common usage of 'borderline case', a borderline case of an *F* can be an *F*. Granted, it cannot be a *clear* F. But the uncertainty is merely empirical. Almost all utterances of 'borderline case' are *boringly* compatible with standard logic.

But there are a few recalcitrant kernels in the corpus. A small percentage of ordinary utterances of 'borderline case' do menace standard logic. Reporters are drawn to some disputes just because of their *intrinsic* resistance to inquiry. For instance, Moslems in New Jersey argue about which way Mosques should face. They all agree that all Mosques must face Mecca. But which way faces Mecca? Does one follow a line through the earth? Or should one follow a line along the surface of the earth?

Reporters signal another philosophical genre with rhetorical queries such as 'Who is to say?' (whether a picture is pornographic rather than merely erotic) and 'Where do you draw the line?' (between schoolyard teasing and sexual harassment). Such rhetoric is aimed at the question itself. In effect, the reporter alleges that the unclarity of the question prevents the fruitful application of *any* investigative procedure. Borderline cases of this philosophical sort are not relative to an answer system. The *question* is missing something. No process or method can get a purchase on such a question.

These absolute borderline cases make many doubt the principle of bivalence. This principle says that each proposition has a single truth-value, true or false. When Plato discusses the proper punishment for crimes of passion, he refuses to describe them as voluntary or involuntary: 'there is a borderland which comes in between, preventing them from touching. And we were saying that actions done from passion are of this nature, and come in between the voluntary and involuntary' (*Laws* 878b). Plato thinks we must hedge and describe the problematic actions as shadows or likenesses of voluntary acts. He suggests an intermediate punishment for crimes of passion to reflect their intermediate status between 'voluntary' and 'involuntary'.

Can Plato be dismissed as illogical? If 'involuntary' is the contradictory of 'voluntary', then an act of passion must fall under one predicate or the other.

Can Plato be dismissed as logical? Trivially, we can square Plato's remarks with the principle of bivalence, by interpreting him as using 'involuntary' and 'voluntary' as *contraries*. Just as comets are neither sane nor insane, some acts are neither voluntary nor involuntary. The principle of charity encourages this effort to construe people as rational by explaining away their apparent violations of standard logic.

When philosophers describe a case as borderline, they normally express *global* pessimism about attempts to learn whether it is an F or a non-F. No one can learn the answer to questions such as *Are prisoners of war residents of an alien country?* and *Are skis vehicles?* In contrast, the pessimism conveyed in most ordinary uses of 'borderline case' is local. We are free to recruit a secondary answer system that can handle the question.

The asymmetry can be explained by the impact question-centered unclarity has on investigation. Ambiguous questions stop inquiry even when the investigators are generously endowed. They must take a break and seek disambiguation. Unclear questions are insensitive to one's choice of an answer system.

The features of answer systems are easiest to recognize in answer systems that have been surgically molded for clarity—formal systems. A statement that is undecidable in one formal system may be provable in another. A system is incomplete to the extent that it fails to answer a question we might expect it to answer. Relative borderline cases are instances of incompleteness.

'Borderline' is typically deployed in the course of epistemic triage. In medical triage, patients are sorted into those who are past helping, those who demand immediate attention, and those who can wait. In epistemic triage, cases are sorted into the Fs, the non-Fs, and the borderline Fs. This quick categorization is an adaptation to scarce intellectual resources. Occasionally, a new answer system will resolve all border-line cases. For instance, DNA testing now perfectly discriminates be-tween twins who have originated from the same fertilized egg and twins who have originated from distinct fertilized eggs. But normally we do not need answers to all our questions. An answer system that *exhaustively* divides the population into the Fs and the non-Fs is apt to be a wasteful luxury.

Some secondary answer systems rely on the screening done by the answer system used in the first phase of the inquiry. For instance, smell tests help diagnose borderline cases of neurological disorders. These olfactory tie-breakers exploit the surprising correlation between schizophrenia and changes in the sense of smell. The smell test is not appropriate at the initial stage of the inquiry because loss of smell is correlated with too many other diseases (depression, Alzheimer's disease, Parkinson's disease).

Borderline cases vary in recalcitrance. We choose a secondary an-swer system that is fairly decisive, well suited to these leftover cases. But as before, it is generally wasteful to use an exhaustive system. Consequently, the secondary system typically has its own borderline cases that can only be resolved with a tertiary system. And yet again, we need to decide whether these leftover leftover cases need to be decided. In principle, we could go on and on in the hope of settling all the cases. But normally such thoroughness is a neurotic violation of the law of diminishing returns.

Here is a second analogue of higher order vagueness: relative border-line cases about relative borderline cases. Many admissions programs restrict preferential treatment to borderline cases. That is, considera-tions of race, gender, and so forth only apply to candidates who neither clearly qualify nor clearly fall short. This leads to the suspicion of bias in assigning borderline status. Those who wish to broaden the effect of preferential treatment will assign borderline status to too many can-didates and those who wish to narrow the effect will assign borderline status to too few candidates. When 'Is this a borderline case?' is ad-dressed by a method that is not wholly decisive, there will be border-line borderline cases.

Absolute borderline cases ensure that thoroughness is sometimes impossible. The persistent inquirer hits a wall: *Does a glass house have any windows? Can you dial on a push button phone? Is chartreuse yellow rather than green?* These questions have grammatical answers: *Yes, glass houses do have windows* and *No, glass houses do not have windows*. However, most philosophers doubt that either of these 'answers' is true (or false).

Since an epistemicist is committed to truth-values for these odd answers, he must hold that there is a function that will take us from the questions to true answers. Therefore, there is a reliable answer system. Even so, it is not an epistemically accessible system. No one could identify this function as the reliable system. If Mr Vagueluck happens to adopt the system, his reliably correct beliefs about the truth-values of vague propositions would not constitute knowledge. For his beliefs would have both a lucky origin and be sustained by luck.

Credible answer systems do not answer questions such as *Is an attached garage part of the house?* The very willingness of ouija boards and oracles to respond refutes their pretensions of reliability. They do not know when to be silent.

Normally, we want to *know* the answer and so turn to the strongest process or method available, one that will provide a correct and informative answer to the question. Consequently, 'That is a borderline case' normally has a performative dimension. It marks a silent zone of the system.

A proponent of the avowal theory of 'I am in pain' (in which the sentence is a kind of groan) might be tempted to view 'That is a borderline case' as a verbal substitute for shoulder shrugging. However, 'That is a borderline case' need not be a confession of *personal* ignorance. The silence of the system is an impersonal property. And ignorance is not inevitable. There are circumstances in which we deliberately restrict ourselves to a weaker answer system. In blind refereeing of scholarly articles, editors conceal the identity of the author. They instruct referees who infer the identity of the author to bracket this knowledge. This forces the referee to make a less informed decision.

Anthropologists even adopt answer systems that they know to be downright unreliable. Evans-Pritchard learned Azande witchcraft to better understand Azande culture. One sign that Evans-Pritchard had learned his witchcraft well was his indecision over certain borderline cases. How quickly must the chicken die in the poison oracle? Can a foreign chicken be employed?

Answer systems need not purport to be reliable. A random mechanism can be the basis for an answer system. The success rate of a random system provides a baseline by which more ambitious systems may be compared. For instance, the *Wall Street Journal* compared the predictions of leading stock analysts against the predictions generated by a dartboard. Since random systems are not lumbered by the objective of securing correct answers, they are impressively decisive, only yielding borderline cases because of mechanical breakdowns or incomplete instructions on how to interpret the results of the random indicator.

Decisiveness need not always come at the price of accuracy. In law and games, disputes are minimized by assigning an adjudicator who has the power to stipulate an answer. The adjudicator is given a rulebook and empirical access to the activity. These normally provide clear answers. But when they do not, the adjudicator can concede that he is faced with a borderline case and answer by fiat. The concession would be incoherent if the borderline case was absolute—for that would be an admission that there is no way at all to answer the question. The borderline case is relative because there is a back-up means of ascertaining the answer: stipulation. Adjudicators are reluctant to rest their decision on nothing but their own authority. However, acknowledging that one is in a gray area can protect a reputation for accuracy and honesty by reducing the amount of perceived disagreement. If people think the adjudicator is mistakenly regarding borderline cases as clear cases, they have reason to doubt his mastery of the rules or his perceptual competence. True, onlookers will also question the adjudicator's competence if he judges a clear positive case as a borderline case. But they have even stronger doubts when they think the adjudicator is judging clear positives as clear negatives.

Decisiveness can also be achieved by regimenting a system so that all questions resolve into a sequence of clear clerical tasks. Formal systems are tidied up in ways that help us to mechanically determine which statements are made by the system. Informal systems have two layers of obscurity. First, there is unclarity about whether the system speaks to the issue at all. Secondly, given that the system does speak, which answer does it give?

Our concern is only with the first layer of obscurity. Logicians have strategies for ascertaining whether a formal system is silent on a proposition. First, you can try to deduce the proposition with the resources of the system. Sometimes you can only prove that there is a proof. But that is enough to show that the system is not silent. If the system is known to be consistent, there is another strategy: add the proposition to the system and check whether the system is still consistent. If a contradiction can be deduced, then the system is not neutral. Indeed, as a bonus we have learned which side the system adopts. For the negation of the proposition is a theorem by *reductio ad absurdum*. If a proposition and its negation can each be added without inconsistency, then the system must be incomplete.

There are incompleteness proofs of informal systems that follow the same pattern. But we also rely on looser evidence. One widely used sign of incompleteness is disagreement among those who have mastered the system. If fishermen quarrel about whether a fish conforms to the size limit, that very disagreement is evidence that the fish is a borderline case. If their only basis for judgment is the official system, then belief that the system is silent on the issue will force each to retract. Their dispute is self-extinguishing.

Well there is one way the fishermen could continue to disagree. The fishermen might be using an unofficial answer system on the side. The answer system we accept for a certain purpose need not be the only one that is in operation. People are pluralistic, bringing a variety of systems to bear on an issue. For the sake of efficiency, they will agree to employ a system with administrative virtues. But they cannot turn off their brains. Many answer systems work involuntarily. Once you learn how to multiply, you automatically solve some addition problems by multiplication.

When extraneous answer systems are afoot, people continue to disagree even after agreeing the case is borderline (relative to the official system). Each acknowledges that the other is not violating the official system; neither side is saying yes when the system says no. For instance, physicians sometimes disagree about whether a patient has appendicitis. Forbidden disagreement arises when one physician has violated the protocol for deriving a diagnosis (overlooking the high white blood cell count, failing to ask about family history, and so on). Permissible disagreement arises when the physicians have reached different opinions on the patient even though each has followed the guidelines for diagnosing appendicitis. The physicians realize that the guidelines do not dictate how much weight to assign each symptom and that there are peripheral symptoms that are below the threshold of official recognition. The patient is a borderline case, so each physician must 'exercise judgment'.

This permissible disagreement is not a license to believe whatever one wishes. The respective answers are based on outside answer systems (or elaborations of the official system) that purport to be reliable. Somebody is making a mistake. Surgery will reveal who is right about the borderline case of appendicitis.

Some philosophers have seized upon permissible disagreement when characterizing *absolute* borderline cases. Crispin Wright speaks of faultlessly generated conflict:

> . . . the normal idea of a borderline case is one on which competent judges may unite in hesitation but about which they may also permissibly differ. If Jones is on the borderline of baldness, that will, of course, make it allowable if we each judge that he is borderline, but also allowable—at least in very many cases—if you regard him as bald and if I do not. (Wright 1995: 138)

If Wright is correct, vague concepts are related to 'essentially contested concepts'. Just as agreement can be semantically relevant, W. B. Gallie argued there are 'concepts the proper use of which inevitably involves endless disputes about their proper uses on the part of their users' (1955–6: 172). Gallie's examples are drawn from perennial debates concerning democracy, art, Christian life, and so on. Gallie's idea is to stand Ludwig Wittgenstein on his head. Wittgenstein emphasized that many of our linguistic practices rest on agreement as to how the world is and how to conduct ourselves. Gallie's audacious thesis is that disagreement can also be constitutive of meaning. In the same spirit, Wright characterizes vagueness as 'permissible disagreement at the margins'.

Wright's limited role for disagreement is more plausible than Gallie's. Yet Wright is still misled by the statistically dominant usage of 'borderline case'. 'Permissible disagreement' makes sense for relative borderline cases because there is agreement on which answer system to employ. But absolute borderline cases are not system relative.

Suppose a third party persuades us that our dispute over whether pudding is a solid is due to the vagueness of 'solid'. This intervention exposes our shared analytic error about the nature of the disputed proposition. The outsider *dissolves* our dispute by showing that pudding is a borderline case of 'solid'. You don't continue to contend that pudding is a solid and I don't continue to contradict you.

Nor do we leave our respective opinions intact by agreeing to disagree. We both *retract* our beliefs and become neutral on the question. Try to think of some belief you have that an absolute borderline *F* is really an *F*. This task is as mis-delegated as a do-it-yourself search for one of your false beliefs. 'Pudding is a borderline case of "solid" but I believe it is a solid' has the same absurdity as the Moorean 'Pudding is not a solid but I believe it is a solid'. You cannot represent your own belief as arbitrary. It is irrational to continue to believe that pudding is a solid after you sincerely concede that the belief has nothing more in favor of its truth than its negation. As a believer, you cannot be willing to assign it the same probability as a proposition about which you are neutral. But to assign it a higher probability is to evince confidence that you are tracking its truth. As a believer, you are picturing yourself as a non-accidental indicator of the truth and hence you are committed to the epistemic accessibility of the supposedly borderline statement. This Moorean thesis does not rest on acceptance of epistemicism. The absurdity is also predicted by, for instance, supervaluationism. The supervaluationist says that borderline statements lack truth-values. Since belief aims at truth, the supervaluationist cannot believe a statement he regards to be borderline. If others believe the statement, the supervaluationist must attribute conceptual confusion to them.

2. Subjective Borderline Cases

Just as a system can appear to answer when it is actually silent (hidden indeterminacy), the system can seem silent when it actually answers (hidden determinacy). This prompts a distinction between subjective and objective borderline cases.

The standard desiderata govern answer systems: consistency, completeness, simplicity, and so on. The statistical phenomenon of regression to the mean suggests that adherents of systems overestimate how well the system satisfies these criteria. The mere fact that you accept an answer system is evidence that some random error has led you to overrate how well it performs. You are more likely to be embarrassed by false determinacy than false indeterminacy.

Interest in false determinacies increased after Gödel's incompleteness results. Ironically, Gödel's result set the stage for a charming example of false *indeterminacy*. Roughly, Gödel proved 'This sentence is not provable in Peano arithmetic' is unprovable in Peano arithmetic. That makes 'This sentence is provable in Peano arithmetic' look like it should also be unprovable. But actually it is a theorem of Peano arithmetic (Boolos and Jeffrey 1974: 188–9)!

Consider the predicate 'bald barber who shaves all and only those who do not shave themselves'. The small percentage of English speakers who are familiar with Russell's barber paradox realize that, on strict logical grounds, this predicate is precise (because it is logically impossible for there to be a barber who shaves all and only those who do not shave themselves). All other speakers regard the predicate as vague. They exhibit characteristic puzzlement when it is inserted in a 'sorites' paradox. They sort cases into positives, negatives, and borderline cases—with just the right shading between the categories. But none of this 'vagueness' behavior suffices to make the predicate vague. This shows that vagueness is not a purely psychological notion. Consequently, there are no purely psychological explanations of the sorites paradox. This point affects even enlightening remarks such as Alvin Goldman's:

That our psychological apparatus should generate logically 'messy' behavior should come as no surprise. The familiar Sorites puzzles are predictable from a psychological perspective. We seem to have two mechanisms for forming categories and making categorization judgments. There is a mechanism that favors (or at least cheerfully accepts) binary, as opposed to graded, categorizations. There also seems to be a principle of 'good continuation', which dictates a preference for co-classifying objects that differ only minutely (on relevant dimensions). This pair of psychological principles leads to the Sorites puzzles. (Goldman 1989: 150)

The psychological principles Goldman cites are germane to the sorites paradox but they cannot fully predict where sorites paradoxes will arise. The predictions would be too broad because *covertly* precise predicates (such as 'bald barber who shaves all and only those who do not shave themselves') trigger the same psychological mechanisms as genuinely vague predicates (such as 'bald barber who shaves all others who do not shave themselves'). The predictions would also be too narrow because the mechanism is not triggered by covertly vague predicates. 'Large shirt that is both inside out and outside in' looks like a contradictory predicate but it is actually equivalent to the vague predicate 'large shirt that is inside out'. A sorites that uses the predicate will have its base step erroneously rejected by the majority of speakers.

The vagueness of some predicates is completely unknowable. Indeed, Alexander Bird has furnished me with a formula for defining them. Let U be any unknowable proposition. Let V be a vague predicate and P a precise one. Then define F as applying to an individual x if both x is V and U is true or if both x is P and U is false. For instance, let a number be birdy if it is small and the continuum hypothesis is true or if it exceeds a billion and the continuum hypothesis is false. 'Birdy' is either co-intensional with 'small number' or co-intensional with 'number greater than a billion'. It all depends on the continuum hypothesis. If psychology were enough to settle whether 'birdy' is vague, the continuum hypothesis could be proved by psychologists. But the continuum hypothesis is provably unprovable. So vagueness is not a purely psychological property.

Other counterexamples to psychologism about the sorites paradox rest on externalist premises about language. Recall Saul Kripke's
contention that 'phlogiston' and 'unicorn' are metaphysically empty
terms. According to Kripke, these terms directly refer if they refer at all.
If they lack referents, then the words are like empty names; they fail to
pick out anything in any possible world. Since vagueness is possession
of possible (absolute) borderline cases, a term which can be known to
be metaphysically empty cannot be vague. Unlike analytically empty
terms such as 'round square', their emptiness can only be discovered
through empirical inquiry. Evolutionary biologists who believed in
Piltdown man tried to situate this 'missing link' in a gradual sequence
that ran from pre-Piltdown man to modern man. Such evolutionary
sequences lend themselves to sorites construction. 'None of the
hominids of this era is a Piltdown man. If a hominid is not a Piltdown
man, then neither is of any of its descendants. Therefore, none the
hominids in subsequent eras is a Piltdown man.' This 'sorites' is
demonstrably sound.

Individualism about vagueness implies that the vagueness of a
speaker's concept arises from the intrinsic properties of his mind. But
this is implausible in view of our practice of borrowing predicates from
other speakers. Suppose I say 'The last word spoken by Fermat applies
to the number fifteen'. If Fermat's last word was 'odd', then my statement is precise and true. If Fermat's last word is 'small', then my statement is vague and of uncertain truth-value. Consequently, the intrinsic
properties of the speaker's mind are not enough to determine whether
the following is a sorites argument or a sound mathematical induction:

1. Fermat's last word applies to one.
2. If Fermat's last word applies to n, then Fermat's last word applies
   to $n + 2$.
3. Therefore, Fermat's last word applies to a trillion and one.

Such pure predicate borrowing is uncommon but one may also wonder
how common purely unborrowed usage is. We learn words from others
and are ready to be corrected when misusing them. I once said 'electron'
is vague because particles are sure to vary in how well they fit the term.
I was then informed that electrons are qualitatively identical. Whoops,
I was wrong about the vagueness of 'electron'! The ill-informed nature
of my use of 'electron' failed to create any borderline cases of 'electron'.

Semantic externalists stress linguistic division of labor. Knowing
what is going on in the mind of an ordinary speaker when he uses the

term 'electron' will not provide knowledge of whether 'electron' is vague. A social form of mentalism does better because it acknowledges the relevance of other minds, in particular, expert usage of 'electron'. But Kripke's examples of 'unicorn' and 'phlogiston' show how the vagueness of a term can turn on aspects of his physical environment. Just as psychology is not enough, sociology is not enough.

When applying the method of empathy, a Kripkean historian may take the perspective of a past chemist and describe 'phlogiston' as vague. For that exercise is aimed at illuminating the scientist's narrow psychology. 'Phlogiston' was indeed *subjectively* vague.

Externalists will agree that narrow psychology cannot predict whether a term is vague. But I want to persuade internalists of the same point. So I revert to examples involving predicates that look vague but which are *analytically* empty.

Diana Raffman (1994) maintains that the sorites victim eventually undergoes a progressive gestalt switch. In a two-faced gestalt switch, like that experienced with the Jastrow duck-rabbit, a single scene is viewed in an alternating way: duck, rabbit, duck, rabbit. In a progressive gestalt switch, there is a sequence of scenes that increasingly favors a second interpretation. For instance, as you view a solar eclipse, you first see the scene as an object losing a larger and larger part. An increasingly large circular portion of the sun seems to be consumed. But as the missing chunk grows, you are increasingly likely to view the missing part as an object in its own right—as the silhouette of the moon. Similarly, when you run down a sorites spectrum from green to yellow, your visual system eventually accepts the invitation to see the shade as yellow rather than green. The new perspective gives you a conflicting interpretation of the shades preceding the gestalt switch. Since the sorites victim always undergoes the switch, he cannot judge the spectrum of cases in a univocal way. Consequently, sorites arguments are inevitably equivocal. Or so says Raffman.

I have several doubts about Raffman's account (Sorensen 1998: 219–20). But the one I wish to press here is that she is confusing speaker meaning as statement meaning. Notice that Raffman's charge of equivocation fares poorly against a 'sorites' concocted with the perfectly precise predicate 'bald barber who shaves all and only those who do not shave themselves'. If logically naive speakers undergo gestalt switches, then those flip-flops might affect the meaning the speaker attributes to the phrase. But that does not amount to changing the meaning of the phrase. The phrase is logically empty regardless of whether people believe it to be empty.

Many vague phrases are too complex to ever be thought about. Iterating 'the mother of' a thousand times yields a grammatical predicate of English. No one will have gestalt switch concerning 'grand^{998}-mother'. Yet we know there are sorites arguments that use 'grand^{998}- mother' as the inductive predicate. The infinite class of sorites argument that are beyond our limits of memory and attention cannot owe their existence to a human penchant for equivocation. Human beings cannot commit the fallacy of equivocation for overwhelmingly complex arguments because they cannot even grasp these arguments.

Pseudo-vague predicates can have the same overwhelming complexity. The contradictions that we can efficiently check are just a small, unrepresentative sample of the total set of contradictions. Most logical falsehoods involve random sequences that do not yield to recursive techniques. They can only be detected through brute force. Super-computers wield far more brute force but still only a finite amount. For any super-computer, there are infinitely many contradictory formulas that are beyond its range. Now consider the predicates that result when we weave in vague predicates (as was done for 'bald barber who shaves all and only those who do not shave themselves'). No super-computer will be able to detect whether these statements are vague or precise. It is physically impossible for there to be an expert who will behave in the way required by sociological accounts of vagueness.

To distinguish a real sorites paradox from a bogus sorites paradox, we must introduce talk about the *correctness* of categorizations. Anyone who applies 'bald barber who shaves all and only those who do not shave themselves' to an individual (whether actual or possible) is making a demonstrable error. In particular, the base step of the barber 'sorites' argument is analytically false.

In a genuine sorites argument, there is no demonstrable error. Indeed, each specific step down the slippery slope is obligatory. Consider the sorites when it is cast as a patient chain argument:

A grave 10 inches deep is shallow.
If a grave 10 inches deep is shallow, then a grave 11 inches deep is shallow.
If a grave 11 inches deep is shallow, then a grave 12 inches deep is shallow.
.
.
.
Therefore, a grave 72 inches deep is shallow.

As the sorites sufferer peers down the slippery slope (from the perspective of the top step), he can see how to satisfy any particular commitment by taking another step down the slope. As the sorites sufferer looks *up* the slippery slope (from the uncomfortable bottom perspective), he sees how he could satisfy any particular step by refusing to take the preceding step. The problem is that his first and last commitments prevent him from satisfying *all* of his obligations. A man caught in a sorites is overcommitted. He is like a handyman who has promised to install a 10 by 10 carpet in a 9 by 9 room. The handyman can make the carpet fit any corner of the room. But he cannot make the carpet fit all the corners.

Knowledge of logic or psychology never puts the sorites sufferer in a position to specify his error and never helps him avoid the mistake in a future sorites. The mis-step is part of our competence, not our performance. It is a forced error and so cannot be traced to inattention, a slip, or confusion.

3. Are Relative Borderline Cases Enough?

Many subjective borderline cases are not borderline cases. All relative borderline cases *are* borderline cases—just ones that are relative to answer systems. The subjective vagueness of 'bald barber who shaves all and only those who do not shave themselves' issues from an avoidable error. In contrast, a relative borderline case is an impersonal property of the answer system.

Relative borderline cases may arise in precise disciplines such as mathematics. Suppose students are punished with the following assignment: list all the composite numbers less than 1,000. The students know that a composite number is any number that has a divisor other than one and itself. They can identify many of the easy cases. All the even numbers after 2 are composite. The students can also identify many large odd numbers, such as 999, as composites because these numbers have obvious divisors. But the students classify the remaining numbers as 'borderline cases' because they require more laborious tests.

'Composite' has relative borderline cases. But it cannot serve as the inductive predicate of a sorites argument. Almost every commentator on vagueness will agree that the sorites paradox requires a different kind of borderline case—what I have been calling an absolute borderline case. This classic conception of a borderline case rests on a contrast between factual ignorance and incompleteness in our representational system. Here is an excerpt from Charles Sanders Peirce's entry for 'vague' in the 1902 *Dictionary of Philosophy and Psychology*:

A proposition is vague when there are possible states of things concerning which it is *intrinsically uncertain* whether, had they been contemplated by the speaker, he would have regarded them as excluded or allowed by the proposition. By intrinsically 'uncertain we mean not uncertain in consequence of any ignorance of the interpreter, but because the speaker's habits of language were indeterminate. (Peirce 1902: 748)

Relative borderline cases arise from incompleteness in the available resources for answering the question. Absolute borderline cases arise from incompleteness in the question.

Characterization of this question incompleteness is the central difficulty. Is the incompleteness meaninglessness? Dr Seuss's children's story *The Thinks You Can Think* exhorts:

> Think! Think and wonder.
> Wonder and think.
> How much water can fifty-five elephants drink?
> You can wonder . . .
> How long is the tail of a ZONG?

The question about the fifty-five elephants is empirically challenging but 'How long is the tail of a zong?' is impervious to all inquiry. No one has any clue as to what would count as progress toward answering the question about the zong's tail. I cannot bring myself to believe that the zong's tail is a meter long because nothing counts as evidence in favor of the claim. The problem is more fundamental than implausibility; I cannot adopt any propositional attitude toward 'A zong's tail is one meter long' (at least if I take it to be meaningless). I cannot even *guess* or conceive of a zong's tail being a meter long. These limits of inquiry are a priori, available to me simply in virtue of my knowledge of English.

The hypothesis that vagueness is meaninglessness does correctly predict the absolute character of borderline cases. However, vagueness is so pervasive that the hypothesis implies that most of what we say is meaningless. This threatens the original contrast between 'How much water can fifty-five elephants drink?' with the meaningless 'How long is the tail of a zong?'. After all, there is a little vagueness in 'How much water can fifty-five elephants drink?'. Scientific utterances tend to be less vague than common-sense observations but both are still vague. Worse yet, the words used to frame the hypothesis that vagueness is meaninglessness are themselves vague, so the thesis implies its own meaninglessness.

We need a more controlled form of semantic shortfall. Intriguingly, key virtues of the hypothesis that vagueness is meaninglessness can be mimicked by the thesis that vague statements have potential meaning. Picture language dynamically, as a living growing thing. Why expect the meaning of each term to be fully mature? Our interests and knowledge change over time. Perhaps meaning comes in developmental varieties and stages. Unlike a meaningless term, a vague term has clear cases that could structure the way borderline cases can become clear cases. When a term is a precisified, there is no brute stipulation. There are natural lines of continuation. The ways in which a term can be given meaning themselves constitute a kind of meaning.

The reaction of those who ask whether a predicate applies to a borderline case is not blank incomprehension. We partially understand what has been asked. The vague query is a near miss of a successful question. The flaw is logical prematurity; we cannot answer the question because the meaning of a key term is not adequately developed. Consequently, applying a predicate to a borderline case yields a statement that is neither true nor false. Supervaluationism gives backbone to the notion of potential meaning. It specifies how terms are to be precisified. And supervaluationism tells us how to handle truth-value gaps in a way that preserves much of standard logic. In particular, all the tautologies of standard logic are endorsed with the help of the principle that a statement is true if it comes out true under all precisifications. For instance, 'A woman wearing only a net is naked' has no truth-value but it is true that 'Either a woman wearing only a net is naked or not' . Thus supervaluationists provide an attractive analysis of absolute borderline cases, one that sensitively courts the intuition that absolute borderline cases are qualitatively different from relative borderline cases. Other suitors should watch and learn.

4. Analyticity and the Absolute

Although many features of absolute borderline cases fit well with contemporary philosophy of language, there are some discordant aspects. Nowadays there is unease about the analytic/synthetic distinction. The notion of an absolute borderline case relies on this distinction by distinguishing between what is true in virtue of meaning and what is not.

This is the basis of Israel Scheffler's attack on 'absolute vagueness'. In the Quine tradition, Scheffler advocates open-minded inquiry. Echoing the flexible Quine of 'Two Dogmas of Empiricism' (rather than the steadfast Quine of *Philosophy of Logic*), Scheffler is willing to change logic to accommodate results from, say, quantum mechanics. Everything is negotiable.

To open this door, Scheffler must close the door on absolute borderline cases. He takes Quine's attack on the analytic/synthetic distinction to show that there is no significant contrast between matters of meaning and matters of fact. Admittedly, we are often unsure about what counts as an answer to a question. But that no more indicts our understanding of meaning than our understanding of the facts. Recall Quine's holistic vision of science:

Science is a unified structure, and in principle it is the structure as a whole, not its component statements one by one, that experience confirms or shows to be imperfect. Carnap maintains that ontological questions, and likewise questions of logical or mathematical principle, are questions not of fact but of choosing a convenient conceptual scheme or framework for science; and with this I agree only if the same be conceded for every scientific hypothesis. (Quine 1951*b*: 134)

Scheffler's own example in 1979 is 'Is there life on Mars?'. At that time, says Scheffler, no one could foresee what constitutes adequate evidence for life on Mars. (My memory of 1979 diverges.)

Like the nihilist, who thinks that vague predicates fail to refer to anything, Scheffler is an eliminativist about absolute borderline cases. Unlike the nihilist, Scheffler believes that ordinary predicates still have plenty of positive cases. Things are more or less as they seem—with the exception of important corrections from science. At certain junctures of inquiry, we do become puzzled about what is at issue. But

The process of advancing inquiry often resolves such indecision, and none should be prejudged as impervious to further investigation and resolution. Here is the positive reason for holding fast to classical logic as a framework capable of accommodating, without structural alteration, any type or degree of resolution of indecision, any elimination of ignorance. Absolute vagueness evaporates as a special category, to be replaced by a contextual counterpart signifying, in each case, a particular indecision theoretically soluble by further inquiry. (Scheffler 1979: 78)

Scheffler's words have a positivistic after-taste. Granted, rejection of the analytic/synthetic distinction eliminates *one* source of unanswerability.

But science itself erects limits. The inevitability of measurement error first became prominent early in the study of thermodynamics. The theory of relativity imposes a speed limit that confines our knowledge to what lies within our light cone. Astronomy shows that the universe is so immense that virtually all of it lies beyond the range of detailed inspection. In addition to these a posteriori limits, computer science furnishes a priori limits (studies of NP-completeness, the measurement of degrees of unsolvabilty, and so on).

Most psychology portrays the mind as a collection of modules. Instead of relying on general intelligence, psychologists explain human abilities as the joint effect of specialized homunculi who work like idiot savants. There is one module for face recognition, another for vision, yet another for language. These in turn are composed of more rudimentary homunculi. Since this cognitive architecture trades rationality for speed, we are prone to illusions in which homunculi disagree, talk over one another, and interact erratically. Since homunculi are dogmatic, the illusions are recalcitrant. On the bright side, these illusions are evidence about how the mind is constituted. Modular psychology implies that the mind is open to study by the same methods as the body. Psychologists can take the mind apart into functional systems. Those systems cleave into subsystems and sub-subsystems.

Philosophers tend to associate illusions with skepticism. But since illusions are signs of modular construction, they are actually reason for scientific hope. Think of how useful illusions have been in understanding vision. By studying how our eyes malfunction in unusual circumstances, we can infer how they function in normal circumstances. Similarly, slips of the tongue, garden-path sentences, and speech pathology furnish linguists with important clues about our language faculty. My speculations about linguistic illusions do not undercut the value of linguistic intuitions or impugn any other aspect of linguistic methodology. As far linguistics go, I am a company man who endorses the cheerful corporate work ethic.

Even so pessimistic implications of modular construction need to be acknowledged. For instance, Noam Chomsky conjectures that much of science builds on innate endowments. Our intellectual ascents require the running starts provided by specialized faculties. Areas of scientific progress and stagnation follow the contour of this underlying bedrock—like the architecture of Manhattan. Jerry Fodor (1983), and more recently and severely, Colin McGinn (1993), have elaborated Chomsky's subterranean themes.

If we take science seriously, we also need to take seriously its implications for the scope and limits of human knowledge. An unromantic survey of scientific implications for human cognition yields little support for the optimistic epistemology we hear at commencement speeches and in science documentaries. Optimistic epistemology may have motivated much scientific progress. But science has not endorsed the empirical assumptions made by the ideal of an unfettered intellect that can boldly strike out in any direction. Instead, science has ungratefully challenged those assumptions. Just as science dethrones us from the center of the universe and dethrones us from a position at the top of the great chain of being, science dethrones us from the center of epistemology.

In short, reservations about the analytic/synthetic distinction do not show that there is something defective in the notion of an absolute borderline case. Of course, there could be other conceptual problems. The distinction between absolute and relative borderline cases resembles the distinction between absolute and relative motion. Everybody in Isaac Newton's era believed that some objects moved relative to other objects. But Newton believed that there was also an absolute form of motion. That is, even if there were only one object in the universe, that lone object could move. Relativists, such as Gottfried Leibniz, believed that all motion was relative motion. (Well, eventually Samuel Clarke forced him to concede that there was some absolute motion.) Strong relativists, such as George Berkeley, believed that absolute motion was conceptually impossible. Similarly, one might suspect that absolute borderline cases are conceptually impossible.

However, my concern is with a weaker sort of relativist. In particular, I am concerned with the eliminativist who merely argues that absolute borderline cases are dispensable: everything worth saying in the vocabulary of absolute borderline cases can be said with relative borderline cases.

Like most vagueness theorists (but unlike the other epistemicists) I am an absolutist. I believe there are two kinds of borderline cases. Only absolute borderline cases constitute vagueness. Part of my job is to challenge the explanatory claims made on behalf of relative borderline cases. I take up this task in the next chapter.

2 Intellectual Embarrassment without Vagueness

Other epistemicists contend that relative borderline cases provide sufficient explanatory resources for vagueness. Consequently, there is no need for research into absolute borderline cases.

I concede that relative borderline cases explain some of the intellectual embarrassment that is widely assumed to be a defining feature of vagueness. But I shall argue that such phenomena have nothing to do with vagueness *per se*. The embarrassment is actually due to limited discriminability rather than vagueness itself. Many of the stereotypical properties of the sorites paradox are actually more generic properties that can be possessed by slippery-slope arguments employing precise predicates.

1. A Walk in the Woods

People are often suspected of judging similar cases dissimilarly. Sometimes this 'inconsistency' can be exposed with a forced march down a slippery slope. Let us audit one of these interrogations as scholarly psychologists.

We could situate this thought experiment anywhere. But in the spirit of academic junkets, we shall go to a French villa. The beautiful Madame Inquisitor will be interrogating Monsieur Suspect. Monsieur Suspect has been chosen because he is suspected of drawing distinctions without differences. The choice of Monsieur Suspect has been influenced by his excellent command of English. We have paid extra to keep everything in English.

Having been apprised of our fondness for the French countryside, Madame Inquisitor escorts all concerned to a cultivated row of trees. Unbeknownst to Monsieur Suspect, the first tree is 1 foot tall and each of the 93 subsequent trees is 1 foot taller than its predecessor. Madame Inquisitor informs Monsieur Suspect that his first task is to distinguish the short trees from the non-short trees.

There is a commotion. Monsieur Suspect protests that 'short' is vague. He will not participate in a sorites paradox!

Mon Dieu! At first we psychologists fear that the interrogation will end before it begins. (Granted, this is a fear of questionable coherence but we psychologists tolerate dissonance.) Madame Inquisitor unexpectedly accommodates the dissident. She graciously agrees to substitute a precise term for 'short', namely, 'less than 50 feet tall'. This avoids the vagueness essential to the sorites paradox. We visiting scholars worry about *notre remboursement*.

Sensing our alarm, Madame Inquisitor takes us aside with a wink: 'Be at ease *mes amis. La configuration psychologique de réponse* would be the same if Monsieur Suspect complied with the request to use "short". You will still learn something about how *les hommes* react to a sorites argument. *En effet,* you will be better off because you will not confound a variable *psychologique* with a variable *de langue.*'

Madame Inquisitor rejoins Monsieur Suspect. From her little purse, she pulls a big list of statements:

1. Tree 1 is less than 50 feet tall.
2. Tree 2 is less than 50 feet tall.

 .
 .
 .

100. Tree 100 is less than 50 feet a tall.

She asks Monsieur Suspect to mark which statements are true and which are false. He has ordinary visual acuity and no access to surveying equipment. Consequently, Monsieur Suspect's knowledge of the tree heights is limited to large intervals. He can know that a tree is between 10 and 20 feet but cannot know that it is between 14 and 16 feet.

Across the English Channel, Professor Williamson analyzes inexact knowledge with the help of margin for error principles. Knowledge requires reliability. If my judgment is reliable, then it would have been right had circumstances been a little different. Otherwise, the judgment was right by luck. Consequently, knowledge requires a margin for error. If Monsieur Suspect says that tree 49 is below 50 feet, then we would conclude that he did not really know that tree 49 was below 50 feet. If he says that tree 10 is below 50 feet, we will credit him with knowledge because the judgment was safely within his range of reliable judgment.

People are sensitive to their limitations and so tend to be less confident as their margin for error diminishes. In the case at hand, Monsieur Suspect believes 1 and disbelieves 100. Neighboring statements in the sequence do not significantly differ in credibility. So it seems that we psychologists can never attribute a belief in statement n without also attributing a belief in statement $n + 1$. Applying this co-attribution principle to our attribution of belief to 1, we attribute belief to 2. And from this attribution of belief to 2, we attribute belief to 3. Continuing the application of the co-attribution principle in this ascending order would compel us to say Monsieur Suspect believes each of the 100 statements.

Oops, that attributes too much belief.

Our reservation about the co-attribution principle is amplified by the reversibility of the co-attribution principle. Attributing *disbelief* to a statement requires that disbelief also be attributed to the negation of its neighbor. Reversing the co-attribution principle leads us to extend disbelief from 100 to 99 and from there to 98 and so on to 1.

Oops, that attributes too much disbelief.

These over-attributions are worse as a pair. Collectively, they force us to attribute both belief and disbelief to each and every member of the list. In addition to being uncharitable, this attribution of directly opposed beliefs to every statement is independently implausible. Monsieur Suspect clearly has unconflicted belief in statement 1 and unconflicted disbelief in statement 100.

Despite the initial plausibility of the co-attribution principle, there must be a statement n that Monsieur Suspect believes and a statement $n + 1$ that Monsieur Suspect fails to believe. Instead of attributing a solid block of directly opposed beliefs, we should instead postulate raw incompleteness.

There is an air of inconsistency in this failure to extend belief to the next case. Monsieur Suspect fails to treat like cases alike. Monsieur Suspect sheepishly acknowledges the overwhelming pairwise similarities. Suppose that Monsieur Suspect believes tree 40 is less than 50 feet tall but believes tree 41 is not. If we were to bring the omission to his attention, he would instantly repudiate either the belief or the disbelief. Moreover, the correction would be involuntary. Suppose I offered him $1,000 for believing that tree 40 is less than 50 feet tall but tree 41 is not. He would not be able to sincerely claim the prize.

I am *not* going to offer Monsieur Suspect $1,000 if, for some n, he believes tree n is less than 50 feet tall while not believing tree $n + 1$ is 50 feet tall. For he could win the prize by demonstrating that he must have formed a belief in this pattern somewhere down the series. Monsieur Suspect cannot say exactly where this belief gap occurs. But the prize did not require that the location be specified; only the existence of the belief gap was required.

Monsieur Suspect's failure to treat like cases alike is involuntary. He cannot choose to believe. Hence Monsieur Suspect cannot choose to believe one proposition and not believe a proposition that is insignificantly different from it. However, Monsieur Suspect can do this unwittingly. The break in belief happens inevitably though there is no need for the break to occur at any particular point. The slippery-slope suspect is like a rigid seesaw that has equally large, overwhelming weights placed simultaneously on both extremes. The seesaw must snap. Reinforcing weak points of the seesaw would only change the place where it snaps.

The location of the error is not stable. If the speaker believes statement 40 but not statement 41, then he cannot be aware of it. Pointing out the omission extinguishes the error but causes another error of omission to pop up elsewhere. The premises for the existence of the omissive error are still intact.

Given the symmetry of the cases, there is no particular reason to end belief at one statement rather than another. Consequently, there is no reason to suppose that people have the same pattern uniformly over time. It may well be that their pattern of belief and unbelief vacillates in response to various non-rational factors. It isn't as if they are flitting between well-worked-out alternatives as to where the line is. Their belief pattern has the ragged character of the absent-minded.

When people 'draw the line' in the course of a warning (or an offer of resolution), they are trying to avoid instability. They may concede that they have no reason to draw the line in this place but will insist that they do have a reason to draw the line somewhere—and reason to stick to that arbitrary decision. These artificial bright lines, created by fiat, are an important defense. Predators and parasites, both literal and figurative, constantly ply the technique of gradual encroachment.

Some people apply the anti-encroachment defense to the slippery-slope paradox. They go down the slippery slope a short way but then dig in their heels. This strategy might be appropriate if the goal were to avoid making inconsistent assertions. However, the strategy does not work at the level of belief because belief is involuntary.

2. *The Normativity of Belief*

We psychologists are reluctant to make value judgments. We should describe, not prescribe. (Oops, there goes one.) Unfortunately, we cannot sustain this neutrality when attributing beliefs.

Belief attribution is normative because it is part of an explanatory enterprise. We postulate beliefs and desires that best explain the subject's actions. The basic idea is that the beliefs and desires lead the agent to choose the alternative that best satisfies the desires relative to his beliefs about the situation. When that is so, the agent is being rational. Irrationalities are deviations from this simple model. As evident from the literature on weakness of will, irrationalities are ill understood even if common. Since simpler, comprehensible explanations are better, there is an explanatory preference for rationality. Theorists vary in their assessment of how strong the preference is but even a mild preference is enough to introduce normative considerations into a belief description. The question of what someone actually believes is influenced by the question of what he ought to believe.

The believer is in the same interpretive position as everyone else; he must attribute beliefs and desires to himself that make the best sense of what he does. So there is pressure to minimize the attribution of inconsistent beliefs by all concerned. Since Monsieur Suspect is opinionated at both ends of the (1)–(100) series, he is caught in a pincer movement. He is squeezed from above and from below toward an inconsistency. The only escape is incompleteness. This is not the judicious incompleteness of a thoughtful 'No comment'. This is the incompleteness of the mental slip, the memory breakdown, and the inferential tic. Since this retreat is the least bad outcome, we should interpret the slippery-slope suspect as incomplete.

Monsieur Suspect is not alone in his jagged incompleteness. We impartial observers, who only wished to accurately report his plight, fall into the same arbitrariness at the interpretive level. The puzzling list for us involves the psychological predicate 'believes':

1.1. Monsieur Suspect believes that tree 1 is less than 50 feet.

1.2. Monsieur Suspect believes that tree 2 is less than 50 feet.

.

.

.

1.100. Monsieur Suspect believes that tree 100 is less than 50 feet.

We want to assign the truth-value true to 1.1 and false to 1.100. We want to treat like cases alike. Statements (1.1)–(1.100) are pairwise alike in belief-worthiness. It would be arbitrary to believe n without believing $n + 1$. But then we would wind up both believing and disbelieving all of the propositions. Better then, to be arbitrary. At some point, we stop believing. This mental process is arational like falling asleep.

We psychologists might become the subjects of a yet higher order study by meta-psychologists. The meta-psychologists will fall into their own arbitrariness. They will need to use the vague predicate 'believes Monsieur Suspect believes' when describing our plight. Meta-meta-psychologists will need the vague predicate 'believes the psychologist believes Monsieur Suspect believes'. And so on. There is no privileged vantage point that is immune from arbitrariness. The project of trying to describe the arbitrariness is infected by that very arbitrariness.

3. The wrong distinction

Could psychologists escape the problem by substituting a precise term for 'belief'? We saw that this strategy failed when the precise 'less than 50 feet' was exchanged for the vague 'short'. What creates the vulnerability to the slippery slope is our limited ability to discern differences, not vagueness itself. So the real escape strategy should focus on the discriminable/indiscriminable distinction, not the precision/vagueness distinction. For instance, a slippery slope can usually be constructed with 'short student' and 'at most 1.7 meters in height' with a class of thirty students. But normally not with 'extremely short student'. Of course, if we turn our attention to *possible* cases, then there will be borderline cases for most vague predicates. But the same goes for most precise predicates. There are possible (relative) borderline cases for 'at most 1.69483722 meters in height'. There are also corresponding slippery-slope arguments.

We psychologists should know better. Experimenters routinely force errors by depriving subjects of resources needed to execute a task. Rushing a subject through a recitation leads to systematic performance errors that illuminate the reading process. Forcing patients to read barely discernible letters helps eye doctors assess their visual acuity.

Forced errors are also a side-effect of demands for decisiveness. Smooth conduct of law and games forbids shoulder shrugging by adjudicators. The judge or umpire must speedily render opinions even when the issues are borderline cases.

People can draw the line between coarse-grained alternatives that are within their power of discrimination. But Madame Inquisitor chooses fine-grained alternatives that are beyond the subject's power of discrimination. The fineness of the alternatives makes the subject pairwise indifferent between neighboring alternatives. Since the subject is also oppositely partisan at the extremes, he cannot complete his belief pattern in a coherent way.

Monsieur Suspect could escape his arbitrariness by enhancing his power of discrimination. With the help of surveying equipment, he could acquire a coherent, complete belief pattern with respect to the trees. This equipment would enable him to detect that tree 49 is the last tree that is less than 50 feet tall. The same applies with vague predicates such as 'tall ship'. With unaided vision, a shoreline observer can see that the first ship in a semi-circle is tall and the last ship is not. But he cannot tell where the tall ships end. With binoculars, he can see that the semi-circle is askew; one segment consists of short, near ships while the remaining segment is composed of a more distant row of tall ships. In both cases of enhanced discrimination, inexact knowledge is supplanted by exact knowledge.

The transformation into exact knowledge is not always possible. When the problem is set beyond our range of any means of discrimination, we are stuck with inexact knowledge. Many problems are outside this range because our powers of measurement are always limited. For instance, measurement instruments themselves affect what they measure.

We cannot distinguish precise slippery slopes from sorites arguments on the grounds that there the precise slippery slopes always offer us an opportunity to switch from inexact knowledge to exact knowledge. Sometimes the switch is physically impossible.

One apparent asymmetry remains. In the case of a precise slippery-slope argument, there is a genuine counterexample to the induction step. There is a last point at which the precise predicate applies. So even if there is no way to detect this last point, there is no temptation to revise logic. In the case of the sorites paradox, there does not seem to be a last point. Hence, there is a real challenge to standard logic.

4. Indiscriminable Concepts

In effect, brother epistemicists have met this challenge by arguing that vagueness only involves relative borderline cases. The logical conservatism that is natural for these borderline cases would then extend to vague predicates.

Timothy Williamson executes this basic strategy in formidable detail. He says that in a sorites argument, the inexactness of one's knowledge issues from unclarity about which concept is being employed. If the inductive predicate is 'noonish', then I cannot tell whether it means 'within 5 minutes of noon' or 'within 6 minutes of noon' or . . .

Thus a vague term introduces a new dimension of difficulty to sorting. If I have a precise predicate, then my uncertainty is confined to the issue of whether a given individual fits the predicate. If I have a vague predicate, then I have a further, underlying uncertainty about which criterion should be employed in the sorting.

Inexact knowledge about which concept lies behind a word is not sufficient for vagueness. When I first learn a new technical term, my understanding is coarse. I cannot discriminate which of many fine-grained alternatives is correct. But I can resolve many of the borderline cases by further immersion in the practices in which the concept plays an important role.

Inexact knowledge about concepts can also ride piggyback on other inexact knowledge. As it happens, Madame Inquisitor's trees have precise phrases carved in them. Tree 1 bears the inscription 'is at most 1 foot in height', tree 2 has the phrase 'is at most 2 feet in height', tree 3 has 'is at most 3 feet in height', and so on.

Madame Inquisitor instructs Monsieur Suspect on his second task. He must sort trees into those that satisfy at least one of the phrases carved on a tree that is less than 50 feet in height. For instance, tree 1 obviously satisfies the phrase carved on tree 10, namely, 'is at most 10 feet in height'. So tree 1 is a clear positive case of a tree that satisfies one of the inscriptions carved in a tree that is at most 50 feet in height.

To abbreviate the process, Madame Inquisitor introduces the term 'arbor-short' to cover exactly those trees that satisfy at least one of the predicates on trees that are at most 50 feet in height. Since Monsieur Suspect only has inexact knowledge of which trees are at most 50 feet tall, he only has inexact knowledge of which trees are arbor-short. Thus there can be a slippery-slope argument using 'arbor-short' which involves unclarity about the meaning of 'arbor-short'. However, 'arbor-short' is a precise predicate. It is intensionally equivalent to 'at most 50 feet in height'.

So what is the difference between 'short' and 'arbor-short'? Intuitively, the difference is that 'arbor-short' cannot be vague because it has a knowable threshold. But this contrast can be rectified with cousins of 'arbor-short' that have unknowable thresholds. They use quantities that involve inevitable measurement errors. Hence they are unknowable to Neanderthals or Martians or any other physically possible beings.

So what is the difference between 'short' and the cousins of 'arbor-short'? Now the tempting answer is: the cousins are known to have (albeit unknowable) thresholds but 'short' is not known to have a threshold. Indeed, some would boldly strengthen the contrast and say that 'short' is known not to have a threshold.

No epistemicist can accept this contrast. Epistemicists claim to know that there is a threshold for 'short'. The cousins of 'arbor-short' show how it is formally possible for words to have unknowable meanings and for these words to give rise to slippery-slope arguments that have stereotypical features of the sorites argument. Unfortunately, these models are artificial. 'Short' does not seem to draw its uncertainty from measurement error (contrary to what I conjecture in *Blindspots*). The epistemicist wants to explain (*a*) how semantic indiscriminability can arise naturally and (*b*) why there is an appearance of boundarylessness.

Williamson appeals to chaos to solve the first explanatory problem. He connects margin for error principles with unstable word usage. If slight differences in word usage affect which concept lies behind the word, then I cannot precisely identify which concept I am using. The factors that determine which concept lies behind 'short' could be analogous to the factors that determine the weather. Meteorologists have a good understanding of the laws that govern weather and have lots of data from satellites and observation stations. This allows for reliable short-term weather prediction. But long-range weather prediction is impossible because of the 'butterfly effect'; very small changes (the air currents produced by a butterfly beating its wings in Tokyo) can have large-scale effects (a hurricane in London). If usage determines the meaning of 'short' in this chaotic fashion, then the threshold of 'short' is humanly impossible to detect because there is no way to discriminate between a range of concepts.

Those holding the traditional attitude toward borderline cases will be displeased by the relativity of Williamson's borderline cases. What is chaotic varies with cognizers. But absolute borderline cases are uniform. Even by terrestrial standards, it is anthropocentric to take human unknowability as the standard for borderline status. As Ian Tattersall (2000) tells us in his *Scientific American* article 'Once We were Not Alone', there have been at least fifteen species of hominids besides *Homo Sapiens*. Our uniqueness is a recent state.

Williamson also needs to weave exceptions into his account to address unpredicted pockets of precision. He grants that natural kind terms are stabilized by natural boundaries and that measurement can stabilize meaning. He also needs to explain how algorithms stabilize meaning. For instance, binary numerals are perfectly precise. But as they become larger and more complex, it is more difficult to figure out what they mean. Eventually we reach numerals so unwieldy that people will disagree or shrug their shoulders or just get their meaning right by luck. Computers have a large range of reliable performance with binary numerals but they will also be overwhelmed. Indeed, Gregory Chaitin (1986) has a theorem modeled on Berry's paradox: no computer can produce a sequence that is more complex than itself. So although there is a numeral for each natural number, only a finite subset of them can be used in a stable way. There is no difference in precision between the stable finite minority and the unstable infinite majority.

Williamson will insist that the meaning of the binary numerals is stable in virtue of the algorithm that assigns a binary numeral to each number. But Williamson also concedes there is a function, which assigns 'noonish' to all the noonish times. Why should only one of these functions stabilize usage? The description of the function linking binary numerals and numbers may be easier to know than the description of the function linking 'noonish' to noonish times. But the comparison also holds between functions for short random sequences of 1's and 0's and functions for large random sequences of 1's and 0's. These unwieldy functions are no less precise than their shorter, easier to know brethren.

5. The Completeness Concern

Timothy Williamson develops parallels between epistemicism and supervaluationism. This is implicit in his 'logic of clarity' (presented in the appendix of *Vagueness* and featured in his later 1999 treatment of higher order vagueness).

Williamson's basic premise is that since we do not know which concept we are using, we do not know which language we are using. This opens a structural analogy:

As a first approximation, for the supervaluationist, definiteness is truth under all sharpenings of the language consistent with what speakers have already fixed about its semantics ('admissible sharpenings'); for the epistem-icist, definiteness is truth under all sharp interpretations of the language indiscriminable from the right one. In both cases, we hold everything precise constant as we vary the interpretation. (Williamson 1999: 128)

The idea is natural for the supervaluationist. An admissible sharpening completes a language in a way that does not contradict the past decisions of the speakers. If there are only ten sharpenings of 'artwork' and

'All artworks are artifacts' comes out true under each of them, then 'All artworks are artifacts' is definitely true.

At first blush, the idea also seems natural for an epistemicist. If there are only ten sharpenings of 'artwork' and 'All artworks are artifacts' comes out knowably true under all of them, then 'All artworks are artifacts' is knowably true.

But there is a hitch: how do I know whether I have considered *all* the sharpenings of 'artwork'? Each sharpening of 'artwork' may be known to be a sharpening that makes 'All artworks are artifacts' true. But if there is no way to know that this set of sharpenings is complete, then no one can know 'All artworks are artifacts'. This uncertainty can arise from the vagueness of 'admissible sharpening'. Some interpretations of 'artwork' are clearly admissible while others are clearly inadmissible. In between are interpretations that are borderline cases of 'admissible sharpening'.

Supervaluationism and epistemicism diverge in the case in which we cannot know (for reasons of vagueness) whether we have exhausted every sharpening but each sharpening can be individually known to make the statement true. In this circumstance, supervaluationism implies that the statement is definitely true while epistemicism implies the statement is indefinite (though true).

Given Professor Williamson's commitment to epistemicism, his account of definiteness is too broad. A statement can fail to be definitely true even though it is true 'under all sharp interpretations of the language indiscriminable from the right one'.

My objection applies equally to a more cautious variation of Williamson's principle. Williamson and I agree that a statement is true if it comes out true under all sharpenings. We disagree over his claim that a statement is definitely true if it comes out true under all sharpenings. We would also disagree if Williamson instead said that a statement is definitely true if it comes out *definitely* true under all sharpenings. For that matter, we would disagree if that italicized *definitely* were iterated any number of times. A statement could be *definitely, definitely, . . . , definitely* true under each sharpening and yet still be indefinite. Or so say I.

In deference to the supervaluationist, let me restate the completeness concern in a way that does not presuppose that there really is a correct interpretation. Suppose it is indefinite whether 'All artworks are artifacts' comes out true under all admissible sharpenings. The super-valuationist says a statement is definitely true when and only when it comes out true under all admissible sharpenings. So the supervalu-ationist would say that it is indefinite whether 'All artworks are artifacts' is definite. In contrast, the epistemicist should say that 'All artworks are artifacts' is *definitely* indefinite. The epistemicist should not require that there be a sharpening under which the statement comes out false.

The epistemicist is a more expansive futilitarian than the supervalu-ationist. If 'All artworks are artifacts' is indefinite, then the supervalu-ationist will infer that there exists a precisification under which it comes out true and a precisification under which it comes out false. For mixed precisifications are the supervaluationist's only basis for assigning borderline status. The epistemicist will regard this inference as hasty. The epistemicist thinks that the statement could be indefinite even if all the precisifications come out true or all the precisifications come out false.

Supervaluationism implies a Barcan formula for the definite operator (read '**Def**p' as 'It is definite whether p'):

$$(p)\mathbf{Def}p \supset \mathbf{Def}(p)p$$

If an epistemicist insists on having a logic of clarity, he should insist that this not be a theorem. After all, everyone agrees that the corres-ponding Barcan formula for knowledge fails:

$$(p)\Diamond Kp \supset \Diamond K(p)p$$

The supervaluationist believes vagueness is a purely semantic phe-nomenon and so sees little resemblance between the two Barcan formulae. However, any theorist who regards vagueness as a species of ignorance should see a damning resemblance. (I include intuitionists —especially those, like Crispin Wright, who closely approximate epistemicism.)

Williamson might hope that knowledge of completeness is *never* needed in the evaluation of sharpenings. After all, universal generaliza-tions can sometimes be known without complete enumeration. I know that all men are mortal on the basis of induction. I know all men are male human beings on the basis of definition. Maybe vagueness creates a special situation in which access to the completeness of the enumera-tion is *never* necessary. As long as each admissible sharpening is such that the speaker can know 'All artworks are artifacts' is true under that sharpening, then he can know 'All artworks are artifacts'. He may not be able to know that he knows. But that's irrelevant because the KK principle (if you know, then you know you know) is false.

The failure of KK is crucial for any epistemicist account of higher order vagueness. A genuinely indefinite definite statement can be known even though it cannot be known to be known. The vagueness of 'know' guarantees that there will be many such cases. But when the completeness condition is violated, the knowledge attribution fails at the first level, not the second.

I have no interest in jacking up standards for attributing knowledge. The completeness concern conforms to our ordinary practice of knowledge attributions. When strangers see me with my two boys, they sometimes ask whether all of my children are boys. The observer sees all of my children. He sees that each child is a boy. Yet he must ask me whether all of my children are all boys. Does the stranger merely fail to know that he knows that all my children are boys? Am I being picky when I say that the stranger does not know?

The completeness requirement can be violated even when one scrupulously acquires justified true belief that one has considered all the alternatives. Suppose the stranger first asks my wife whether I have any further children. In an unusual moment of absent-mindedness, she misconstrues the question to be about my friend who, as it happens, also has exactly two children—both boys and both in view. So she answers 'He has no further children'. The epistemically responsible stranger winds up with a justified true belief that all of my children are boys. For the stranger, there is no epistemic possibility of there being further children. Yet the stranger does not have knowledge that all of my children are boys.

The completeness concern does not over-intellectualize knowledge. The completeness concern defeats knowledge that p only when the alternatives to p have been exhausted by luck. A reliabilist could incorporate the completeness concern by demanding that the knower be designed in a way that ensures an exhaustive elimination of alternatives. Engineers design coin-counting machines to satisfy the completeness concern. The machines must be free of pockets and adhesive surfaces that might prevent all the coins from dropping into coin-detecting mechanisms.

Let me convey the gritty character of the completeness concern with a scene from the 1971 movie Dirty Harry. The tough San Francisco police detective 'Dirty' Harry Callahan has just foiled a bank robbery. There has been much shooting. He has a pistol pointed at a wounded robber. The robber thoughtfully eyes his loaded rifle which is within reach. Harry smiles and says

I know what you are thinking: Did he fire six shots or only five? Well, to tell you the truth, in all the excitement I kind of lost track myself. But being that this is a .44 Magnum, the most powerful handgun in the world and which could blow your head clean off, you've got to ask yourself one question: Do I feel lucky? Well, do you punk?.

We demand knowledge of completeness even when attributing knowledge to animals. Recall the clever monkey who stays up a tree until the hunter leaves. The hunter tries to outsmart the monkey by entering the jungle with a partner and then having the partner depart. But the monkey counts. Two hunters went in, only one went out, so one remains. The smart monkey waits in the tree. The next day, the hunter recruits an additional partner. The monkey sees three hunters enter but sees only two leave. He is not fooled. The hunter adds a further partner after each failure. On the seventh day, the monkey loses count. He climbs down, and is captured. Turn your attention from the monkey's seventh day plight to the happier sixth day. After all six hunters had left, the monkey climbed down and was not captured. Although each hunter was known by the monkey to have departed, the monkey did not know that all the hunters had departed. For the misfortune on the seventh day demonstrates that the monkey was not able to reliably execute a complete enumeration of the hunters.

Concerns about completeness apply to interpretations. Hunter-gatherers regularly make deals with each other. As in all contractual reasoning, hunter-gatherers must be vigilant against loopholes and misunderstandings. Hence, our ancestors had an interest in checking whether key conditions of the pair of promises hold under all admissible interpretations.

This quality control effort goes well beyond contracts. Hunter-gatherers give each other directions, contrive jokes and compliments, craft proposals and recipes. They need to recover from miscommunications and diagnose verbal disputes. Interpretation is not just for French intellectuals conversing in cafés.

Williamson does picture precisifications in a heady way. He assigns each predicate *infinitely* many interpretations. This magnitude of alternatives would stop us finite beings from knowing 'All artworks are artifacts' by enumeration. Our knowledge of the generalization would have to be explained in the same way we know arithmetic truths that have infinite domains.

Whatever the details, such knowledge is just as sensitive to completeness concerns. Here is an illustration. A perfect number is a number whose positive divisors (except for itself) sum to itself. For instance, 6 is perfect ($1 + 2 + 3 = 6$) as are 28 ($1 + 2 + 4 + 7 + 14 = 28$) and 496 ($1 + 2 + 4 + 8 + 16 + 31 + 62 + 124 + 248 = 496$). Euclid proved that $2^{n-1}(2^n - 1)$ always yields an even perfect number if the parenthetical expression is a prime. Two thousand years later, Leonard Euler proved that Euclid's formula is exhaustive—that it yields *all* the even perfect numbers. Euler's result sets in motion a further line of thought. Primes that fit the parenthetical expression are known as Mersenne primes. A Mersenne prime is a prime of the form $2^n - 1$ such as 3, 7, 31, and so on. In light of Euler's result, mathematicians know that there are exactly as many even perfect numbers as Mersenne primes. Mathematicians conjecture that the number of Mersenne primes is infinite. If this conjecture is correct, then there is also an infinity of even perfect numbers. More ancient is the conjecture that there are no odd perfect numbers. (It has been proved that any odd perfect number must exceed 10^{300} and must be divisible by a prime power exceeding 10^{20}.) If there are no odd perfect numbers, then each perfect number is such that it is known to have the form $2^{p-1}(2^p - 1)$ and yet it is not known that all perfect numbers have this form. If both conjectures are true, then there are infinitely many perfect numbers each of which is known to have the form $2^{p-1}(2^p - 1)$ even though it is unknown that all perfect numbers have the form.

Infinity does not inhibit the logicians' completeness concerns. Consider a deductive system that has the axiom schema $n = n$ but no inference rules. In this system, one can prove $1 = 1$, $2 = 2$, and so on but cannot prove that $(n)(n = n)$. This 'omega incompleteness' can be remedied by introducing a rule that would entitle the inference from a set of infinitely many premises. But this omega rule is a significant departure from the classical conception of a proof which is restricted to derivations of a finite length. The completeness concern is a rugged, universal feature of knowledge and demonstration.

Supervaluationism overgeneralizes from one kind of predicament—having too many possibilities. This 'embarrassment of riches' is the most colorful obstacle. Witness how epistemologists focus upon skeptical 'counter-possibilities'. However, epistemologists concede that inquiry can be blocked by a wide variety of phenomena: circularity, unbelievability, inexpressibility, Gettier defeaters, and on, and on. True, these duller obstacles do not normally suffice for vagueness. But the same goes for counter-possibilities. The inquiry resistance that constitutes vagueness must be absolute. But no epistemic obstacle has a monopoly on recalcitrance.

The scruffy nature of knowledge leads me to predict that there are further divergences. For instance, I have doubts that knowledge collects over conjunction. Consider a student who knows each answer to a hundred question logic test. Does he thereby know the conjunction of these answers? When the student learns that he answered perfectly, he is pleasantly *surprised*. Although confident of each answer, he was not confident in the conjunction. This suggests that one could know that 'All artworks are artifacts' comes out true under each sharpening, know that the set of sharpenings is exhaustive, and still not know whether 'All artworks are artifacts' is true. This failure of knowledge to collect over conjunction need not be due to idiosyncratic limitations of memory and attention span. (This kind of case is developed in Ch. 6.)

Of course, Professor Williamson will want to idealize this limitation away as an accident of human psychology. Maybe an ordinary student fails to know but an *ideal* student does know. This maneuver competes with Williamson's desire to put a human face on vagueness. The more he idealizes to save principles of epistemic logic, the less basis he has to preferentially relativize borderline cases to human beings. Fondness for a tidy logic of clarity is in tension with Williamson's anthropocentrism.

My view is that vagueness inherits the untidiness of knowledge. The logic of clarity will not reveal the structure of higher order vagueness. Epistemology has more to teach about higher order vagueness than modal logic.

6. Who is Right?

So far, I have only argued that epistemicism and supervaluationism diverge with respect to the Barcan formula for definiteness. There remains the issue of whether the formula is desirable—even to the supervaluationist.

The supervaluationist is inspired by Peirce's conception of borderline cases in terms of inquiry resistance. This inquiry resistance issues from our representational apparatus rather than empirical sources. The supervaluationist is trying to model this representational inquiry resistance. The motivation disappears from the work site when they construct their semantics. But it is still the invisible hand that guides construction of the theory.

Now consider the 'All artworks are artifacts' example. The supervaluationist says that the vagueness of 'admissible precisification' makes it indefinite whether the statement is definite. So it is indefinite whether inquiry could correctly answer whether all artworks are artifacts.

Consequently, this particular aesthetic research project falls under a cloud of indeterminacy. The research could not 'fix belief' on the issue. Thus we have just the sort of inquiry resistance that Peirce had in mind when he characterized vagueness. The source of the inquiry resistance need not be an ineliminable alternative interpretation. *Any* representational source of inquiry resistance will do.

In the end, supervaluationists should be embarrassed by the Barcan formula for definiteness. Unhappily for them, they are forced down the wrong road. Epistemicists should not follow them.

Only epistemicism can do comprehensive justice to the futilitarian aspect of vagueness. For epistemicism is the only position that builds inquiry resistance into the notion of a borderline case. Non-epistemic theories are only guided indirectly by Peirce's conception of inquiry resistance. They use the conception to select something that appears to entail inquiry resistance (truth-value gap, intermediate truth-value, truth-value glut, and so on) But these semantic notions lack the complex structure of knowledge and so are doomed.

3 Forced Analytical Error

Our interlude with Madame Inquisitor took an embarrassing turn. Although we psychologists were just auditing her interrogation, we emerged as co-confessors to the 'inconsistency' of an arbitrary failure to believe. For the limits of discrimination affect both Monsieur Suspect and the describers of Monsieur Suspect.

But the describers of Monsieur Suspect are in a predicament that removes the scare quotes from 'inconsistent'. The indiscriminability relation only forced errors of omission—the failure to treat like cases alike. Vagueness forces commissive errors about analytical statements. Consequently, there is a clear sense in which our beliefs are massively contradictory. The contradictions are inescapable because they issue from linguistic competence itself.

I am not alleging that *language* is inconsistent. Language is a means of making assertions that makes no assertions of its own. English cannot disagree with French; both are unopinionated. My thesis is that, none the less, all speakers are inconsistent by virtue of their mastery of a natural language.

The coercion can be traced to the vague part of language. When the predicates are precise, we can play the odds. But when the predicates are vague, we fall under the command of a simplifying epistemology. This system confers focus by preventing mental and conversational clutter. Under the weight of these clarifying epistemic obligations, we are forced to accept some contradictions as analytic truths. Well, let us not understate. We are forced to accept a wide plume of contradictions.

This plume is not functional. The contradictions are like the heat radiating from a light bulb. The heat is a side-effect that can be stopped only by turning off the light.

1. Madame Inquisitor Encircles a Contradiction

The inconsistency induced by linguistic competence is universal, massive, and mandatory. Anyone who understands this sentence believes infinitely many contradictions. That means *you*.

And me. Since falsehoods cannot be wittingly believed, I can only roughly locate the language-induced contradictions. Consider my beliefs about which times are noonish. The definition of 'noonish' is 'near noon'. I last used the term for setting a lunch date. Madame Inquisitor relativizes 'noonish' to that appointment:

0. One second after noon is noonish.
1. If 1 second after noon is noonish, then 2 seconds after noon is noonish.
2. If 2 seconds after noon is noonish, then 3 seconds after noon is noonish.

.
.
.

10,000. If 10,000 seconds after noon is noonish, then 10,001 seconds after noon is noonish.
10,001. Therefore, 10,001 seconds after noon is noonish.

The conclusion is analytically false (10,000 seconds after noon is 2.46 p.m.). Premise 0 is analytically true. Therefore, there must be a conditional in the chain that has an analytically true antecedent and an analytically false consequent. Call this conditional X. The material conditionals preceding X have analytically true antecedents and analytically true consequents. Therefore, they are all analytically true. The conditionals coming after X have analytically false antecedents, and so are also analytically true. Thus conditional X is the only false premise. It is an analytic falsehood.

Each of premises (1)–(10,000) seem analytically true because they manifest our understanding that 'noonish' is tolerant (Wright 1975). Whenever we believe that n seconds is noonish, we are compelled to believe that $n + 1$ seconds is noonish. This is a psychological compulsion. But it is not a mere psychological compulsion. The compulsion is part of the psychology of language and hence has a normative aspect. We can only be inducted into a language in so far as we submit to conditionals such as these. We have a conditional *obligation* to believe each of these tolerance conditionals: if you wish to use 'noonish', then you must cooperate by ignoring insignificant differences. (But like Monsieur Suspect, we are doomed to violate our obligation because the obligations are not jointly satisfiable.)

Tolerance conditionals fit the negative conception of a priori statements. Each of (1)–(10,000) is incorrigible in the sense that none of them can be corrected. Each is irrefutable, undeniable, and irrevisable. Belief in a tolerance conditional does not require empirical investigation. Speakers are entitled to believe each tolerance conditional without any backing.

Wait! Recall that Madame Inquisitor previously demonstrated that not all of (1)–(10,000) are analytic truths. In fact, she showed that one of them is an analytic falsehood. Although each tolerance conditional is incorrigible, their conjunction is corrigible. Incorrigibility fails to agglomerate when some of the incorrigible statements are also fallible. 'Incorrigible' only means that no one is ever in a position to *show* that the statement is mistaken. Tolerance conditionals can be false; they just can't be shown to be false. These claims commit me to a controversial proposition: some a priori statements are analytic falsehoods. The epistemology of language collides with its semantics. In particular, true threshold statements are false (without being made false by the world) and yet incorrigibly believed (without the benefit of empirical warrant). There are independent grounds for thinking that there can be a contradiction which one justifiably believes to be a logical truth. Consider a student who is given a test in sentence logic. He is required to pick as many truths as he can from a list. He knows the list is composed solely of logical truths and logical falsehoods. The student believes each of his answers, $p_1, p_2, \ldots, p_n$. However, he also believes that at least one of these answers is false, that is, he believes $\sim(p_1 \,\&\, p_2 \,\&. \ldots \&\, p_n)$.

Here is a direct proof (by constructive dilemma) that the student believes a logical falsehood. If any of his answers $p_1, p_2, \ldots, p_n$ are false, then the student believes a logical falsehood (because the only falsehoods on the question list are logical falsehoods). If all of his test answers are true, then the student believes the following logical falsehood: $\sim(p_1 \,\&\, p_2 \,\&\ldots\& \, p_n)$. For if $p_1, p_2, \ldots, p_n$ are true, they are all logical truths. A conjunction of logical truths is itself a logical truth. And the negation of any logical truth is a logical falsehood. Hence, if all the student's test answers are true, then his belief that $\sim(p_1 \,\&\, p_2 \,\&\ldots\& \, p_n)$ is itself a belief in a logical falsehood.

The student could be aware of this proof that he believes a contradiction. And he could also know that this contradiction is such that he believes it to be a tautology. The student could reasonably resign himself to this belief in a contradiction. This may be the best he could do given the time available.

The student's contradiction could be cleared by learning the test answers from the instructor. However, he might develop the more general belief that at least one of his beliefs is a logical falsehood. This meta-belief is self-fulfilling; anyone who believes that he believes a contradiction must believe a contradiction. For if the rest of his beliefs were not contradictions, he would believe of a set of consistent propositions that at least one of them is inconsistent. Such a belief is itself inconsistent.

Belief in one's logical fallibility is self-fulfilling. This meta-belief is a more stable source of contradictory beliefs than the belief concerning items on the logic test. Since the meta-belief ranges over infinitely many beliefs, it cannot be overturned by eliminating a finite number of contradictions. I elaborate in the Cartesian Chapters 8, 9, and 10.

2. An Empathic Explanation of Inconceivable Thresholds

The belief that one has inconsistent beliefs becomes even more stable if our language faculty itself forces belief in contradictions. Language is the infrastructure that permits human beings to reason in a sophisticated way. If that infrastructure imposes contradictory beliefs on its users, then there is no human exit from contradiction.

Nor would there be an inhuman exit. A non-human thinker must understand us by embedding our perspective. To step into our shoes, this thinker must use human conceptual apparatus. And it is that apparatus which forces analytical errors. Of course, the thinker would not need to escape if it never enters our perspective. But then the alien cannot know the threshold of a vague predicate. If '15 minutes after noon is the last noonish minute' is true, then it can be known only by someone who is competent with 'noonish'. But if 'noonish' is in the alien's vocabulary, then the alien intelligence must follow the rules for using the term. Those rules make a virtue of necessity by forbidding the speaker from believing any threshold statement. Since knowledge implies belief, the alien cannot know which minute is the last noonish minute.

The alien might chafe under our rules. Consider the child's game of five-letter scrabble. Words longer than five letters are illegal. The reason for the restriction is that young children have trouble with long words. The limit makes the game accessible to a wider group of players. Older children hate the game. But if they begin to play with words longer than five letters, they are no longer playing five-letter scrabble. The five-letter word limit is a constitutive rule.

A minority of linguists think English syntax is like five-letter scrabble. They require that each sentence of English be intelligible to a normal human speaker of English. That makes the peculiarities of memory and parsing relevant to grammar. A superhuman might have a much better memory and sentence parser. He would long for a higher powered language. But when he speaks English, he must abide by rules that are tailored to his less gifted interlocutors.

The human language organ has evolved. Proto-humans who possessed a substantially different language organ would have substantially different rules. Even if we regarded their language organ as rudimentary, we would be curious about their language. To learn their language we would have to submit to rules tailored for their psychology, not ours. We might not like the rules but would be obliged to follow them on pain of changing the topic.

Any thinker who does not enter our perspective does not understand our subjective side. It is tempting to infer that the alien could at least understand people in the way autistics seem to—as physical objects. But even that is too generous. 'Physical object' is vague. Consequently, the alien thinker would also fail to grasp our objective side. This would impugn the alien's understanding of himself. For the alien would not be able to appreciate an important difference between himself and human beings.

An inflexible alien cannot step into our shoes. Theologians worry that God may be such an alien. God cannot feel pain because pain is endured against one's will. God is all powerful and so suffers nothing against His will. To understand pain, one must experience pain. And to understand the human condition, one must understand pain. So God's power walls Him off from us.

People often try to understand epistemicism by taking God's point of view; God sees the threshold for noonish but the human beings are, for some special reason, blind to it. But a threshold is not the sort of thing that can be known. God's point of view is impossible because it implies that all truths are co-knowable. But the truth is that ignorance of some facts is implied by knowledge of others. There is no point of view from which the threshold of noonish is accessible. For all points of view must reach noonish via our point of view. Our psychology forms an epistemic bottleneck. Consequently, the ignorance associated with vagueness is absolute ignorance. (This is *one* reason for absolute ignorance, not the only reason. In the final chapter, I speculate on an independent source of absolute borderline cases.) When I say that the price of competence in a human natural language is inconsistency, I mean to include all cognizers whatsoever.

If '15 minutes after noon is the last noonish minute' is unacceptable to a competent speaker, then so is ' "15 minutes after noon is the last noonish minute" is true'. Thus a Martian commentary on English will not escape the tolerance norms of English. If the Martian language is precise, then the commentator cannot even express knowledge that 'noonish' is roughly synonymous with 'within 15 minutes of noon'. For 'roughly synonymous' is vague. If the Martian language is vague, then it is possible to *roughly* translate vague predicates into precise predicates. But this is as pointless as roughly translating vague Chinese sentences into precise English sentences. A proper translation preserves meaning. Thus a proper translation of a Chinese sentence into an English sentence matches Chinese vagueness with English vagueness. The same principle applies for paraphrases within a language. As far as meaning preservation is concerned, 'A puppy is an immature dog' is a better definition than 'A puppy is a dog less than 12 months old'.

3. The Inferiority of Tolerance Conditionals

My justification for belief in the single false tolerance conditional, X, is almost optimal. However, it cannot be perfect because my justification for its converse is better. All tolerance conditionals share this inferiority. For instance,

> (932) If 932 seconds after noon is noonish, then 933 seconds after noon is noonish.

is not as epistemically good as 'If 933 seconds after noon is noonish, then 932 seconds after noon is noonish'.

The inferiority of tolerance conditionals persists even when they have a probability of 1. Consider the infinite class of tolerance conditionals of the form 'If n seconds after noon is noonish, then there is a time later than n seconds after noon which is also noonish' where n equals a rational number between 1 and 10,000. At most one of the conditionals in this infinite set is false, so the probability of each statement is 1. (Members of an omega-inconsistent class of propositions can each have a probability of 1 even though the probability of them all being true is 0 (Zaman 1987).) These tolerance conditionals have the same probabilities as their converses but are not as epistemically good as their converses.

Although imperfect, tolerance conditionals are worthy of assent. This applies even to conditional X (the single false conditional lying somewhere between (1) and (10,000) of the noonish sorites). Thus my belief in conditional X is a highly stable belief in an analytic falsehood. No amount of further inquiry can show that I ought not to believe that conditional X is an analytic truth.

Conditional X perfectly mimics members of the immense class of analytic truths that express the tolerance of 'noonish'. Their form is 'If n seconds after noon is noonish, then $n + 1$ seconds after noon is noonish'. I could avoid believing conditional X by not believing any tolerance conditional. But that would mean sacrificing a huge number of true beliefs to prevent a single false belief. I could try to merely assign probabilities to the tolerance conditionals. But that would overwhelmingly complicate my belief system. The more efficient arrangement is to extend epistemic entitlement to all the statements.

Appropriate resemblance to an entitling feature is itself a source of entitlement (Driver 1992). When a wife gives birth to a daughter, then the presumption is that the girl is her husband's daughter and so enjoys rights against him. If the husband does not challenge the presumption, the girl counts as his daughter whether or not the husband actually sired her. What makes the girl his daughter is her appropriate resemblance to someone who was sired by him. Conditional X is like the girl who acquires rights by resemblance. Conditional X is a priori because it has an appropriate resemblance to an analytically true statement. 'If one minute after noon is noonish, then two minutes after noon is noonish' is clearly an analytic truth and so, trivially, resembles an analytic truth. Thus tolerance conditionals actually have two sources of apriority.

Overdetermination of apriority can be mechanically illustrated with a sprawling disjunction such as:

> Either $1 = 1$ or all bachelors are male or nothing is both red all over and green all over.

The first disjunct is a priori in virtue of its syntactic analyticity. The second disjunct is a priori in virtue of its semantic analyticity. And the third disjunct is a priori in virtue of being a synthetic a priori truth. Since a disjunction is a priori if any of its disjuncts are, the apriority of the disjunction as a whole is overdetermined by three separate sources of apriority.

The apriority of conditional X is disquieting because X is actually analytically *false*. Apriori contradictions would be numerous. There are infinitely many distinct sorites arguments. (A sorites can be constructed from each of '1-ish', '2-ish', '3-ish', and so on.) Hence, there are infinitely many contradictions that I ought to believe to be tautologies. I do as I ought. Therefore, I believe infinitely many contradictions.

An analytic sorites argument imitates the virtues of a mathematical chain argument; it is an obviously valid argument based on *a priori* premises. In mathematics, there is an intimate connection between understanding and belief. The simpler the statement, the more intimate the bond—and the more difficult it is to make sense of error. Those who say $2 + 3 = 6$ are construed as mis-speaking rather than mis-believing. But if no one makes obvious errors, then how can they make unobvious errors? Unobvious conclusions are linked to obvious premises via obvious inference rules. In so far as obviousness agglomerates, mathematical debates take on the air of verbal disputes.

The sorites inherits this indisputability. Anyone who understands a link in the chain must believe it. I had a bright Russian student who insisted that 900 seconds after noon is the last noonish second. In the course of class discussion, the student explained that a friend once translated '-ish' as 'within fifteen minutes'. So he calculated $15 \times 60 = 900$ seconds. His classmates promptly tutored him on the inappropriateness of drawing sharp lines for words with an 'ish' suffix. Despite my epistemicist loyalties, I spontaneously joined the defense of the 'ish' norm. The Russian quickly fell into line.

I also had a student who insisted that 1,000 seconds after noon was the last noonish second. He was perfectly fluent in English. However, he had a scientistic fetish about powers of 10. When quantities got murky, he narrowed the candidates down to 10, 100, 1,000, and so on. My conclusion about this student was that his theoretical beliefs were interfering with his linguistic competence.

In *Through the Looking Glass*, Alice is given an oral examination. The White Queen asks 'What's one and one and one and one and one and one and one and one and one and one?' Alice confesses she does not know. She lost count. The Red Queen concludes Alice cannot add. Linguists disagree with the Red Queen on the grounds that Alice's ignorance is best explained as arising from a limit on her short-term memory rather than an inability to add. My point in saying that any competent speaker is entitled to believe each premise of the chain argument is that refusal to assent must be subsumed under one of the categories of performance failure. In particular, if a philosopher refuses to assent to a tolerance conditional, the best explanation is that his theoretical beliefs block the manifestation of his competence. The philosopher's competence is apt to reassert itself when he leaves the lectern. He relies on tolerance conditionals when teaching his children color words or assigning course grades to students. Conflict between competence and theory is a rich source of contradictions.

But my thesis is that linguistic competence *internally* generates contradictory beliefs. There are some analytic falsehoods which we are entitled to believe *a priori*. The justificatory credentials of these chameleon contradictions are as strong as the analytic truths they mimic. For instance, it is just as reasonable to believe conditional X (the false tolerance conditional lying between premises 1 and 10,000) as it is to believe the analytic truth (932).

When I describe (932) as an analytic truth, I am taking a tiny risk. For (932) might be conditional X and so actually be a contradiction. Switching to nanoseconds (billionths of a second) reduces the risk:

(932,000,000,000)   If 932,000,000,000 nanoseconds after noon is noonish, then 932,000,000,001 nanoseconds after noon is noonish.

The probability of (932,000,000,000) is higher than the probability of many propositions that I firmly believe. Ditto for (932). However, ordinary speakers rarely base their belief in (932) on probabilities. They are under no obligation to provide a probabilistic rationale for their assent to (932). Speakers assert it without any backing.

The tension between these two observations can be addressed by extending R. M. Hare's (1981) distinction between two levels of moral thinking. The intuitive level consists in the application of entrenched rules. The critical level concerns the basis for the rules. As a utilitarian, Hare believes that the basis for moral rules is the promotion of optimal consequences. Since good consequences are often best promoted by forgoing the cost of computing them, we develop rules to simplify our deliberations. This picture extends to the epistemology of language. Our beliefs about language acquire a deontological character when acceptance rules have been institutionalized.

Rules can be pitched at different levels of detail. This looseness has generated attempts to collapse rule utilitarianism into act utilitarianism (Lyons 1965). Even those who accept the rule utilitarian framework worry about the appropriate trade-off between efficient implementation and accuracy. For the moral rules can be judged by how well they fit an independent standard (the production of good consequences).

Moral systems are made correct by factors beyond our subscription to them. However, subjectivism is correct for language. What makes a language my language is just my psychological relationship with it.

The development of acceptance rules is normally too gradual to observe. However, the legal profession is under steady pressure to explicitly change rules of evidence to reflect scientific advances. Lawyers prefer not to present evidence at the critical level because it is too demanding on juries. Hence, when scientists develop new methods of crime detection, lawyers regulate its presentation. That way the jury is entitled to accept the conclusion of what is actually a complicated chain of reasoning. For instance, lawyers who pioneered the use of fingerprint evidence at first had to present complicated arguments and qualified conclusions. Rules of evidence were then reformed in a way that permitted the lawyer to flatly assert that a certain set of fingerprints belong to the defendant. The same process of simplification is now under way for DNA evidence.

Doubt about (932) is wrong-headed at the intuitive level. We ought not to burden our thoughts and conversation with insignificant possibilities. This presumption against attending to outlandish scenarios can be overridden. When propounding the statistical theory of heat, James Clerk Maxwell emphasized the possibility that his tea will grow hotter rather than cooler as it sits on a cold table. At the critical level, we see that there is an epistemic possibility that (932) is false. Indeed, our available evidence does not completely preclude the possibility that (932) is an analytic falsehood. It is important for us to recognize this epistemic possibility when diagnosing the sorites.

Note that my earlier attribution of compulsory belief was conditional; if you believe that n minutes after noon is noonish, then you are obliged to believe that $n + 1$ minutes after noon is noonish. The near-perfect symmetry between the antecedent and consequent forces us either to believe them both or not believe them both. Theoretically, one can escape inconsistency by abandoning belief in favor of probabilities. The resemblance between the antecedent and consequent of the tolerance conditional is not quite perfect. Hence, the probability assigned to the antecedent can be slightly different than the probability assigned to the consequent. This probabilistic form of epistemicism has the same difficulties as the probabilistic solution to the preface paradox (Makinson 1965). An author who, in the preface of his book, reports his belief that the text contains some errors must have jointly inconsistent beliefs. For if the beliefs expressed in the text are correct, then the belief expressed in the preface is incorrect. Theoretically, authors can escape by not believing anything they write. They can just assign probabilities.

The problem is that probabilistic thinking is computationally expensive—coherent probability assignments generate a combinatorial explosion of tasks. The explosion is harmless when only a small number of propositions are involved. So for special purposes, we can temporarily think probabilistically. This talent can be magnified with the help of computers. But even super-computers are soon overwhelmed. As the computer scientists say, the problem is 'NP-complete'.

We're stuck. Other beings, even if free of this sweeping limitation on computability, get stuck behind us.

4 Inconsistent Machines

> There are three kinds of people in the world;
> those who can count and those who can't.

Forced analytical errors are prominent in my epistemology of language. I say language systematically passes off contradictions as tautologies. I say there are infinitely many of these pseudo-tautologies. And I say competent speakers *ought* to be fooled by them. Permanently.

I shall appeal to precedent to justify and clarify my attribution of functional, massive inconsistency. I will compare and contrast my attribution of analytic error with other forms of inconsistency.

1. Motivation

The inconsistency of a self-deceived person arises from a motivated belief. The self-deceived wife wants her husband to be faithful. Her desire sustains her belief in his fidelity even as her belief in his infidelity is nurtured by mounting evidence. In contrast, linguistic inconsistency is dispassionate and is not a form of cognitive malfunction.

Nor does the linguistic inconsistency have the magical air that accompanies the behavioral inconsistencies of athletic performers. Bowlers tend to direct the ball even after they release the ball. They know these control movements cannot affect the course of the ball and yet seem to believe that they do. Perhaps some of the bowlers are merely being expressive. But many are not, at least not all the time.

The bowler's irrational belief that he can control the ball after it is released seems weaker than the belief that he cannot affect the course of the ball after its release. Psychologists who study blind sight may wish to challenge this. The patient with blind sight says he cannot see the figure before him but will accurately 'guess' the shape of the figure. One hypothesis is that beliefs run along separate channels, one oriented to talk, the other oriented to action. The blind-sight patient has the action-oriented belief that the shape is a square but lacks the discursively oriented belief. Likewise, one may say that the bowler has the action-oriented belief that the ball can be controlled after release and the discursive belief that it cannot. The bowler uniformly says that the ball cannot be controlled but continues to act on the belief that it can be controlled. Why don't actions speak louder than words? Or at least as loud?

Unlike the inconsistency I attribute to speakers, the inconsistency of bowlers is not constitutive of their practice. So let me turn to a possible illustration of constitutive inconsistency. Colin Radford (1975) contends that emotional reactions to fictions do essentially involve inconsistency. I pity Anna Karenina only if I believe something bad has happened to her. But I know nothing bad has happened to her because I know Leo Tolstoy's story about her is false. Radford contends that some normal people lack the inconsistency and so are never moved by the fate of fictional characters. However, all the normal people I have met are moved by fictions. If one of my children failed to be moved by fairy tales, I'd consult my pediatrician. Suppose the pediatrician said 'The bad news is that the child cannot be moved by fictions. The good news is that he is consistent. If you give him a dose of this drug, he'll enjoy stories like the other children—though at the expense of his consistency.' I would head straight to the pharmacy. If Radford is right about there being an inconsistency involved in being moved by a fiction, then it is an example of an inconsistency that enables us to participate in a desirable practice. It would also be an example of a hardy inconsistency that can recover after exposure. When people want to suppress the emotions felt at the cinema, they make progress by reminding themselves that they are only seeing a movie. However, after this special effort ceases, the audience member reverts to a state in which he can be moved by fictions.

Similarly, people can make a temporary, special effort not to believe the tolerance conditionals associated with a particular sorites argument. They can merely assign high probabilities to each tolerance conditional. A short reprieve is available elsewhere in philosophy. Some people can temporarily ease skeptical tension by merely assigning high probabilities to statements such as 'I have hands'. But they lapse back into the belief because they cannot sustain the costs of complicated mental representations.

2. Mechanical Contradictions

The relevance of economics to consistency is evident in cheap hand-held calculators. The old calculator I use to compute grades for my students is demonstrably inconsistent. If I divide 1 by 3 and then multiply by 3, my calculator answers 0.99999999. Thus my calculator says $(1 \div 3) \times 3$ = 0.99999999. Some defend the result by saying the calculator really has the sophisticated belief that $1 = 0.99999999. \ldots$ But the error builds as I increase the size of multiplier. In particular, it says $(1 \div 3) \times$ $99,999,999 = 3,333,329.$

The calculator manual forthrightly notes that false answers such as these arise because the calculator rounds off. My calculator only remembers the first eight digits of the answer. This explains the error for other functions involving internal continuous calculations. For instance, my calculator says that the square root of 2 is 1.412135. It also says $1.412135 \times 1.412135 = 1.999998.$ Thus my calculator is inconsistent in two senses. In addition to providing mathematically impossible answers, it gives extensionally different answers to synonymous questions.

I have been accused of abusing machines: 'You are deliberately asking questions that your little calculator is apt to get wrong!' I wish my mother had displayed the same protectiveness: 'Teacher, please do not abuse the boy! He was not designed to do algebra. His hunter-gatherer ancestors evolved in the African savanna during the Pleistocene Era. A little low level arithmetic was as much as their environment required back then.'

People are less motherly when I show off my new calculator that does not make the same mistakes. Rounding errors can be avoided by remembering the history of a calculation. This new calculator is better than the old one because it is more accurate. So the old one must really have been making mistakes.

Talk of what a machine ought to do is often criticized as an intrusion of value into the mechanical world of cold facts. However, Marvin Minsky tenderly contends that the notion of a machine is value-laden:

[Newton's mechanics] is supposed to be a generalization about some aspect of the behavior of objects in the physical world. *If the predictions that come from the theory are not confirmed, then (assuming that the experiment is impeccable) the theory is to be criticized and modified,* as was Newton's theory when the evidence for relativistic and quantum phenomena became conclusive. After all, there is only one universe and it isn't the business of the physicist to censure *it*, much as he might like to.

For machines, the situation is inverted! The abstract idea of a machine, e.g., an adding machine, is a *specification* for how a physical object *ought* to work. If the machine that I build wears out, I censure *it* and perhaps fix it. (Minsky 1967: 5)

Minsky's distinction is reminiscent of distinctions drawn in terms of word to world fit. A *description* such as 'The mouse is trapped' has a direction of fit that runs from words to the world. With *imperatives* such as 'Trap the mouse!', the direction of fit is from the world to words. Mousetraps are normative in that their direction of fit runs parallel with the mouse-catching imperative. The designer of the mousetrap gives the machine a sense of what *ought* to be. By natural design, human beings are built to answer questions (and walk and eat and so on). Just as we assess the consistency of people, we assess the consistency of machines.

The inconsistencies of my old calculator are large scale. Almost all decimal numbers require more than eight digits. (Indeed, the number 1/3 requires infinitely many decimal places.) Hence, relative to a random sample of purely arithmetical questions, my calculator gives the wrong answer to over 99 per cent of possible questions. Even knowing this, I rely on the inconsistent machine to do the serious business of assigning grades.

True, some calculators refuse to operate after you enter more than eight digits as input. (They will report an input overflow error.) But they will operate when the output is more than eight digits. If the calculator refused to output, its scope would be intolerably limited.

Happily, the sort of questions I ask the calculator are far from random. Like most human beings, I hover near 0. I never do sums such as

$$201983476050165209650325263346261698820562 +$$
$$292489016367407348535720871869873984 = ?$$

A question-answer machine can afford to be mostly wrong as long as it correctly answers the questions it is apt to be asked. Marvin Minsky neglects this point because he assumes that inconsistent machines will make *relevant* errors:

In any case, when a realization of one of our machines fails to do what our logic and mathematics predict of it, we are quite sure that either it must be defective or broken, or else our logic must be inconsistent. And surely most people would agree that it would be disastrous, and *as unthinkable, for an adding machine to err but not be defective* as it would be for 2 + 2 to occasionally equal 5. (Minsky 1967: 6)

A machine that says 2 + 2 = 5 is unacceptable because we are apt to ask questions involving integers near 0. However, arcane errors are acceptable and inevitable. (Incidentally, Minsky should disentangle uniformity from consistency. A machine that acts randomly can be consistent. And a machine that acts uniformly can be inconsistent.)

Flaws are common even in advanced computation. In 1994 engineers at the Intel corporation discovered that the floating-point arithmetic of the new Pentium processor had a glitch which would, in rare cases, yield an incorrect addition of integers. Corporate officers agreed to replace the processor for technical users but refused for non-technical users on the grounds that the glitch was insignificant. From an engineering perspective, this policy was sensible. It is wasteful to pursue unneeded accuracy.

The Intel policy was a public relations disaster. Their customers were incensed that Intel refused to replace 'defective machines'. There was an entire web site devoted to ridiculing the Pentium processor. ('How many Pentium designers does it take to screw in a light bulb? Answer: 1.999904274017, but that's close enough for non-technical people.') The company withdrew the policy and agreed to replace Pentium processors on demand.

There are theorem-proving computers that will generate useless results if fed inconsistent premises. Paraconsistent logics are often promoted as a way of reining in the machine by reining in the logic. But machines tend to be idiot savants that lack the power to do runaway deductions. Think of a miscalibrated slide-rule. All of its answers are inconsistent. But it does not give conflicting predictions about the weather or incoherent alibis. The slide-rule answers are restricted to a narrow domain of questions (even though there are infinitely many questions within the domain).

The inconsistencies of idiot savants do infect people who rely on their results. If an engineer's slide-rule warps in the sun, he can under-estimate the diameter of the cords needed for his suspension bridge. Thus a contradiction can lead to a bridge collapse.

The engineer might be driven mad by the disaster. But not by run-away deductions from the contradiction. His brain supports a system of homunculi. Each of these calculator-like entities is protected by its limited representational power. Collectively, the homunculi constitute a much more powerful system that enjoys the protections afforded by modular construction. Redundancy within the system helps detection of conflicting answers. Deductions consume energy, so there are inde-pendent reasons why lengthy deductions will be terminated. The com-putational theory of the mind has the resources to explain how the mind copes with massive inconsistency. Just as it does not need to tinker with logic to handle false beliefs, the computational theory of mind need not tinker with logic to handle inconsistent beliefs.

3. Deviant Conceptions of Incoherence

Some philosophers think that propositions can be incoherent in a way that is neither captured by standard logic nor by standard logic as supplemented with an enriched list of logical words (as when 'necessary' is added to obtain modal logic). Dialetheists believe that some propositions are both true and false. In standard logic, a contradiction entails any and all propositions. All hell breaks loose. Paraconsistent logics are designed to stop these runaway deductions. Only a little hell breaks loose. Graham Priest (1998) maintains that this makes room for reasonable belief in the contradictions. He gives the example of someone in a doorway. Is he in or out of the room? Given that in and out are mutually exclusive and exhaustive, and given that neither in nor out is the default position, then the man is both in and not in.

Stephen Schiffer (1998) has a less transparently deviant conception of incoherence. In a 'happy face solution' to a paradox, one arranges the elements of paradox into a set that involves jointly inconsistent propositions. One then solves the paradox by refuting one member of the set. In an 'unhappy face solution' to a paradox, one is unable to gain consistency by refuting a member of the paradoxical set. For one is rationally obliged to accept each member of the paradox. Anyone who managed to become consistent by rejecting a member of the paradox would be violating a conceptual norm. The only 'solution' to this kind of paradox is the modest one of understanding why there is no legitimate escape from the inconsistency. Waxing meta-philosophical, Schiffer opines that most, perhaps all, philosophical problems only have unhappy face solutions. He has argued, in particular, that there are only unhappy solutions to the problem of free will, skepticism about knowledge, and the sorites paradox.

We can contrast Schiffer's conception of inevitable error with the forced error that arises from expressive inadequacy (Cummins 1996: 23–7). Non-spherical maps of the earth must distort. A Mercator map is faithful for areas near the equator but exaggerates regions near the poles. Indeed, a Mercator map cannot include the poles because they would require an infinite amount of paper. Hammer maps and cylindrical maps are just as distortive but distribute the distortion differently. Judicious switching between maps minimizes the harm.

The human perceptual system appears unable to represent a nose as concave rather than convex. If you look at the concave side of a Halloween mask, you see the features as convex. Your visual system is helpfully biased toward common situations and so uses expressive inadequacy to rule out certain situations a priori. If a certain kind of situation will never actually arise, then there is a prophylactic advantage in a system that refuses to let the issue be formulated. By preventing the issue from getting on the agenda, one saves the time needed to rule it out.

Expressive restriction is also at play with language learning. There are large classes of mathematically possible languages that human beings are unable to learn. This incompetence is to our advantage because it spares children the trouble of eliminating these languages as candidates for the language that is actually being spoken in their community.

However, there is no limit on what a natural language can express. So the sorites paradox is not due to the poverty of our expressive resources. In the case of the liar paradox, Alfred Tarski (1929: 164–5) thought the *richness* of natural language was the problem. English is 'semantically closed'; anything can be said in English. In particular, the liar paradox can be expressed in English because English permits a sentence to assert or deny its own truth. Tarski's solution to the liar paradox is to drop natural language in favor of a hierarchy of languages which are each expressively incomplete, considered separately. Taken collectively, the hierarchy of languages purports to be complete in the sense that it lets us say everything that is scientifically worth saying. This does not include the liar sentence. Tarski considers the hierarchy's inability to express the liar sentence as a desirable.

In a similar spirit, Rudolph Carnap (1950, ch. 1) looks forward to the day when science will have precisified language to such an extent that the sorites paradox cannot be formulated. Could these future scientists celebrate their precision? No, for 'precise' is a vague term. ('Precise' is the contrary of 'vague' and the contrary of a vague term is itself vague.) No precise language contains 'precise'. However, precision is just the property scientistic philosophers such as Carnap want to talk about. Hence, the precise language envisaged by Carnap is expressively incomplete. Schiffer concurs. Schiffer agrees that the sorites paradoxes arise from vague terms but condemns any program for their elimination as too repressive.

Schiffer accepts Tarski's characterization of language as semantically closed. So he is not saying that the sorites paradox arises from our *limited* power of representation. We are not boxed in. Indeed, the source of our consternation is the enormous power of natural language. For the power is obtained by forgoing defensive measures. This is a familiar military theme. When the Israelis wanted to maximize air power during the Six Day War, they sent all of their planes out on the attack, leaving their homeland defenseless to an air attack. In hockey, the trade-off creates a characteristic stage of the game. During the final minutes, the trailing team substitutes an extra skater for the goalie in a desperate attempt to tie the score. Similarly, if we want full representational power, then we cannot encumber ourselves with Tarski's safety restrictions. Schiffer agrees with Tarski that there is a trade-off between offense (expressive power) and defense (protection from inconsistency). But Schiffer disagrees about the value of defense. He thinks Tarski overestimates the damage done by inconsistency and underestimates the opportunity costs that accrue from fortification. Schiffer thinks that the full power of natural language is needed to say what we want in philosophy. He also doubts that philosophers have any real option to restrict language in the way Tarski envisages. When philosophers shut down part of the system for the sake of consistency, they violate conceptual norms. According to Schiffer, most inconsistency avoidance in philosophy is futile. Perhaps all.

An unsolvable problem is still a problem. Schiffer is not adopting Wittgenstein's position that there are no genuine philosophical problems. Nor does he go in for the romantic defeatism that can be found in Immanuel Kant's treatment of the antinomies of pure reason. According to Kant, we have a natural tendency to succumb to transcendental illusion—the illusion of applying principles appropriate for phenomenal reality to noumenal reality. While under the spell of the illusion, we fall into intractable debates about free will, infinity, and so on. Both sides of the debate muster arguments which, if considered on their own, would be decisive. Each side of the argument would be compelling were it not confounded by the existence of the other. The only way out is to reject the presupposition shared by both sides of the argument—that phenomenal principles apply to noumenal reality. Although Kant is forceful about the necessity of rejecting this natural presupposition and withdrawing from traditional metaphysics, he also speaks warmly of our futile efforts to solve the antinomies of space and time. He compares the traditional metaphysician to a bird fluttering its wings against the cage. The bird has an admirable drive for free flight.

Schiffer offers no consoling comparison to noble creatures. He does offer a more egalitarian explanation of the futility of metaphysical musings about free will. Whereas Kant attributes an attractive but false presupposition to traditional metaphysicians, Schiffer endorses key metaphysical presuppositions. Schiffer refuses to adopt an elitist perspective. He has no insight to lord over his colleagues. He is deep in the trenches with his fellow philosophers—both live and long dead. Schiffer is just unusual in his resignation; he denies there is any way out of the trench. Unlike World War I infantry, Schiffer thinks trench life is not bad. (The eminent biologist J. B. S. Haldane admitted he loved fighting in World War I.)

Schiffer's conception of incoherence is itself incoherent. Language and concepts are the means used to assert propositions but they do not assert any propositions. Therefore, language and concepts cannot imply any inconsistent propositions. To attribute incoherency to something that is necessarily not incoherent is itself incoherent. Since Schiffer's notion of an unhappy face solution implies that concepts can be incoherent, his notion of an unhappy face solution is itself incoherent. Therefore, there are no unhappy solutions. Not one. Nor could there be.

But Schiffer is driving at an interesting idea. He draws an analogy with Charles Chihara's (1979) lovely example of Secretary Liberation. Secretary Liberation is a club for all and only those secretaries who are not permitted to join the clubs for which they are secretaries. Suppose the club grows so large that it hires a secretary, Miss Fineline. Is Miss Fineline permitted to join Secretary Liberation? It seems that the club's constitution forces us to say she is permitted and forces us to say she is not permitted. Anyone who fails to feel the force of each horn of the dilemma either misunderstands the club's constitution or fails to draw a valid inference. So the inconsistency appears to be part of the very meaning or essence of the institution. If language is a system of rules such as the institution of Secretary Liberation, then language itself will be inconsistent. And isn't it plausible that language should have this kind of architectural inconsistency? Language is not even planned. Language is a sprawl that arises without foresight or concern for consistency.

The first step of Schiffer's analogy is mistaken. There is no such thing as Secretary Liberation in the sense Charles Chihara defined for it. Nor could there be such a club. For the existence of such a club would imply a contradiction, that is that there could be a secretary of Secretary Liberation. There can be clubs that are nearly indistinguishable from Secretary Liberation as officially defined. These make an exception for their own secretaries. Their own secretary is outside the domain of discourse of the club's central rule that all and only those who are club secretaries excluded from their own clubs can be members of the club. These look-alike clubs are free to exclude their secretaries, include them, or say nothing at all. Since we generally prefer to alter our opinion about the nature of a thing rather than alter our opinion of whether it exists, there would be pressure to say that Secretary Liberation is identical to one of the 'look-alikes'.

A persistent paradox monger might try to *stipulate* that their central rule does cover Secretary Liberation's own secretary. However, given that our other assumptions are still in force, this stipulation would fail to put the secretary in the domain of discourse. For if it succeeded, there would be a contradiction. End of story.

Dialetheists find such loyalty to the principle of non-contradiction dogmatic. But I deny that dialetheists have a more permissive attitude toward *contradiction*. The meaning of 'contradiction' is spelt out by its role in *reductio ad absurdum*. The whole idea behind a reductio is that contradictions are absolute stopping points. To show that a proposition entails a contradiction is to reject that proposition. Unlike *modus tollens*, reductio is a premiseless form of deduction. We make an assumption tentatively, deduce a contradiction, and then infer the negation of the assumption. Open-mindedness about the truth of the contradiction is just closed-mindedness with respect to its status as a contradiction. Dialetheists are inadvertent skeptics about contradictions. They believe there are no contradictions; there are just propositions of various degrees of attraction and repugnance. Graham Priest ranks the absurdity of 'I am a fried egg and it is not the case that I am a fried egg' equally with 'I am a fried egg'. When you uniformly translate the dialetheist in terms of what he really means, you will discover him to be disappointingly sober. If you want to hear something startling, then listen to the guy who uses 'contradiction' in the standard sense.

Although I have criticized Schiffer's conception of incoherence as incoherent, I have been inspired by it. View me as fixing his broken picture of incoherence. The first stage of the salvage operation has been epistemological. I have tried to make room for rationally mandatory belief in inconsistencies with some claims about apriority (which I shall substantiate in Ch. 6). The next chapter continues the salvage effort in psychological terms. The goal is to show how contemporary views about the modularity of mind fit the attribution of inconsistency to language users.

5 Sainsbury's Spectra and Penrose's Triangle

Have I created an impossible problem for myself? I want to reconstruct genuine vagueness, the kind involving absolute borderline cases, from only those resources permitted by bivalent logic. Am I like an engraver who sets out to create shades of gray by scratching sharp black lines into a white surface?

Well I hope so! Take a close look at George Washington's picture on a one dollar bill. His face is gray. Washington's face looks gray even after you notice that the picture is composed solely of fine black lines. All engraved portraits exploit the 'spreading effect': at a sufficiently fine scale, black and white are optically fused into gray. Shadows and shades of gray are rendered by varying the density of the lines.

Many report that the optical fusion does not wipe out the perception of black and white. The same surface is seen *simultaneously* as gray all over and as black and white all over. Unlike the Necker Cube, there is no alternation between consistent interpretations. There is a single inconsistent interpretation.

L. M. Hurvich (1981) has a neat explanation of the inconsistent perception. Basically, one feature detector analyzes the fine lines as just fine lines. Another feature detector averages the black lines with the white spaces to obtain the feature 'gray'. These parallel processes do not trigger intervention by a consistency censor. Consequently, the viewer sees the same surface both ways.

A parallel explanation can be offered for the waterfall illusion. If you stare at a waterfall and then look at neighboring rocks, the rocks appear to move while remaining stationary. Staring at the waterfall adapts some position detectors but not others. When your eyes turn to the rocks, these adapted detectors indicate that a movement in the opposite direction of the waterfall is taking place. However, your unadapted detectors declare that the rocks are not moving. Absent the intervention of a censor, we see the rocks both ways at once.

Logic dictates an underlying reality that is black and white. A model of vagueness must work within this restricted medium. Like an

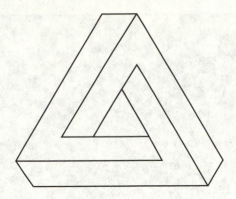

FIG. 5.1 Penrose triangle

Source: Penrose and Penrose (1958: 31).

engraver, an epistemicist can render shades of gray by appealing to psychological mechanisms that average out bivalent complexities.

1. The Nature of Impossible Figures

I say the color spectrum is an impossible figure like the Penrose triangle (see Fig. 5.1). The impossible appearance arises from the operation of ill-coordinated homunculi. One homunculus tells me that there are three sides. A second says that each of the angles formed by these sides is a right angle. A third says that side 1 connects to side 2 and says side 2 connects to side 3. The homunculi jointly form the representation of the Penrose triangle. After realizing that a triangle cannot be composed of three right angles, I scrutinize the so-called triangle and try to figure out what when wrong. Even if I succeed, my homunculi will continue to sing their incoherent song. I will still 'see' the impossible triangle even if I do not believe what I am seeing. Even if I believe the edge connection assumption is false, the sides still look connected to me. The illusion is irresistible.

Much of our visual system is cognitively impenetrable; new knowledge cannot overturn what we seem to see. We continue to see a single spiraling cord in the Frasier twisted-cord illusion (see Fig. 5.2) even after tracing a finger around the separate concentric rings in the picture. We know that there are boundaries between the outer and inner loops but continue to see an undivided continuous strand. As with the sorites,

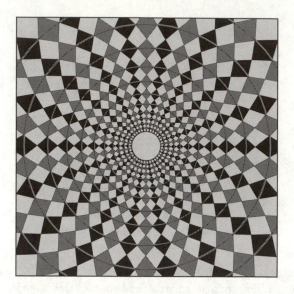

FIG. 5.2 Frasier twisted-cord illusion

there is a failure to see discontinuities even after their existence has been established.

Cognitive impenetrability is standardly cited as evidence of the modularity of the perceptual system. The system is a committee of autonomous subsystems that do not heed each other. Instead of pooling their information, the systems just vote on the information they have. Since natural selection has opportunistically installed lots of redundancy, the overall system is generally reliable for the settings hunter-gatherers confront.

I invoke homunculi to explain our perception of spectra. Homunculi are rudimentary agents, highly specialized and uneducable. Whereas intelligent people change their opinions after being refuted, our stupid homunculi are dogmatic. In the case of the color spectrum, the compartmentalized homunculi dogmatically persist with their jointly inconsistent representation of a change from red to non-red that at no point makes a transition from red to non-red. They'll never learn.

An impossible figure is a figure that generates an impossible appearance. After the publication of the Penrose triangle in 1958, M. C. Escher developed the aesthetic aspect of the Penrose triangle in a number of

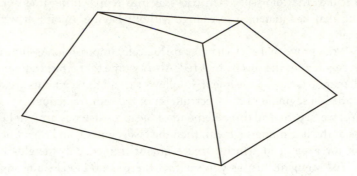

FIG. 5.3   The 'truncated pyramid'

famous works. Over 160,000 copies have been sold of Escher's 1961 lithograph *Waterfall*.

There is a difference between an impossible appearance and an apparent impossibility. The impossibility of an appearance might be unobvious. People rarely notice the common mistakes artists make with perspective, mirrors, and shadows. Unapparent impossible appearances are the rule with computer-generated impossible figures. The software exploits the fact that large-scale impossible figures can be cobbled together from snapshots of parts of the Penrose triangle (Ernst 1986: 58). These montages are geometrically impossible but their complexity overwhelms our modest consistency checkers. There is no visual dissonance (which leaves these busy giants less aesthetically stimulating than Escher's lithographs).

The impossibility of an appearance is sometimes concealed without overloading our critical capacities. This simple figure looks like a truncated pyramid but it is impossible to continue the edges in such a way as to obtain a complete pyramid.

The color spectrum is more like the 'truncated pyramid' than the Penrose triangle; there is an impossible appearance but no appearance of impossibility. But there is a difference. Once the pseudo-pyramid is exposed, we meekly acquiesce to correction. Only fools bridle against trigonometry. But wise men do try to modify logic to validate the appearance of red shading seamlessly into orange.

Non-representational art could have impossible figures. The impossibility associated with spectra is logical rather than algebraic or geometrical. Unlike the Penrose triangle, spectral inconsistency cannot be escaped by viewing the spectrum as a two-dimensional figure. In particular, the color spectrum tricks us into representing it as something that has managed to change without having a point at which it changes.

We can prove that such changes are logically impossible. Assume the first segment of the spectrum is red. Also assume that if one segment is red, then so is the next segment. It follows that all the segments are red. Yet the last segment of the spectrum is not red. Contradiction.

Yet we 'see' that all three elements of the inconsistency are true! Just look at the beginning segment, then the last segment, and then finally look for a point at which a red segment immediately neighbors a non-red segment. Just as you see that there is no blood stain on the spectrum, you 'see' that there is no boundary between the red and non-red segments.

Let us consider the position of an eminent philosopher who advocates removing the scare quotes around 'see'.

2. Boundarylessness

My favorite episode of *King of the Hill* features a boy, Bobby Hill, suffering eerie psychological side-effects of the drug Ritalin. Bobby is seated at the kitchen table. He sniffs the air and prophesies 'There is some milk in the refrigerator that is about to go bad'. He takes another sniff and announces 'There it goes'.

The absurdity is that the vagueness of 'bad milk' prevents anyone from detecting the exact moment at which milk turns bad. But most people think there is a deeper absurdity that explains the indetectibility: there just is no boundary to detect.

Most vagueness theorists try to accommodate this intuition by replacing sharp boundaries with 'unsharp boundaries'. For instance, the promoter of fuzzy logic says that the threshold to bad milk is a transition of *degrees* from non-badness to badness. At noon 'The milk is bad' is 0.99 true but then one minute later the statement becomes true to degree 1. Supervaluationists prefer truth-value gaps. There is a step from 'The milk is bad' being neither true nor false to it being true.

In his inaugural lecture at King's College, 'Concepts without Boundaries', Mark Sainsbury dismissed these replacements as futile half-measures. For Sainsbury, the problem is not that the classical logician makes a mistake about the *nature* of the boundary. Rather, the problem is that the classical logician postulates a boundary at all. Sainsbury thinks that in the color spectrum, there is a change from red to non-red without there being a point at which a change takes place. There is no natural boundary between red and non-red. Nor have speakers established a convention that serves to demarcate red from non-red. Since there is no further source for a boundary between red and non-red, Sainsbury endorses the perception that there is no boundary. He thinks deviant logicians are too conservative with respect to boundaries. The supervaluationist just replaces the classical true/false dichotomy with a trichotomy of true/false/neither. The fuzzy logician's replacement involves extra truth-values. These views accept the presupposition that concepts partition objects into sets. Instead of doubting the classical assumption that concepts pigeonhole reality, they just disagree on the number of pigeonholes.

Sainsbury concedes that deviant logicians have attempted to further soften the boundary by iterating their more complicated partitions. For instance, supervaluationists say that the trichotomy true/false/neither is itself vague. But even if the iteration proceeds infinitely, the end state will be three sets. The members of the first are individuals to which the predicate applies without falling under the shadow of vagueness at any level. The members of the second set are those individuals to which the predicate falsely applies without falling under the shadow of vagueness at any level. And the remaining set consists of those individuals who are under some shadow of vagueness at some level. This is just the sort of sharp division that motivated the search for an alternative to classical logic.

Sainsbury contends that most concepts do not partition objects into sets. Instead, they order objects in the way a magnet organizes iron filings. Most of the particles cluster at the opposite poles but some occupy intermediate positions. 'Not bad milk' and 'bad milk' generate opposite fields of influence. Particular cases cluster around paradigm cases. There is no need to find a dividing line to understand how a spectrum works. To organize things along a spectrum is itself a perfectly standard way of classifying things.

I agree that classification along a spectrum is perfectly standard. But perfectly standard schemes can be inconsistent.

3. Overlooked Boundaries

The neurophysiologist, Vilayanur Ramachandran, has an example involving a disk separating a green band and a red band. A version of this example is reproduced on the book jacket. Hold the figure about a foot from your face. Now close your right eye. Focus on the dot to the right of the bars. Slowly move the illustration toward you. At a certain critical distance, the textured disk will fall into the region of your blind spot and completely disappear. We 'fill in' this blind spot in an interesting way. According to Vilayanur Ramachandran,

Subjects reported that when the disk falls in the blind spot, the line appears continuous even though, paradoxically, they could not actually see the border between the green and red segments. The paradox arises presumably because part of the visual system is signaling that the line is continuous while another part is unable to discern a border between the red and green colors. (Ramachandran 1992: 87)

The 'little man' who says that the bar is continuous does not discuss his opinion with the little man who says that there is no boundary. And they do not discuss their opinions with the third little man who says that the bottom part of the bar is red while the top bar is green. The little men just talk at once without concern for keeping their collective story straight. The result is the depiction of a scene involving an object that is red on the bottom, green on top, but which at no point changes from red to green. Since nothing can be both red and green, the representation is incoherent.

Similarly, the boundarylessness of the color spectrum should be explained as an illusion generated by segregated homunculi. There is a little man who spots the difference between red and orange in the color spectrum. A second little man spots the connectedness between the red segment and the orange segment. And, finally there is the third man. He says that there is no boundary between the red and orange portions.

4. Illusory Boundaries

The fallibility of our boundary detectors runs in both directions. In addition to mistakenly saying that there is no boundary, the homunculus sometimes mistakenly says that there is a boundary (see Fig. 5.4). Consider the square that begins this sequence. Although it looks brighter than its background, the area within the 'square' reflects only as much light as the area in the background. These illusory contours show that boundary attribution can be stimulated without objective gradient differences.

The superimposed edges are cued by four black 3/4 circles. In the first figure, they look like black circles that each have a quarter blocked by a

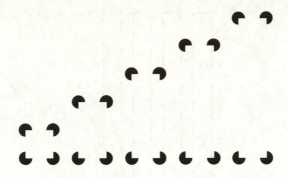

FIG. 5.4 Illusory contour sequence

Source: R. Sorensen, 'Sharp Boundaries for Blobs',
Philosophical Studies, 91/3 (Sept. 1998): 275–95.

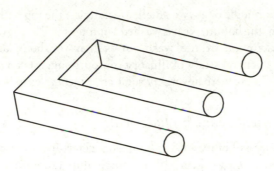

FIG. 5.5 Devil's tuning fork

square. This triggers one element of the visual system into a representation (or schematic representation) of a square.

The subsequent figures 'stretch' the illusory square into longer and longer rectangles. Eventually the middle begins to 'wash out'. In the devil's tuning fork (Fig. 5.5), there is a compulsory disappearance of the boundary between the middle fork and its neighbors. But here (Fig. 5.4) the wash-out is not forced. Our visual system is responsive to some kind of quota on the proportion of explicit to implicit boundary drawing. But there is no inconsistency in extending the boundaries indefinitely for ever larger rectangles. Instead one is limited to a few alternatives. One can see the last figure as a single big rectangle with a

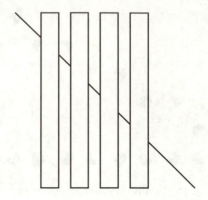

FIG. 5.6 The iterated Poggendorff illusion

washed-out middle or as two smaller rectangles, the top with a washed out bottom, the bottom with a washed out top.

One description of the wash-out is that the boundary erodes. However, a general study of illusory contours suggests an alternative description: there were never any squares or rectangles to begin with.

5. *Inconsistent Boundary Judgments*

The two-way fallibility of our boundary detector can be dramatized by its inconsistent verdicts within a single illustration. In the illusion shown in Figure 5.6 (an iterated version of the Poggendorff illusion), the homunculus reports that there are discontinuities each time the oblique line passes behind a rectangle. On close inspection, each segment of the long oblique line seems slightly lower than a straight continuation. However, there is a second report that contradicts these misalignment verdicts. For overall, the line looks straight. Thus the homunculus making the long-range colinearity judgment contradicts the homunculus making the local judgments.

Is this one homunculus contradicting himself or is this two homunculi disagreeing? Psychologists prefer their homunculi to be individually consistent. For only then can they reduce the inconsistency of a human being to a mere disagreement amongst his homunculi. This 'divide and conquer' strategy only works when contradictions are compounds of self-consistent propositions. Stereotypical contradictions such as P & ~P satisfy this condition. However, the inconsistency 'Something is not identical to itself' does not contain propositions as components. The inconsistency is derived at a sub-propositional level by predicate logic with identity. Therefore, 'Something is not identical to itself' is a counterexample to the logical myth that all contradictions are compounds of consistent propositions.

This logical point shows that an eliminative reduction of human inconsistency is impossible. Psychologists can explain a joint n-way inconsistency as a disagreement among n individually consistent homunculi. Since any truth function can be expressed with negation and conjunction, the strategy seems feasible for contradictions at the level of sentence logic. It can also work for many formulas in predicate logic such as '$(x)Fx$ & (x)~Fx'. But when an existential quantifier binds variables inside the contradiction, such as '$(\exists x)(x \neq x)$' the contradiction is indivisible. This shows that inconsistency cannot always be analyzed as disagreement amongst consistent believers.

Homuncular models of inconsistent belief are still valuable. For instance, they explain the incorrigible inconsistencies at the perceptual level. However, a complete homuncular model of inconsistency must have some homunculi that are individually inconsistent.

Often there is a trade-off between postulating one inconsistent homunculus or two consistent homunculi that disagree. Consider the iterated Poggendorff illusion. If we were willing to postulate separate homunculi to perform two very similar tasks, each homunculus could be consistent. For instance, one homunculus might be dedicated to local continuity judgments and another makes global continuity judgments. But once we become resigned to having a single homunculus believing an indivisible contradiction, we have less motive to postulate distinct homunculi each time we confront an inconsistency. It is simpler to postulate a single boundary detector that makes inconsistent boundary attributions.

In any case, only the global judgment is correct. The local discontinuities are an illusion. A straight edge will verify that all the line segments are objectively co-linear.

The color spectrum is a dual of the iterated Poggendorff illusion. In the iterated Poggendorff illusion, each pairwise judgment of *discontinuity* is mistaken while the global judgment of continuity is correct. The pattern is reversed for the color spectrum. Almost all of our pairwise judgments of sameness of color are correct. The only specifiable mistake is the global 'judgment' that all the shades are the same color.

There are people who can consistently view impossible figures. Instead of seeing the devil's tuning fork as a three-dimensional figure, some see it as a two-dimensional pattern of lines. These two-dimensional viewers can more accurately draw the impossible tuning fork from memory than three-dimensional viewers.

The color spectrum should puzzle even two-dimensional viewers. For the contradiction does not turn on depth perception. Nor does it rely on picture perception.

There is nothing special about vision. Consider Roger Shepherd's ever rising tone. You can listen to this auditory counterpart of the ever rising staircase at the Illusion Works web site (www.illusion-works.com) As you listen, it eventually becomes evident that the tone repeats. So your judgments of which tone is higher than its predecessor fail to be transitive. Similarly, if you listen to a tone that imperceptibly rises, you eventually realize that your judgments of sameness of tone fail to be transitive.

When I look at the color spectrum, I see it just the way Professor Sainsbury sees it. Not only do I fail to discern any boundary, I also see the spectrum as unbounded. I can see this absence just as I can 'see' an absence of a seam in an automotive repair—even when I know the weld necessitates a seam.

If you agree that the color spectrum is an impossible figure, then you believe that there can be a boundary in just those sequences which are most compelling without boundaries. This belief neutralizes a strong inhibition against adopting the epistemic solution to the sorites paradox.

6. The Case of Language

Language, like perception, is an ancient, stratified structure of reflexes (Fodor 1983). The modularity of the perceptual system is more salient because we have easy cross-checks. I can quickly measure the lengths of the Müeller–Lyer lines with a ruler (see Fig. 0.1). I do not need to rely on abstract arguments to demonstrate an illusion.

Phonological illusions are also amenable to easy empirical demonstrations. The impression that the 'p' in 'pet' is pronounced the same as the 'p' in 'pat' can be overturned by holding a moistened hand to your mouth as you say the words. The aspirated 'p' in 'pet' is detected by a puff of air on the hand.

Some syntactic illusions also yield to easy proof. Garden path sentences such as 'The prime number few' are judged ungrammatical because they are exceptions to the heuristic strategies of our unconscious sentence parsers. However, people quickly grasp their error when primed on the right syntactic structure: 'The mediocre are many but the prime number few'.

Other syntactic illusions require abstract argumentation. Most people mistakenly judge 'Misery loves company' as grammatical and 'The maid the cook the footman the butler fired kissed scolded left in tears' as ungrammatical. Substantial coaching is needed to reverse these judgments. To exclude 'Misery loves company' as a mere idiom, the linguist shows how general rules which would license 'Misery loves company' would also license 'Poverty adores cheese' and 'Virtue bought a pet kitten'. A special rule could be designed which licensed only 'Misery loves company'. But this legislation of a particular case would be ad hoc. The linguist demonstrates the grammaticality of 'The maid the cook the footman the butler fired kissed scolded left in tears' in stages. What did the butler do? The butler fired the footman. What did the footman do? The footman (whom)[the butler fired] kissed the cook. What did the cook do? The cook (whom)[the footman the butler fired kissed] scolded the maid. And what did the maid do? The maid (whom) [the cook the footman the butler fired kissed scolded] left in tears. After you ascend the ladder of intermediate sentences, you can understand the complex sentence. So there is a meaning that can be decoded. The grammaticality of long and complex sentences is a side-effect of characterizing grammars with recursive rules. Since the rules can be applied over and over, a theory which blesses the short and simple grammatical sentences will also bless long and complex sentences whose meaning can only be captured with pencil and paper calculations. We cannot screen out the long and complex sentences with restrictions on how many times the rule can be applied because any particular number will be arbitrary:

The unacceptable grammatical sentences often cannot be used, for reasons having to do, not with grammar, bur rather with memory limitations, intonational and stylistic factors, 'iconic' elements of discourse. . . . and so on. Note that it would be quite impossible to characterize the unacceptable sentences in grammatical terms. For example, we cannot formulate particular rules of grammar in such a way as to exclude them. Nor, obviously, can we exclude them by limiting the number of reapplications of grammatical rules in the generation of a sentence, since unacceptability can just as well arise from the application of distinct rules, each being applied only once. (Chomsky 1965: 11)

Chomsky's remarks can also be used to criticize those who try to solve the sorites paradox by limiting the number of times an inference rule can be applied. For instance, Paul Ziff (1974) says that *modus ponens* is a good inference rule as long as it is not pushed too far. But this threatens chain arguments such as: a billion is a large number. If a billion is a large number, then a billion and one is a large number. Therefore, a billion and one is a large number. If a billion and one is a large number, then a billion and two is a large number. Blah, blah, blah. Therefore, two billion is a large number.

Short valid arguments must add up to long valid arguments. For corresponding to each valid argument is a necessary truth. The truth is a conditional whose antecedent is the conjunction of the premises and whose consequent is the conclusion. Necessity collects over conjunction: $(\Box p \,\&\, \Box q) \supset \Box(p \,\&\, q)$. Thus there must be a necessary truth corresponding to the long argument. And that necessary truth guarantees the validity of the long argument.

The length of a proof is relative to the resources of the deductive system in question. A deductive system that contains the inference rule of mathematical induction will allow us to validate a sorites argument in a single step. If the same system lacks *modus ponens*, then the 'short' argument 'If John goes, Mary stays. John goes. Therefore, Mary stays' could require thousands of steps to prove. The psychological ease with which I wield *modus ponens* makes me 'translate' mathematical induction into a sequences of *modus ponens* inferences. Similarly, the psychological ease with which I wield English makes me translate French, under my breath, into English. But I ought not to confuse this psychological primacy with logical primacy.

Semantic illusions tend to require abstract, complicated demonstrations. However, the illusion of semantic boundarylessness can be exposed with an argument that is unusually simple and powerful. Given (a modest fragment of) standard logic, there is only one plausible solution to the sorites paradox: reject the induction step. That entails there must be a last F where F is the predicate featured in the sorites argument. Hence, some sentence of the form '*n* is the last noonish second' must be true.

The only hitch is that sentences of the form '*n* is the last noonish second' must always be rejected as (semantically) contradictory by competent speakers. Your linguistic boundary detector is sensitive to gestalt principles like good continuation and common fate. The similarity between '*n* seconds after noon is noonish' and '*n* + 1 seconds after noon is noonish' is always nearly optimal. Our symmetry-sensitive homunculi will always indicate that there is no difference between the two sentences. Our intuitions about the sentences are the voices of homunculi. Their siren song is powerful. Pilots still perish because they trust the 'seat of their pants' more than their gauges.

The pilots at least have the advantage of a *specific* independent check on whether their homunculi are misleading them. In the case of the 'n is the last noonish second', the only check is a generalization: there is a unique n such that n is the last noonish second. There is no indication of exactly which number n equals. Thus there is little counter-pressure against our homuncular intuitions in favor of the falsehood of, say, '1,000 seconds after noon is the last noonish second'. Given the overwhelming probability that it is indeed false, why fight our gut feeling that the sentence is false? I am not going to crash and die. I am playing for small stakes. If I wish to optimize my number of true beliefs, I am well-advised to go with the flow. I will gain a huge number of true beliefs at the expense of just one false belief.

Of course, I cannot choose what to believe. I am merely trying to rationally reconstruct the policies under which I in fact form beliefs. The preface paradox shows that the policy for human beings does not require joint consistency for beliefs. Indeed, it shows that inconsistency is rationally mandatory. You are irrational if you fail to believe that you have at least one false belief.

We are instead built according to a compromise strategy. Instead of devoting all resources to preventing error, we allot part of the budget for eliminating easy errors, another portion for recalcitrant errors, and then resign ourselves to the intractable errors.

Well, 'resign' is misleadingly passive. We sometimes make a virtue of necessity by exploiting error. After road engineers absorbed the lesson that perceptual illusions mislead motorists about speed, the engineers redesigned approaches to hazards to harness these illusions (Denton 1973). Consider roundabouts at the end of long fast sections of the road. Transverse bars are painted across the road at decreasing intervals to create an illusion of acceleration. Even the engineers who design the illusory approaches will slow down in response to their gut fear of losing control. The extent of one's conformity to a speed limit is influenced by how one perceives the road. Little wonder that road engineers increase conformity by manipulating perceptions. All normative systems opportunistically adapt to people's perceptions. Perceptions of boundarylessness provide a natural opportunity to increase the efficiency of natural languages.

Kant believed that the transcendental illusion responsible for the antinomies of reason persists in a weakened form even after the truth is known. Similarly, I think there will be 'residue' (Bernard Williams's term for lingering regret by victims of moral bad luck) after epistemicism is accepted. Intellectual historians in the year 2100 will readily appreciate why people felt in their hearts that epistemicism is wrong, wrong, wrong. But they will assimilate epistemicism to other veridical paradoxes such as the Copernican paradox that the earth orbits the sun.

7. Homunculi and Inconsistent a priori Judgments

Perceptual psychologists study illusions because they reveal empirical assumptions made by our visual system: the light source is from above, the scene is uniformly illuminated, objects are staying the same size, and so on. The system needs to make empirical assumptions to narrow the range of possible answers to the question of what is responsible for the image it is receiving. Geometrically, a square image can be caused by an infinite range of trapezoids presented at various angles.

Different modules in the visual system will make different empirical assumptions. There is no guarantee that these supplemental premises will be jointly consistent. A module will stick with any assumption that is sufficiently fruitful. Often, a variety of distinct assumptions will work well enough. If one system uses an inverse square law for gravity and another uses an inverse cube law, then there will be little difference in their predictions. This means that we should expect modules to make conflicting assumptions about the world.

These supplemental assumptions are innate and are also good candidates for being a priori. Many animals see objects as soon as they are born. If a newborn sees its mother withdraw, then the newborn knows its mother withdrew (rather than shrank or seamlessly passed out of existence in favor of a smaller creature) by virtue of the supplemental assumptions that help it see. The newborn is entitled to make these assumptions about the world. Its entitlement does not rest on previous empirical demonstration. Since these assumptions are associated with different homunculi, they are derived independently of one another. Just as we expect a scientist to disagree a bit with other scientists when each is working independently, we should expect an isolated homunculus to make supplemental assumptions that are at some variance with the supplemental assumptions of other homunculi. In so far as we grant a priori status to the supplements, we have an example of inconsistent a priori judgments.

Like perceptual homunculi, linguistic homunculi also face under-determined problems which can only be solved by making supplemental assumptions. A large range of grammars can generate the sentences heard by a child. Different linguistic homunculi solve the problem with different assumptions and with little coordination. Hence, it is likely that linguistic homunculi also make conflicting assumptions. Consequently, there should also be inconsistent linguistic a priori judgments.

The modular theory of mind provides a nurturing setting for my postulation of inconsistent a priori judgments with respect to tolerance conditionals. But all this psychological support will collapse if inconsistent apriorities are conceptually impossible. In the next chapter, I will argue that oxymoronic appearance of 'inconsistent apriorities' is due to mistakes about the nature of apriority.

6 Does Apriority Agglomerate?

Must a valid syllogism with a priori premises have an a priori conclusion? Only if apriority collects over conjunction: $(\mathbf{A}p \,\&\, \mathbf{A}q) \supset \mathbf{A}(p \,\&\, q)$. Philosophers have presupposed this agglomeration principle rather than argued for it—or even asserted it. Historically, supporting arguments could have been quickly mustered. Apriority has long been closely associated with analyticity and necessity. They both agglomerate. Therefore, any account which implies that apriority is co-extensive with either of these notions also implies that apriority agglomerates. Agglomeration could have also been supported by appeals to the certainty, irrevisability, or the infallibility traditionally (and disastrously) associated with apriority.

However, recent commentators would consider all of these arguments as outdated. They think traditional rationalists imposed an overly ambitious epistemology on a humble but useful concept. Once we pare away the extraneous, mistaken claims about apriority, we find a concept that a scientific naturalist could welcome (Goldman 1999). Recent progress in the psychology of mathematics may change this 'could welcome' into 'should welcome'. I contend that this spare conception of apriority correctly undermines all the positive arguments in favor of agglomeration. It also paves the way for a re-examination of agglomeration that illuminates the sorites paradox.

1. The Logic of Apriority

Agglomeration needs to be appraised in relation to other inference rules involving apriority. Picture these rules as constituting a branch of epistemic logic:

| AI: | $\dfrac{\vdash p}{\mathbf{A}p}$ | ADE: | $\dfrac{\mathbf{A}(p \supset q)}{\mathbf{A}p \supset \mathbf{A}q}$ | AD&: | $\dfrac{\mathbf{A}(p \,\&\, q)}{\mathbf{A}p \,\&\, \mathbf{A}q}$ |

AEI: $\dfrac{\mathbf{A}p}{\mathbf{A}q}$ [Where (p & q) $\supset$ r $\quad$ $\dfrac{\mathbf{A}q}{\mathbf{A}r}$ is a truth of logic]

AA: $\dfrac{\mathbf{A}p}{\mathbf{A}\mathbf{A}p}$ $\qquad$ AE: $\dfrac{\mathbf{A}p}{p}$ $\qquad$ AC: $\dfrac{\vdash \sim p}{\sim \mathbf{A}p}$

AI makes all logical truths a priori. Unlike the other principles, AI would not be rendered vacuously valid by the non-existence of a priori statements. ADE entitles distribution of apriority over material conditionals. From ADE and AI we can derive AD& and its converse, the agglomeration principle. Hence, any successful challenge to the agglomeration principle must also militate against the joint exercise of AI and ADE. Indeed, since ADE is plausible, AI should be singled out as a prime suspect. Suspicion also falls on AI from other directions. For instance, AEI can also be derived from ADE and AI. Consequently, an effective refutation of AEI must also dispose of AI.

Could a refutation of the deductive transmissibility of apriority proceed without raising the issue of whether apriority collects over conjunction? In conversation, Alexander Bird has sketched a line of attack that makes no initial mention of AD&. Let the conclusion of an argument be any necessary truth that is not a priori. Let all the premises be irrelevant a priori propositions. The resulting argument is vacuously valid because its conclusion is a necessary truth. But the apriority of the premises fails to make the conclusion a priori.

One might try to exclude Bird's vacuous cases by further requiring that the thinker know that the argument is valid. But this will not help when the conclusion is a necessary a posteriori truth. Only empirical investigation can demonstrate the necessary truth that 'Water is H_2O'. In this sense, 'All bachelors are male. Therefore, water is H_2O' is valid a posteriori. To exclude Bird's cases, the defender of the deductive transmissibility of apriority must require that the validity of the argument also be a priori.

This qualification makes the agglomeration principle AD& necessary for even single premise arguments. If the apriority of premises cannot be pooled with the apriority of the inference, then the conclusion might fail to be a priori. So although AD& looks like it only applies to the transmissibility of apriority through multiple premise arguments, it indirectly applies to single premise arguments as well.

AA tells us that apriority is itself an a priori matter. Like KK (if you know, then you know you know) in classic epistemic logics, AA plays a dark role in skeptical arguments against apriority. It also plays a dark role in suppressing empirical investigation into apriority. For AA encourages the belief that the scope and limits of armchair inquiry is itself an armchair inquiry. I hate AA. But my main motive for listing it here is to simply mark the distinction between AA and the agglomeration principle.

AE represents the principle that apriority entails truth. Traditional rationalists assume apriority entails certainty. This has made them easy targets for skeptics of apriority (Quine 1951a; Kitcher 1983). But recent rationalists are fallibilists (Bonjour 1998: 110–19). These new rationalists also concede that a thinker can be aware that his a priori beliefs are jointly inconsistent. Their standard example is a math student torn by conflicting results. The student's proof gives him warrant for p, the textbook's proof gives him warrant for q, and the student's incompatibility result gives him warrant for $\sim(p \ \& \ q)$. The student wisely responds by rejecting the weakest member of the inconsistent triad. This shows that a priori warrants can be ranked. Not all apriorities are equal.

Rankings make sense from an evolutionary perspective. Natural selection solves cognitive problems pluralistically and incrementally— by amassing a bag of tricks. Individually, these heuristic devices are only modestly reliable. But collectively, the motley of quick and dirty criteria comprise a rugged system that copes well in real-life circumstances. In laboratory conditions, the stupid rules can be prised apart and channeled into embarrassingly poor performance. But in circumstances approximating our hunter-gatherer past the tricks are mutually reinforcing. Each homunculus systematically errs but in different directions. (The real problem with stupidity is that there is not enough to go around.) This modular conception of apriority predicts that our language faculty is vulnerable to illusions just like our perceptual system is vulnerable to illusions. Competing homunculi will generate conflicting judgments. Thus our various sources of apriority will need to be measured against each other.

From fallibilism about apriority, we quickly conclude that apriority comes in degrees (Plantinga 1993: 109). Since a priori judgments can vary in warrant, some a priori judgments lack maximal warrant. When there is no minimum degree of warrant, we reach Paul Moser's (1987: 2) 'minimal a priori' in which P need only be more probable than not P.

Bayesians demonstrate that a self-correcting agent can build an imposing edifice of near-certain knowledge from numerous beliefs that are only slightly more probable than not. However, this cumulative process cannot rely on agglomeration: p and q can each be more likely than their negations without $p \ \& \ q$ being more likely than $\sim(p \ \& \ q)$.

Once we deny that apriority entails truth, we must countenance the possibility of jointly inconsistent apriorities. For instance, if p and q each have independent probabilities of 0.7, then $(p \ \& \ q)$ only has a probability of 0.49. Hence, its negation would be somewhat more than minimally a priori. This yields a set of apriorities that are indirectly inconsistent: $\{Ap, Aq, A{\sim}(p \& q)\}$.

Apriorities cannot be *directly* inconsistent. It is impossible for p to be more probable than ${\sim}p$ while ${\sim}p$ is more probable than p. Hence, ${\sim}(\exists p)(Ap \& A{\sim}p)$ even though $(p)Ap \& A{\sim}(p)p$ holds for some domains of statements. I shall argue that this second possibility is exemplified by the induction step of the sorites paradox. Endorsing jointly inconsistent apriorities sets the stage for acceptance of apriorities that turn out to be contradictions.

Adding a truth condition to apriority, AE, will prevent inconsistent apriorities. And raising the threshold of acceptable probability will reduce the frequency of agglomeration failures. But the threshold must be raised to 1 merely to avoid counterexamples based on the rule for calculating the probabilities of conjunctions.

Since our topic is the transmission of apriority via valid inference, the more pertinent instance of inconsistent apriority is the surprising a priori proof. From a priori premises that I accept, I am led to a conclusion that I previously had a priori warrant to reject. It is just this reversal of a priori judgments that characterizes the most striking mathematical results. These proofs of the 'impossible' include the Tarski–Banach paradox, Cantor's diagonal proof, and Russell's refutation of Frege's principle that there is a set for each property. If apriorities were always jointly consistent, one could only argue to conclusions that merely correct an error of omission or which fortify a pre-existing belief.

There is a tendency to assimilate all surprising a priori proofs to rebuttals of fallacies. For apriority is often regarded as universally *robust*; if p is a priori, then *no* further evidence can undermine P. The Gettier problem led some epistemologists to initially claim that knowledge is universally robust. But they retreated once the pervasiveness of misleading evidence was appreciated. Knowledge is robust but only with respect to *accessible* evidence. Localized robustness is also appropriate for apriority. The mere fact that I could acquire evidence by sufficient reflection does not make it accessible.

If there are inconsistent apriorities, then the agglomeration principle would let one infer a counterexample to AC (the prohibition against a priori contradictions), for the conjunction of the jointly inconsistent a priori propositions is a contradiction. I do not think that this derivation can be used to form a sound objection to the agglomeration principle.

For in addition to the surprising arguments in mathematics, there are surprising arguments in logic. These show that logicians sometimes have a priori warrant for logical falsehoods. So I reject AC. Indeed, the only principles I accept are ADE and AD&.

2. Inductive a Priori Reasoning

Following Tyler Burge, I take apriority to be an entitlement to have an attitude toward a proposition without empirical investigation. Experience may be needed for me to *understand* the proposition but it is not playing an essential role in justifying the proposition. Experience may also be needed to *preserve* results from earlier stages of a priori reasoning (Burge 1993). Experience can provide ancillary services without being on stage.

The non-empirical aspect of apriority is compatible with some a priori reasoning being inductive. The role of induction in mathematics can be dramatized by showing how Goodman's projectibility problem can arise within number theory.

Consider Goldbach's conjecture that every even number greater than 2 is the sum of two primes. Goldbach probably acquired his first evidence for the conjecture by simply checking many even numbers. Let us suppose that he checks all even numbers up to 2,000. Since the property does hold for these numbers, our hypothetical Goldbach concludes, by enumerative induction, that the next even number, 2,002, is also the sum of two primes. Although this argument may not suffice to give him knowledge that 2,002 is the sum of two primes, it does give him some degree of justification.

There are more sophisticated illustrations of inductive reasoning in mathematics presented by Imre Lakatos, George Polya, and Tyler Burge. My simple example has been contrived to show how the grue paradox arises within mathematical reasoning. Let the domain of discourse be the even numbers greater than 2. Now consider the following gruesome predicate:

> x is *goldbachgrue* iff either x is the sum of two primes and $x < 2,001$ or x is not the sum of two primes and $x > 2,001$.

Every even number up to 2,000 is goldbachgrue. Thus one can argue that the next even number, 2,002, is goldbachgrue. This conclusion conflicts with the one made by our hypothetical Goldbach. As in the classic grue paradox, conflicting predictions arise from using different predicates in arguments of the same form (here, the shared argument form is enumerative induction).

This mathematical case causes indigestion for some 'solutions' to the new riddle of induction. The predicates of the perverse induction cannot be screened out because they are time sensitive or because they fail to pick out natural kinds. But the important lesson for us is that Goodman's new riddle of induction is not about empirical reasoning *per se* but about induction. This releases a priori reasoning from the chains of deduction.

3. The Relativity of Apriority

The primary bearer of apriority is the propositional attitude (believing, knowing, guessing, and so on) rather than the proposition itself. A proposition could be a priori to *Homo Sapiens* but a posteriori to Neanderthals. This sensitivity to reference groups is disguised by absolute locutions of the form '*p* is a priori'. Perhaps fittingly, the '*Ap*' notation inherits this oversimplification.

The relativity of apriority tends to be recognized by theorists who provide a positive theory of what makes a proposition a priori. For instance, Alvin Plantinga's (1993: 109) proper functioning account of warrant makes apriority species relative. Relativization is even more fine-grained in scientific studies of apriority. Psychologists studying mathematical, logical, and linguistic competence, will in effect ask 'A priori to whom?' and 'A priori when?'. There is now experimental evidence that many species have rudimentary mathematical awareness (Dehaene 1997, ch. 1). It has been known longer that mathematical beliefs in children mature in stages. To make sense of developmental acquisition of a priori beliefs, we need to make contrastive apriority attributions within a single individual's lifetime. Agent-less apriority is scientifically irrelevant. And illogical. Propositional attitudes must have bearers as well as objects. Free-floating apriority 'drops a variable'.

Although we should not thin the notion of apriority syntactically (by turning the apriority relation into a one-place predicate), we should follow Burge's example of thinning the notion semantically. Apriority does not entail knowledge or truth or perhaps even justification. An entitlement is a right that need not be earned by knowledge of that right. The right to believe can even survive failure to exercise the right or even the title holder's renunciation or denial of that right. Rights do not agglomerate. I have a right to vote for the legalization of marijuana and a right to vote against the proposal but these rights are not co-exercisable. I am entitled to buy any liter of water but am not entitled to buy every liter of water (Sorensen 1986).

Deontological conceptions of warrant raise the possibility that the deontic logicians' (Sinnott-Armstrong 1988: 127–35) concerns about the agglomeration of 'ought' carry over to epistemology. However, my case against agglomeration does not presuppose acceptance of Burge's deontic characterization of apriority. Interestingly, the common terms uses to analyze apriority (immunity, justification, knowledge, probability, and tractability) are non-agglomerative. The same goes for sources of apriority. For instance, methodological conservatives assign a (slight) warrant to a belief simply by virtue of it being an established belief. When I believe p and believe q without believing p and q, methodological conservatives assign warrant to the conjuncts, not the conjunction.

Every attribution of apriority to a proposition is tacitly an attribution of a cognitive ability to some thinker. In particular, the ability to justifiably believe without reliance on experience is a privational ability like the ability to safely fly an airplane without looking out of a window. I am not back-pedaling on the normativity of apriority when saying a priori beliefs involve an ability. After all, the ability to *safely* fly without relying on visual information presented through the windows is a normative notion. Pilots even receive official certification for 'instrument flying'. The entitlement behind a priori beliefs is earned by the abilities composing linguistic competence and the operation of the senses. Ability attributions are normally non-agglomerative. I can hear without my left ear and can hear without my right ear but I cannot hear without both. With just a glance I can know that on the page lie scattered three pennies. A glance also suffices for three nickels or three dimes or three quarters. But I cannot know with just a glance, that on the page lie scattered three nickels, three dimes, and three quarters.

In sum, there are a priori grounds for suspecting that apriority does not agglomerate. Let me now try to stitch these patches of evidence into an argument.

4. *Agents with Upper Bounds*

The authors of *Precalculus Mathematics* conclude their preface by posting a reward: 'In spite of all efforts to root out errors, some may still remain. But we believe these are so few that we safely offer for its first detection in a book of this series $5 per typo and $10 per serious error to students and staff at institutions using this book' (Flanders and Price 1981, p. viii). The modest size of the rewards betokens a lack of confidence in the conjunction of all their (a priori) answers. This suggests that the apriority of their warrant would fail to agglomerate *if* the authors were fortunate enough to have an error-free text.

Suppose this good fortune is enjoyed by Professor Ambitious. He has written a mathematics book and has a priori warrant for each statement in his text. However, Professor Ambitious refrains from believing the conjunction of those statements. Indeed, he is willing to bet *against* the conjunction. His basis need not be an a posteriori assessment of past a priori errors. We can suppose that he has an a priori appreciation of the limited nature of his a priori warrant.

The best explanation of the asymmetry between his attitude toward the conjuncts and his attitude toward the conjunction is that the individual warrants do not constitute a collective warrant. Professor Ambitious is a counterexample to the *personal* agglomeration principle: If statements p and q are each a priori to x then they must both be a priori to x, that is, $(x)[(Axp \& Axq) \supset Ax(p \& q)]$.

The first assumption behind the counterexample is that conjuncts are easier to warrant than their conjunctions. The second assumption is there is an upper bound on the Professor's abilities. The reasoning is that wherever that upper bound is, there are some just barely accessible conjuncts whose conjunctions are not accessible. Any finite improvement of the Professor that increases his access to a conjunction also increases his access to new conjuncts. Therefore, the Professor's warrants cannot be made agglomerative by improving him. Each solution to an agglomeration failure creates a new failure of agglomeration.

Other counterexamples to the personal agglomeration principle exploit other asymmetries. For instance, if there is an upper bound on the length of understandable sentences, then two understandable sentences can have an unintelligible conjunction. The basic idea is that the capacity of bounded agents can be overwhelmed by the sum of burdens that can be shouldered individually.

Upper bounds do not defeat an *impersonal* agglomeration principle: $(x)(Axp \& Axq) \supset (\exists y)Ay(p \& q)$. This weaker principle merely says that whenever two propositions are a priori to an individual, then their conjunction is a priori to someone or other. Consider an infinite sequence of finite thinkers each with a greater upper bound than his predecessor. If these thinkers are arranged like the natural numbers (reflecting their increasing power), then each thinker has an upper bound. But there is no limit on the population as a whole. Consequently, if p and q are each a priori to x, there will be some individual y such that the conjunction is a priori to y.

Impersonal agglomeration would be relevant to the deductive transmission of apriority if apriority were primarily a property of statements rather than a property of the attitude toward that statement. Analyticity and necessity *are* primarily properties of statements. Perhaps the tendency to lump apriority with analyticity and necessity makes impersonal agglomeration appear germane. In any case, only the personal agglomeration principle licenses the transmission of apriority from premises to their conclusion. Focusing on a single agent is essential when studying the agglomeration principle because a single agent must make the inference that spreads the apriority from the conjuncts to the conjunction. After all, the following argument is invalid:

1. Someone has a warrant for p that does not rely on sense experience.
2. Someone has a warrant for q that does not rely on sense experience.
3. Therefore, someone has a warrant for p and q that does not rely on sense experience.

The conclusion is true only if the same someone satisfies both premises.

This requirement may seem satisfied when the reasoner is pictured as an arbitrary individual. An arbitrary F has all and only those properties shared by all Fs. Hence, the arbitrary man is finite (because all men are finite). Yet the arbitrary man has no upper bound on his power. This generic thinker seems ideally suited for the study of how apriority passes from premises to conclusion.

But as George Berkeley (1710) first emphasized in his criticism of John Locke's theory of abstract ideas, arbitrary objects are incoherent. An arbitrary F has all and only those properties that are shared by all Fs. Hence, an arbitrary number is either odd or even. Yet it is not odd and it is not even. Therefore, the principle of bivalence implies that arbitrary individuals are logically impossible.

In a lonely defense of arbitrary individuals, Kit Fine (1985: 11) boldly recommends that we spare arbitrary individuals by instead rejecting bivalence. One might resort to deviant logic if standard logic offered no solution to the problem of generality. But Gottlob Frege's theory of quantification dispensed with arbitrary individuals. The theory, now entrenched in standard logic, captures all the relevant inferences involving universal quantifiers. The only complaint is that the inferences are more cumbersome and less intuitive. Arbitrary individuals are more natural than flagged variables. Similarly, naive set theory is more natural than Zermelo-Fränkel set theory. Zermelo-Fränkel set theory has awkward limitations on set formation that are designed to avoid Russell's paradox. For heuristic purposes, one may choose to work with an incoherent notion like an arbitrary individual or a naive set. It is pedantic to always insist on consistency in one's methods of discovery. But the results can only be vindicated by reinterpretation into a coherent theory.

Various species of ideal thinkers are useful in epistemology. There might be circumstances in which arbitrary individuals ought to be employed despite their handicap of inconsistency. But arbitrary individuals ought not to be employed for an investigation of apriority. Arbitrary individuals discourage us from distinguishing between global robustness and local robustness. They make a mystery of surprising a priori arguments. And they lay the groundwork for skepticism about apriority by misleading us into accepting an overly strong logic of apriority.

Standard quantification theory undercuts the temptation to think that impersonal agglomeration is relevant. The point of defending the agglomeration principle is to ensure that the individual apriority of the premises is transmitted to conclusion by the process of valid inference. That inference must be performed by a single reasoner.

5. AI and Non-demonstrative Apriorities

A complete refutation of the agglomeration principle requires an attack on AI, the principle that all logical truths are a priori. For AI and the plausible ADE suffice to derive agglomeration:

1.	Ap	Assume
2.	Aq	Assume
3.	$p \supset (q \supset (p \,\&\, q))$	logical truth
4.	$A[p \supset (q \supset (p \,\&\, q))]$	3, AI
5.	$Ap \supset A(q \supset (p \,\&\, q))$	4, ADE
6.	$A(q \supset (p \,\&\, q))$	1, 5 modus ponens
7.	$Aq \supset A(p \,\&\, q)$	6, ADE
8.	$A(p \,\&\, q)$	2, 7 modus ponens

My specific objection to AI is that every finite agent has an upper bound on the logical truths to which he has access. Logical truths that are too complex for one agent may be accessible to another agent. But this does not help the agent who must transmit the apriority of his premises to his conclusion. Thus the point about upper bounds that was used to attack agglomeration also affects AI.

Allegiance to AI is historically deep. Leibniz (and later Frege) thought a priori propositions consisted of the laws of logic plus anything derivable from those laws. Hence Leibniz endorses AI as well as its converse. Leibniz was inspired by Euclid's axiomatic geometry. This system suggests every known mathematical truth is either a self-evident certainty or can be derived from self-evident certainties through self-evident steps. Certainty can only be transmitted by deductive inference. Hence, no a priori proposition is the conclusion of an inductive argument or the conclusion of an inference to the best explanation.

However, there do appear to be many a priori beliefs that are non-demonstrative (Burge 1998). Euclid's unsystematic predecessors had a priori warrant for many geometrical propositions. Historians generally credit these early geometers with the *discovery* of these propositions and portray much of Euclid's work as regimenting these pre-existing results. Isaac Newton lacked any *demonstrative* knowledge of the principles of calculus. But he knew enough to engage in the notorious priority dispute with Leibniz. Normally a mathematician acquires a justified belief in a conjecture before attempting a proof. The grounds for these conjectures are often difficult to articulate. But they form the basis for recreational bets (which range from foolish to wise) and for professional investment in which years of labor are at stake.

Proofs themselves develop in stages. As more gaps in the proof sketch are filled, the probability of a successful demonstration increases. This shows that there can be a priori evidence of there being other a priori evidence. The finished proof is an important cognitive advance but it is not the first stage of justification.

The Euclidean myth has helpfully raised standards in mathematics; instead of settling for modest support, mathematicians have demanded rigorous proof. Surprisingly often, the excessive demand has been satisfied. But this axiomatic model has been undermined by two famous developments. First, efforts to prove the parallel postulate backfired. Instead of proving the proposition by *reductio ad absurdum*, Gerolamo Saccheri inadvertently inaugurated non-Euclidean geometries. The usefulness of Reimannian geometry in relativity theory led mathematicians to retract the claim that the axioms are always self-evident certainties. It is now thought permissible to have axioms that merely have a sufficiently high degree of a priori plausibility. This kind of self-evidence does not agglomerate. Two propositions can satisfy the quota of plausibility without their conjunction satisfying the quota.

The second development was Kurt Gödel's incompleteness results. Gödel showed that for each finite, consistent, axiom system strong enough to express the truths of arithmetic, there will be a truth that cannot be proved. If these truths are logical theorems (as logicists contend), then they are direct counterexamples to AI. Once again, we must be careful to relativize. Each system has an unprovable theorem but there is no theorem that is unprovable in all the systems. After all, one can prove any proposition by simply adding it to the list of axioms of the original system. Every truth of arithmetic is provable in the perverse, 'impersonal' sense of being provable in some system or other. When Leibniz and Frege associated apriority with provability, they intended provability within a single system.

Most mathematicians concede that we have justified belief in the consistency of arithmetic despite the impossibility of proving the consistency of arithmetic. Similarly, there is a consensus that scholars have justified belief in Church's thesis, the axiom of choice, and so on. There is indeed a long list of unprovable propositions. Each have some degree of a priori warrant. But the a priori warrant does not extend to the conjunction of the members on this long list of disparate propositions.

The list of unprovable but a priori beliefs can be extended by going outside of mathematics. There are a priori justified beliefs undergirding morality, aesthetics, and empirical investigation. Many, if not all, of these beliefs are non-demonstrative.

The generality of non-demonstrative methods is encouraged by Nelson Goodman's methodology of reflective equilibrium. In a classic commentary on logic, Goodman (1954) notes that we work back and forth, adjusting principle to intuitions and adjusting intuitions to principles. This process of testing inference rules by their instances uses induction, inference to the best explanation, and perhaps some further modes of non-deductive inference that we have yet to articulate. Hence, logical opinions can acquire a priori non-demonstrative warrants that fail to agglomerate.

6. A Posteriori Sorites Arguments and Relative Apriority

A statement *p* is a priori relative to empirical basis b if, and only if, anyone who knows b is entitled to believe *p* without further empirical investigation. Generally, we point out these apriorities when the thinker is in a position to make a surprising inference on just the evidence at hand. For instance, I can know a priori that there are at least two philosophers who have the same three initials. I antecedently know that there are only 26 letters in the alphabet and so am in a position to know that there are only $26 \times 26 \times 26 = 17{,}576$ initials. I also know that there are over 17,576 philosophers with initials. Since there are more philosophers than possible initials, some philosophers must share the same initials. Surprisingly, I can learn this fact without leaving my armchair. Normally, we must gather new empirical information to answer questions such as these. Claims of relative apriority mark exceptions to this rule of thumb. The exceptions are not entirely higgledy-piggledy. Any law attributing endless exponential growth (of computer memory, scientific literature, and so on) can be known to be false a priori. For given the background assumption of a finite domain, the process will exhaust its resources.

Absolute apriority and relative apriority are inter-definable. On analogy with the deduction theorem, absolute apriority can be considered a limit case of relative apriority. The base of empirical propositions to which we are relativizing can be made smaller and smaller. When this set of empirical propositions is the empty set, we have absolute apriority. Some skepticism about apriority just amounts to doubt that the set can be empty. Don't I need experience to learn the language? Don't I need schooling to become mathematically literate? Psychologists even speculate that I must manipulate objects to learn spatial concepts. Defenders of absolute apriority say that experience is only needed to *trigger* conceptual development (as exposure to the sun is needed to trigger the skin's innate tendency to tan). But even those who grant there is genuine learning of concepts from experience, tend to avoid skepticism about absolute apriority. They say a statement is a priori as long as it is based on topic-neutral experiences. Relative apriorities, in contrast, use empirical premises relevant to the conclusion.

Relative apriority can be defined as the absolute apriority of a conditional. For instance, the whole conditional 'If there are over 17,576 philosophers with initials composed of three letters, then at least two of them share initials' is absolutely a priori. Those who believe that experience is always needed for knowledge of substantive statements are free to concede that many *conditionals* are absolutely a priori.

Since absolute apriority does not agglomerate, relative apriority does not agglomerate. That means the anti-agglomeration diagnosis applies to some arguments that have a posteriori premises. All a posteriori arguments have some a priori component but normally this portion is trivial or not naturally separable. A posteriori sorites arguments differ in that the conceptual aspect of the argument is in the foreground and the empirical features are in the background.

Suppose that we have been treated to the spectacle of a heap of sand being destroyed grain by grain. Each of the following conditionals is a priori relative to this empirical basis:

1. If removing the first grain of sand from the heap left it a heap, then the removal of the second grain of sand left it a heap.

2. If removing the second grain of sand from the heap left it a heap, then the removal of the third grain of sand left it a heap.

            .
            .
            .

10,000. If removing the 10,000th grain of sand from the heap left it a heap, then the removal of the 10,001st grain of sand left it a heap.

Although each of these a posteriori conditionals is a priori relative to my observation of the heap's gradual destruction, one of them is false. The conjunction of these conditionals is a priori false relative to the destruction. So is the corresponding generalization:

For each n, if removing n grains of sand left it a heap, then removing $n + 1$ grains of sand left it a heap.

A syntactic distinction can be drawn between wide and narrow apriority. The Barcan formula for apriority would entitle an inference from narrow scope apriority to wide scope: $(x)AFx \supset A(x)Fx$. The invalidity of this inference can be used to elaborate the epistemic solution to the sorites paradox. The paradox is most compactly expressed as a mathematical induction of the form: F_1, $(n)(Fn \supset Fn + 1)$, therefore, $(n)Fn$. As an epistemicist, I affirm the narrow scope apriority of the induction step, $(n)A(Fn \supset Fn + 1)$, while denying its large scope apriority, $A(n)(Fn \supset Fn + 1)$. This syntactic point allows me to capture data which (falsely) suggest that vague language is inconsistent.

Speakers are tempted to infer wide apriority from narrow apriority. Whether or not they actually make this inference, the fallacy blocks most of them from gaining a priori knowledge that a threshold exists. So although they all have access to a sound proof from known premises that there is a threshold for 'heap', almost none of them gains knowledge of the conclusion from this proof. Those who most patiently and perceptively study the proof also tend to be the ones with philosophical views of language that are incompatible with the conclusion.

7. Does Conceivability Distribute over Disjunction?

We are immobilized by two opposed arguments. The first appears to show that the induction step is an a priori truth. The second argument appears to show that the negation of the induction step is an a priori truth.

Each speaker has a right and a duty to ignore insignificant differences. This makes each step of the sorites individually a priori. Yet the negation of the conclusion is also a priori. Hence, our apriorities are jointly inconsistent. Language commands assent to propositions that cannot be true as a conjunction.

Once we detect the inconsistency, we backtrack and reconsider the premises. The only premise that seems vulnerable is the induction step: 'For each n, if n seconds after noon is noonish, then $n + 1$ seconds after noon is noonish'. However, each counter-model is believed by a competent speaker to be a contradiction. Hence, a competent speaker 'does not understand what it is like for the induction step to be false'.

I am appealing to the connection between inconceivability and perceived contradiction. Given that the usual acceptance rules are in force, the speaker must regard the negation of any tolerance conditional as a contradiction. Just as he cannot imagine how there could be evidence for 'The penultimate man is the last man', he cannot imagine how there could be evidence for '12.15 is the last noonish minute'. If I perceive a proposition as a contradiction, then I cannot conceive of how it could be true or how there could be the least bit of evidence in its favor. Nor can I imagine anyone else doing the conceiving. Perceived contradiction is a kind of stopping place in thought. In a *reductio ad absurdum* proof, the reasoning ends as soon the contradiction is derived. To the extent that I perceive a threshold statement as a contradiction, I think of further inquiry on the matter as impossible and therefore misconceived. I am at a limit. In this sense, perceived contradictions shape the area in which reasoning can take place.

However, the shaping done by *perceived* contradictions differs from that done by contradictions. Contradictions shape thought both locally and holistically because any disjunction of contradictions is itself a contradiction. However, if each proposition merely has a high probability of being a contradiction, then their disjunction need not have a high probability of being a contradiction. A disjunction of perceived contradictions could even have a high probability of being a tautology. What is inconceivable considered severally may be inevitable considered collectively. Such is the case with the negation of the induction step of an analytic sorites argument.

My claim that inconceivability does not collect over disjunction is restricted to the epistemic sense of 'conceive'. This is the sense that entails belief: if I conceive that p, then I believe that p is possible. Possibility collects over disjunction: $(\Diamond p \vee \Diamond q) \supset \Diamond(p \vee q)$. Belief in possibility does not. The point can be put in terms of a conceiving operator, C. A disjunction can be conceived without any of its disjuncts being conceived: $C(p \vee q)$ does not entail $(Cp \vee Cq)$. The point will flow over to existential generalization: $C(\exists x)Fx$ does not entail $(\exists x)CFx$. For instance, I can conceive of there being something I cannot conceive even though I cannot conceive of a particular thing that is inconceivable to me.

Indeed, I actually believe that there are things I cannot conceive. Evolutionary theory and psychology give me ample grounds for believing human beings have limited cognitive ranges. But other limits to conceivability are species neutral. Under the influence of a causal theory of directly referential terms, I believe that there are propositions about future individuals which I cannot now entertain. One year before my son Zachary was born, I could not think thoughts about *him*. As a believer in planned pregnancies, I had general thoughts about having a child, having it in the winter, hoping that it would be a sound sleeper, and so on. I could even have thoughts about *the* sibling of my extant son Maxwell. But my planning could not include thoughts about Zachary himself. For he was not around to be thought of. As far as *de re* thoughts go, every pregnancy is unplanned.

Ditto for Martian pregnancies. Extra-terrestrials may be smarter than us. But the range of their *de re* thoughts is equally hemmed in by the structure of causal chains. As smart as these aliens may be, they cannot have *de re* thoughts about future individuals or merely possible individuals. If we are outside their light cone, then we cannot figure in their thoughts.

Since conceivability does not collect over disjunction, thought experiments can succeed without specificity. John Hick (1957, ch. 7) tries to cope with the problem of evil by demanding a specific description of a better world than the actual world. But an atheist could conceive of a better world without having the resources to uniquely describe the possible world. Just as I can see an apple without seeing every part of it, I can conceive a scenario without conceiving each part of the scenario.

Just as there is a non-epistemic sense of 'see', there is a non-epistemic sense of 'conceive'. This sense has no implication of belief. Bertrand Russell (1948: 112) conceived of someone having justified true belief without having knowledge. His example featured a man who reads the time off of a broken clock that is coincidentally correct. However, Russell did not believe it was possible for someone to have justified true belief without knowledge. For Russell's example was merely intended to illustrate why true belief did not suffice for knowledge. Edmund Gettier (1963) was the first to *epistemically* conceive a counterexample to the justified true belief analysis of knowledge. Non-epistemic conceiving is atheoretical. Non-epistemically conceiving *p* entails the possibility of *p*. Consequently, non-epistemic conceiving agglomerates.

Some philosophers profess skepticism about intensional concepts, especially those concepts in the 'intensional circle' isolated by W. V. Quine: analyticity, apriority, and necessity. The skepticism comes in degrees, trailing off into mere discomfort. The next chapter is an effort to keep everyone unskeptical and comfortable. The strategy is to formulate my results in terms acceptable to Quine. In particular, I will rely solely on syntactic analyticity. The point is not merely to persuade Quine and fellow travelers. I think my contortions within the Quinean strait-jacket create novel evidence against epistemicism's rivals.

7 Analytic Sorites and the Cheshire Cat

(Logicians do it) or [not (logicians do it)]

I shall construct a slippery-slope argument that begins with a logical truth and concludes with a logical falsehood. Since logical truths can be deleted from an argument without affecting its validity, this sorites argument has superfluous premises. Indeed, I shall contend that all but one of the links in the chain are dispensable.

1. Borderline Cases of 'Logical Truth'

Suppose an instructor in sentence logic asks the class for a sample sentence so that she can display its logical form. Mr Vague volunteers

(A) If it is both the case that either $1 = 1$ or not, and $2 = 2$ or not, then it is not the case that either $1 = 1$ or not, or $2 = 2$ or not.

Under the exclusive reading of 'or', (A) is a tautology. Under the inclusive reading of 'or', (A) is a contradiction. Let 'v' stand for inclusive 'or' and '≢' stand for exclusive 'or':

Exclusive reading:

$$[((1 = 1) \not\equiv {\sim}(1 = 1)) \,\&\, ((2 = 2) \not\equiv {\sim}(2 = 2))] \supset$$
$${\sim}[((1 = 1) \not\equiv {\sim}(1 = 1)) \not\equiv ((2 = 2) \not\equiv {\sim}(2 = 2))]$$

Inclusive reading:

$$[((1 = 1) \lor {\sim}(1 = 1)) \,\&\, ((2 = 2) \lor {\sim}(2 = 2))] \supset$$
$${\sim}[((1 = 1) \lor {\sim}(1 = 1)) \lor ((2 = 2) \lor {\sim}(2 = 2))]$$

The instructor asks Mr Vague whether he meant the inclusive or exclusive reading of (A). She makes the question clear with the help of truth tables. Mr Vague understands the truth tables and admires the distinction. Yet Mr Vague confesses that at the time, he did not clearly intend one meaning rather than the other.

The absence of a clear intention makes his utterance vague rather than ambiguous. If Mr Vague's utterance were merely ambiguous, then Mr Vague would know which reading he intended. But Mr Vague was never in a position to know which reading he meant. His utterance of (A) is borderline between 'utterance using the inclusive or' and 'utterance using the exclusive or'. Utterance (A)'s borderline status does not make (A) vague. 'There are infinitely many prime numbers' is a borderline case of 'short sentence' but that does not make the utterance vague. If we know an utterance is borderline between expressing precise proposition X and precise proposition Y, then we know it expresses a precise proposition—even though there is no telling which of the two propositions it really expresses.

Since it is more charitable to attribute beliefs in tautologies rather than beliefs in contradictions, one might urge the exclusive reading of Mr Vague's utterance of (A). But he did not *assert* (A). Mr Vague was only uttering a sample sentence. The principle of charity is not triggered.

Even if charity were triggered, the principle would not be able to adjudicate between cases that are borderline between distinct logical truths. Suppose Mr Vague had asserted

(B) Either $1 = 1$ or it is not the case that $1 = 1$.

The statement is a logical truth under both the inclusive and exclusive readings. Although (B) is true by virtue of its logical words, there is vagueness as to which logical form it has.

Methodological hunger for simplicity always creates pressure *against* attributing ambiguity (Wertheimer 1972, ch. 2; Kripke 1977: 268). So does responsible metaphysics: to postulate an extra meaning is to postulate an entity and such postulations must always be backed by evidence. (Physicists also believe in quantitative parsimony (Nolan 1997).) Mr Vague has been depicted in a way that ensures that there can be no evidence that overrides the presumption of univocality. The situation has been tailored for an application of Paul Ziff's (1960: 44) favorite tool: 'Occam's Erasure'.

2. The Cheshire Sorites

Sometimes an exclusive 'or' gradually develops into an inclusive 'or'. Consider a restaurant with a blackboard used to post the daily specials. One day, the manager writes 'Free coffee or juice!' on the blackboard. The offer begins as a clearly exclusive choice. Pick! Either but not both!

The offer increases business. Thus a new inscription of 'Free coffee or juice!' is written on the blackboard the following day. And the next. And the next. Under the pressure of competition, more and more customers are given both coffee and juice if they request both. This is initially a supererogatory courtesy that goes beyond the terms of the offer. But as the manager's permissiveness gradually becomes common knowledge, 'Free coffee or juice!' gradually develops into an *inclusive* offer. What had been supererogatory is now obligatory; the waiter *must* give both coffee and juice upon request. Thus the meaning of the manager's 'or' in his daily inscriptions of 'Free coffee or juice!' develops from the exclusive to the inclusive reading. But no inscription is the first clear offer containing an inclusive 'or'.

Inscriptions of (A) could develop in the same way. Suppose speaker 1 clearly intends the 'or' in his utterance to be exclusive (thereby making utterance A1 a logical truth). At the opposite end of the spectrum is speaker 1,000 who clearly intends (A) to be read inclusively (thereby making utterance A1,000 a logical falsehood). In between are speakers who have less clear intentions.

Suppose each speaker writes his assertion of (A) in a log book. This log book is used as a 'dictionary' by a logician. In particular, the logician assigns the name An to the proposition expressed by speaker n. He then constructs a sorites argument—the Cheshire sorites:

(C)   A1, A1 $\supset$ A2, A2 $\supset$ A3, . . . , A999 $\supset$ A1,000, therefore, A1,000

A standard deductive system that is strong enough to validate A1 as a logical truth is strong enough to validate the Cheshire sorites. It is also strong enough to validate the argument that results when A1 is deleted from the premise set. After all, the inference rules of such a system can simply reintroduce A1 by deriving it from the empty set (since A1 is a logical truth). A logician may hope for a more elegant proof. But the simple reintroduction tactic illustrates the key point that inference rules have the power to do the job normally accomplished with a premise (when that premise is a logical truth). The edited sorites shows that the sorites paradox cannot always be solved by rejecting the base step. For the trimmed sorites lacks a base step.

Although the early utterances of (A) use the exclusive or, the latter utterances are progressively better candidates for 'is using the inclusive "or" ' (the reading under which (A) is a logical falsehood). Consequently, any precisification of this vague predicate must cut the sequence in a way that preserves the numerical order of the statements. That is to say, there is some n such that all the speakers up to n are using 'or' exclusively and all of the speakers after n are using 'or' inclusively. The inclusive reading of (A) makes the utterance a logical falsehood, so we know the conclusion is a logical falsehood. We also know that the first premise was a logical truth (since that inscription clearly involves an exclusive reading of (A)). Since the partition of exclusive uses from inclusive uses must preserve numerical order, every precisification of 'uses "or" inclusively' ensures that exactly one premise in the argument is a logical falsehood. The false premise has a logical truth as its antecedent and a logical falsehood as a consequent. More specifically, the antecedent is a proposition that was expressed by someone using 'or' exclusively and the consequent is a proposition that was expressed by a neighbor who used the 'or' inclusively.

Epistemicists, like me, view vagueness as ignorance. We accept the previous sentence without qualification. Epistemicists believe that each utterance in argument (C) expresses a proposition. But we think that there is a great deal of repetition; many sentences in the premise set express the same proposition. For instance, many of the early conditional utterances express the conditional proposition whose antecedent and consequent consist of the exclusive reading of (A). This conditional is lengthy:

$$[((1 = 1) \not\equiv {\sim}(1 = 1)) \,\&\, ((2 = 2) \not\equiv {\sim}(2 = 2))] \supset {\sim}[((1 = 1) \not\equiv {\sim}(1 = 1)) \not\equiv ((2 = 2) \not\equiv {\sim}(2 = 2))] \supset [((1 = 1) \not\equiv {\sim}(1 = 1)) \,\&\, ((2 = 2) \not\equiv {\sim}(2 = 2))] \supset {\sim}[((1 = 1) \not\equiv {\sim}(1 = 1)) \not\equiv ((2 = 2) \not\equiv {\sim}(2 = 2))]$$

Efficient arguers try to express distinct propositions with each assertion made in the course of their argument. Circular reasoners are notorious for failing to achieve this goal; the proposition expressed by their conclusion is also expressed by one of their premises. Ordinary arguments also tend to have this kind of redundancy—even when non-circular. Whether in haste or for emphasis, everyday arguers state a small number of propositions in different ways. In the case of argument (C), only four distinct propositions are expressed: the exclusive reading of (A), the conditional which uses this exclusive reading as both antecedent and consequent, the conditional which uses the exclusive reading in the antecedent and the inclusive reading in the consequent (this is the sole logical falsehood in the premise set), and the conditional that uses the inclusive reading in both the antecedent and consequent.

Other views of vagueness mimic the epistemic analysis of (C). Supervaluationists accept statements that are true under all their precisifications. For instance, they regard 'An hermaphrodite is a sibling of its brother' as true even though the hermaphrodite is borderline between being male and female. In the same spirit, supervaluationists accept the attribution of a logical falsehood to the Cheshire sorites. Although the supervaluationists echo the epistemicists' diagnosis of the Cheshire sorites (and sorites arguments in general), the supervaluationists do not share the epistemicist's realism about the proposition that is the single false premise in the Cheshire sorites. For them, it is *as if* a single logical falsehood was expressed by one of the sentences.

Normally an argument is said to equivocate when there is a change in meaning that invalidates the argument. However, some changes in meaning preserve validity. Read the following argument as using 'or' in the exclusive sense in the premise and in the inclusive sense in the conclusion: 'Either Jack took the E train or Jack took the F train, therefore, either Jack took the E train or Jack took the F train'. The argument is formally valid because it has the valid form E ≢ F, therefore, E v F. The argument would also be valid if the premise were expressed by an utterance that was borderline between being an inclusive use of 'or' and an exclusive use of 'or'. For it would be valid under all precisifications of the relevant meta-linguistic predicates, that is, 'uses "or" inclusively' and 'uses "or" exclusively'.

The change in meaning in the Cheshire sorites does not invalidate the argument. Just the opposite! The change of meaning *guarantees* the validity of the argument because it ensures that one of the premises is a logical falsehood. The meaning switch will be from an exclusive reading of (A) in the antecedent of a conditional (which expresses a logical truth) to an inclusive reading of (A) in the consequent of a conditional (which expresses a logical falsehood). Even so, the shift in meaning is damaging because it guarantees that the Cheshire sorites is necessarily unsound.

In textbook examples of equivocation, it is easy to identify the exact point at which the meaning changes. Ordinary cases tend to be murkier; we can tell that the meaning shifted either here or there but it is not clear exactly where. The Cheshire sorites involves an extreme degree of this murkiness. There is no telling which of very many premises has this mixed usage. Surprisingly, we can identify the *proposition* expressed by the single false sentence in the premise set of the Cheshire sorites. The proposition consists of a material conditional that uses an exclusive reading of (A) in the antecedent and an inclusive reading in the consequent:

$$[((1 = 1) \not\equiv \sim(1 = 1)) \& ((2 = 2) \not\equiv \sim(2 = 2))] \supset \sim[((1 = 1) \not\equiv \sim(1 = 1)) \not\equiv$$
$$((2 = 2) \not\equiv \sim(2 = 2))] \supset [((1 = 1) \vee \sim(1 = 1)) \& ((2 = 2) \vee \sim(2 = 2))] \supset$$
$$\sim[((1 = 1) \vee \sim(1 = 1)) \vee ((2 = 2) \vee \sim(2 = 2))]$$

The single false sentence in the Cheshire sorites is the premise that expresses this proposition. But is this premise A500? Is it A501? A502? There is no way to tell because of the vagueness of the meta-linguistic predicate 'utterance using the inclusive or'.

The early premises of the Cheshire sorites are logical truths that have logical truths as consequents. The late premises are logical truths that have logical falsehoods as their antecedents. Since logical truths can be suppressed without affecting the validity of the argument, we may erase these superfluous premises. It is natural to begin erasing the clearer logical truths at both ends of the chain and work toward the middle. Each erasure is a precedent for moving another step inwards from both directions. But the disappearances cannot continue without limit. There must be exactly one premise that has a logical truth as its antecedent and a logical falsehood as its consequent. This premise is not a logical truth and so remains after all the logical truths disappear. The recalcitrant premise lingers like the grin of the Cheshire Cat.

We cannot identify exactly which inscription figures as the single premise of the radically reduced sorites. Is it A500? Or A501? Or what? However, we can identify the argument in the sense of identifying the *proposition* that serves as the premise. Since the proposition expressed by the conclusion is already known, we can identify the whole argument in its propositional form:

$$[((1 = 1) \not\equiv \sim(1 = 1)) \& ((2 = 2) \not\equiv \sim(2 = 2))] \supset \sim[((1 = 1) \not\equiv \sim(1 = 1)) \not\equiv$$
$$((2 = 2) \not\equiv \sim(2 = 2))] \supset [((1 = 1) \vee \sim(1 = 1)) \& ((2 = 2) \vee \sim(2 = 2))] \supset$$
$$\sim[((1 = 1) \vee \sim(1 = 1)) \vee ((2 = 2) \vee \sim(2 = 2))]$$

Therefore,

$$[((1 = 1) \vee \sim(1 = 1)) \& ((2 = 2) \vee \sim(2 = 2))] \supset$$
$$\sim[((1 = 1) \vee \sim(1 = 1)) \vee ((2 = 2) \vee \sim(2 = 2))]$$

This argument is degenerately valid because its premise is a logical falsehood.

Sentence logic suffices to diagnose the Cheshire sorites; it is formally unsound because one of its premises is a logical falsehood. Deviant logicians must concur because their systems are designed to converge with classical logic when the components of the arguments are precise propositions. For instance, supervaluationists accept all the tautologies of classical logic. Hence, they must agree that the Cheshire sorites has a single logical falsehood amongst its premises. All many-valued logics yield classical logic as a special case when all the truth values of the propositions are the extreme values of 1 or 0. Statements have the same truth-values as the propositions they express. Hence, the many-valued logician must agree that the Cheshire sorites has one premise that is fully false and the rest of the premises are fully true.

Although a single premise sorites is instructively easy to rebut, it is a genuine sorites argument. A sorites argument minus its superfluous premises is still a sorites argument. Hence, this limiting case of a sorites is a counterexample to the charge that all sorites are invalidated by their excessive length (as measured by the number of premises or the number of steps in the derivation or the number of times it employs an inference rule).

3. Bypassing the Analytic/Synthetic Controversy

Commentators on the sorites have not bothered to distinguish between analytic and synthetic sorites. Both species have long been in circulation. However, all of these analytic sorites have featured base steps that are *semantically* analytic:

1. Base step: 1 second after noon is noonish.
2. Induction step: for each n, if n seconds after noon is noonish, then $n + 1$ seconds after noon is noonish.
3. Conclusion: 10,000 seconds after noon is noonish.

Deleting the base step does not affect the *semantic* validity of the argument: it is impossible for the premises to be true and the conclusion false. However, the argument is not *syntactically* valid; the conclusion cannot be derived from the induction step using only rules of inference.

Both semantically and syntactically baseless sorites are interesting. But the syntactic variety has greater dialectical significance. Quine's (1951a) influential critique of the analytic/synthetic distinction is confined to semantic analyticity. His objection is that there is no extensional reduction of semantic analyticity to syntactic analyticity. The objection, whatever its merits, presupposes contentment with the status of logical truths and logical falsehoods (Quine 1953).

Nihilists (Horgan 1995; Heller 1990; Unger 1979) contend that the sorites has a purely metaphysical solution. One simply rejects the base step of all positive sorites (those that apply a vague predicate to something and then comprehensively extend that application) and accepts the soundness of all negative sorites (those that deny the application of a predicate to something and then comprehensively extend that denial). This policy was formulated with synthetic sorites in mind. Rejecting the base step then amounts to an ontological thesis. The implications are more complex for analytic sorites arguments:

1. For all x, if x is 1 second after noon, then x is noonish.
2. For all x and for all y, if x is n seconds after noon and y is $n + 1$ seconds after noon, then if x is noonish, so is y.
3. For all x, if x is 10,0000 seconds after noon, then x is noonish.

If all our predicates are like 'round square', then the premises and conclusion are vacuous necessary truths. Hence, this kind of nihilist would be in the peculiar position of affirming the soundness of this positive sorites argument. If only vague predicates are logically empty, then the first premise is a necessary falsehood. If 'noonish' is meaningless, then the above inscription is a pseudo-argument that has the misleading appearance of being valid. And if 'noonish' is merely metaphysically empty (say in the fashion Saul Kripke envisages for 'unicorn'), then the first premise is necessarily false in a metaphysical way. None of the above complications wrought by semantically analytic sorites are damaging to the nihilist's position.

However, syntactically analytic sorites arguments poses a problem for nihilism. Since the base step can be derived from the empty set of premises, the only option for the nihilist is to reject any rule of inference that leads to the conclusion. But if the nihilist rejects a classical rule of inference, he becomes a deviant logician. Classical nihilism is an incomplete solution to the sorites because it is silent on syntactically analytic sorites arguments.

4. Requiring Clarity leads to Ineffabilism

One might dismiss (A) and (B) on the grounds that a speaker who uses 'or' without clearly meaning one reading rather than the other fails to make a statement. This proposal must be distinguished from the familiar ban on applying logic to vague statements. (A) and (B) are vague between precise propositions. To exclude (A) and (B), the policy must focus on the process rather than the product sense of 'statement' (Sorensen 1990). The objector must be alleging that speaker unclarity between precise alternatives procedurally nullifies the statement.

This is a formidable requirement. Most college students are like Mr Vague. They need a logic course to even formulate the distinct interpretations. Logicians, chiefly in the twentieth century, have uncovered numerous indeterminacies in our ordinary usage of other logical words. Once we leave the classroom, these fine points recede from consciousness and we lapse into patterns of speech and inference that are uninfluenced by logical training. As underscored by experimental studies of reasoning, this modularity of mind extends to the instructors themselves. Unless cued, logicians fall into the same patterns as everyone else.

Logic will make further progress in the twenty-first century. Future logicians will expose yet more alternatives and thereby expose unclarities we have not envisaged. This indeterminacy is with us as we now speak. It might pervade all of our discourse.

I shall illustrate the specter of global unclarity with a hypothetical language community. The Ors are an isolated, primitive group who have so far coined words for only three sentence connectives: 'and', 'or', and 'not'. Happily, these connectives are enough to express all of sentence logic. Each line of a truth table can be described in disjunctive normal form with connectives drawn just from $\{\sim, v, \&\}$. Since A & B can be defined as $\sim(\sim A \; v \sim B)$, the smaller set $\{\sim, v\}$ also is expressively complete (Hunter 1996: 67). In addition, $\{\sim, \not\equiv, \&\}$ is an adequate set because $(A \not\equiv B) \not\equiv (A \; \& \; B)$ is equivalent to A v B. The Ors are so-called because they maximize their usage of 'or' (perhaps for religious or philosophical reasons—like devotees of Søren Kierkegaard's *Either/or*). They use 'or' even when they are conveying information that could be expressed with a single atomic statement. This is logically feasible; A is equivalent to A v A and equivalent to $A \not\equiv (A \; \& \sim A)$. Now suppose a logic missionary, Dorothy, visits the land of Ors and carefully distinguishes between inclusive and exclusive 'or'. Like Mr Vague, the Ors admire Dorothy's distinction but confess to having never clearly meant one reading over the other. They have just muddled through. According to the requirement of clarity, the Ors never made a statement prior to the arrival of Dorothy. And according to the global ineffabilist, we may be in the same predicament right now.

But if our unclarity prevents us from expressing any propositions, then we cannot propound arguments. Hence, the nihilists would have never thought of a sorites argument. Moreover, there would be no logical doctrine that 'forces' the nihilist to deny that vague predicates apply to anything. Nihilists might be temperamentally attracted to global ineffabilism. But if they defect to ineffabilism, they occupy a position that has nothing to say about the sorites. Or anything at all.

5. Supervaluating Logical Constants?

Supervaluationists (Fine 1975; McGee and McLaughlin 1995) apply logic to vague statements by counting a statement as true if it comes out true under all of its precisifications. This technique is inspired by the substitutional criterion of logical truth: a statement is a logical truth just if it comes out true under all interpretations of its non-logical words.

A precisification is an intermediate species of substitution in which the clear cases are held constant but the borderline cases are varied. Supervaluationists have generally assumed that vagueness only affects predicates and not logical constants. Hence, they have claimed that their method preserves all classical logical truths. Their flagship example is the law of excluded middle: every statement of the form 'Either p or not p' is true. Supervaluationists carefully distinguish this law from the law of bivalence: every proposition has exactly one of two truth-values.

This convergence with classical logic is jeopardized if supervaluationists supervaluate 'or'. Given the substitutional criterion of logical truth, the decision to vary the interpretation of 'or' commits them to regarding 'or' as a non-logical word. They would then be forced to deny that utterances of the form 'Either p or not p' are logical truths. The supervaluationists could still maintain that utterances of the form 'Either p or not p' are *semantically* analytic. Substitution instances would be like 'If there is a most popular sentential connective, then it is definable with a Sheffer function'. This statement expresses an analytic truth about a sentential connective under every precisification of 'most popular sentential connective'. (*Every* connective is definable with a Sheffer function.) But it is not a logical truth.

6. Trickle-Down Vagueness?

(A) and (B) are borderline between 'statement using "or" in the inclusive sense' and 'statement using exclusive "or" in the exclusive sense'. A supervaluationist may reason that since (B) comes out true under every meta-linguistic precisification, (B) is true. He may go on to reason that since (A) comes out true under one precisification and false under the other, (A) is neither true nor false.

This trickle-down theory of vagueness confuses language levels. Just as the vagueness of 'cloud' cannot make clouds vague, the vagueness of 'short word' cannot make short words vague. 'Prime' is a borderline case of 'short word' but that does not make 'prime' possess its own borderline cases.

An object language cannot be vague simply in virtue of the vagueness of a meta-language that is used to describe it. Some of the meta-languages used to describe algebraic chess notation are vague, for instance, the informal commentary in chess instruction booklets. But other meta-languages are precise, for instance, the various programming languages used to computerize chess. Vagueness does not pass down to lower language levels.

Consider a code in which mathematical sentences composed of fewer than 20 characters use the dot as a decimal point while those that have at least 20 use the dot to convey multiplication. A code-breaker may be told that the dot in short sentences of the code should be read as a decimal point and the dot in non-short sentences should read as multiplication. This decoding key is vague because some of the mathematical formulas are borderline cases of 'short sentence'. However, all of the unclear statements in the object language express precise propositions.

7. *Ambiguity versus Meta-linguistic Vagueness*

Ambiguity differs from vagueness in being pre-propositional. Propositions may be vague but can never be ambiguous. After all, propositions play the role of dis-ambiguators; they are the things between which utterances are ambiguous. There is an unclarity about which propositions (A) and (B) express. Hence they resemble ambiguous utterances. However, the unclarity does not arise from any ignorance that the speaker was ever in a position to remedy. Mr Vague's utterances of (A) and (B) owe their unclarity to their status as borderline cases of 'utterance using the inclusive or' and 'utterance using the exclusive or'.

The meta-linguistic predicates which map utterances into propositions are vague. Hence, there are a priori grounds to expect that some utterances that only have precise terms will be borderline cases of these predicates. Given the compositionality of precision, utterances which have only precise terms must be precise as a whole. The conjunction of any precise utterance with another precise utterance yields a precise conjunction. Hence, there are a priori grounds to expect that a sorites can be constructed solely from precise statements.

'Statement' has a process/product ambiguity. It can refer to the process of expressing a proposition or the product of that process—the proposition. (A) and (B) are vague statements in the process sense but not the product sense. When Mr Vague uttered (A) he expressed a precise proposition but there is vagueness as to which precise proposition he expressed.

An utterance can be a borderline case of a vague meta-linguistic term without having any vagueness of its own. Suppose the instructor is illustrating how Gödel numbers can be decoded into logical formulas. In a British-American accent, Mr Vague says

(C) The formula with Gödel number three billion is a logical truth.

The instructor notes that 'billion' means 10^9 in the American dialect but 10^{12} in the British dialect. She asks Mr Vague whether he is British or American. Mr Vague replies that he is an even mix: he has a British mother and an American father, he spends half his time in London, half in New York, he eats scones for breakfast, bagels for lunch. Like most speakers, Mr Vague never realized that the American and British dialects have systematically divergent numeral systems after one million. He confesses that although he knows a million is 1,000,000, he does not know how many zeros come after the rarely used numerals that come after a million: billion, trillion, quadrillion, quintillion, and so on. Mr Vague was just guessing when he asserted (C).

Nevertheless, the logic instructor works out which formula (C) amounts to when 'three billion' is treated as 3×10^9 and which formula (C) amounts to when treated as 3×10^{12}. To her chagrin, the formula corresponding to 3×10^9 is a logical truth although the formula corresponding to 3×10^{12} is a logical falsehood. This combination of Gödel numbering and dialect variation shows that for any pair of propositions, there is a possible utterance that borderline expresses each of them.

Logicians were right in thinking that the sorites is driven by vague predicates. But they were wrong in thinking that the vague predicate must appear within the argument itself. It suffices to have vague predicates in the meta-language that describes the sorites argument.

The Cheshire sorites teaches two lessons about the pain of contradiction. First, there are painless contradictions. Some logical falsehoods can perfectly mimic logical truths. In particular, there is no way to detect the contradiction that must figure as a premise of the Cheshire sorites. The second lesson is diagnostic. The plausible premises of the Cheshire sorites entail an obvious contradiction and so the argument causes the normal pain of contradiction. However, this is referred pain. The source of the suffering is not *in* the argument; for the vague predicate responsible for the source of the discomfort is in the meta-language, not the object language.

8   Believing the Impossible

> Bones, I want the impossible checked out too.
>
> (Kirk to McCoy, in *The Naked Time*)

Apart from the sorites, what reason do you have for thinking that you are as profoundly inconsistent as I allege? What independent reason do you have for believing that you believe any contradictions at all?

There is a long philosophical tradition, dating back at least to Plato, which denies my presupposition that it is possible to believe the impossible (and, in particular, the contradictory). Many of the philosophers you most respect belong to this honorable lineage: Donald Davidson, Daniel Dennett, Ruth Marcus, Robert Stalnaker, Ludwig Wittgenstein, and on, and on. So why believe me?

Well, you probably already believe me. Only the minority of philosophers who make a close study of belief become skeptics about belief in the impossible. I also have an unprecedented dialectical advantage.

1.   Belief in Believable Impossibilities is Infallible

Here is a debate I cannot lose. I argue that it is possible to (at least unwittingly) believe the impossible, say, that there is a largest prime number. The *impossibilist* objects that I am mistaken. Wrong move! By trying to correct me, the impossibilist concedes that I believe a false proposition. The proposition in question (i.e. that impossibilities can be believed), if false, is necessarily false. Thus, the impossibilist would be conceding that an impossibility can be believed.

If believing the impossible is impossible, then so is believing one can believe the impossible, and believing one can believe one can believe the impossible, and so on. The 'and so on' elevates my debating point beyond the status of a rhetorical zinger. Most transcendental arguments can be circumvented with judicious rephrasing. Claims about essential preconditions have a notorious tendency to beg the question. However, the soundness of 'I believe that it is possible to believe an impossible proposition, therefore, it is possible to believe an impossible proposition' can only be challenged in ways that also undermine its intended adversaries. For example, a skeptic about modalities might judge the premise as false on the grounds that my thesis, $\lozenge(\exists p)(\exists x)(\sim\lozenge p \ \& \ Bxp)$, is meaningless. However, the impossibilist can only accept skepticism about modality by undermining his own thesis. For the negation of a modal proposition is itself a modal proposition. Or to emphasize a related symmetry, the negation of any meaningful sentence must itself be meaningful, so the impossibilist must view his adversary's position as meaningful. This prevents him from portraying me as a 'believer' who lacks an object of belief. If the impossibilist can get into the belief relation with 'No one can believe an impossibility', then I can get into the belief relation with its negation.

I take myself to be in a debate that philosophers normally only dream about. To win, I need only believe my thesis. (Indeed, later it will be demonstrated that I need only appear to believe it.) The reason is that belief in 'Some impossibilities are believable' guarantees its own truth. Believing so makes it so. (*Self-intimation* is the converse where being so makes it believed so.) This logical entailment ensures that the argument does not rely on dialectical hocus pocus. Those who affirm $Bp \supset \lozenge p$ tend to subscribe to substantive modal logics such as the highly popular S5. Therefore, no question is begged by recasting my argument for the infallibility thesis with the help of an asocial, though heart-warmingly quick and dirty proof:

1. $Ba[\lozenge(\exists p)(\exists x)(\sim\lozenge p \ \& \ Bxp)]$ — Premise.
2. $\sim\lozenge(\exists p)(\exists x)(\sim\lozenge p \ \& \ Bxp)$ — Assume for the sake of a *reductio ad absurdum*.
3. $\sim\lozenge\lozenge(\exists p)(\exists x)(\sim\lozenge p \ \& \ Bxp)$ — 2, Whatever is impossible is not possibly possible.
4. $\sim\lozenge\lozenge(\exists p)(\exists x)(\sim\lozenge p \ \& \ Bxp) \&$ $Ba[\lozenge(\exists p)(\exists x)(\sim\lozenge p \ \& \ Bxp)]$ — 3, 1 Conjunction.

Intermission: Notice that line 4 gives us a concrete example of believing the impossible. To make the point a matter of principle, we need only name the bracketed proposition and apply existential generalization. So let m name $\lozenge(\exists p)(\exists x)(\sim\lozenge p \ \& \ Bxp)$. And on with the show:

5. $\sim\lozenge m \ \& \ Bam$ — 4, Synonymous redescription of the proposition with a name.
6. $(\exists x)(\sim\lozenge m \ \& \ Bxm)$ — 5, Existential generalization.
7. $(\exists p)(\exists x)(\sim\lozenge p \ \& \ Bxp)$ — 6, Existential generalization.

8. $\Diamond(\exists p)(\exists x)(\sim\!\Diamond p \ \& \ Bxp)$ 7, Whatever is actual is possible.
9. $\sim\!\sim \Diamond(\exists p)(\exists x)(\sim\!\Diamond p \ \& \ Bxp)$ By *reductio ad absurdum* from 2
                                          through 8.

If we venture from the modal system S4 to S5, we can go on to invoke the principle that whatever is possible is necessarily possible. This yields the modest but fertile necessary truth: $\Box\Diamond(\exists p)(\exists x)(\sim\!\Diamond p \ \&$ Bxp). If no one actually happened to believe $\Diamond(\exists p)(\exists x)(\sim\!\Diamond p \ \& \ Bxp)$, then my thesis would still be rendered true by a *possible* believer. 'Some impossibilities can be believed' may look contingent because the natural demonstration is prompted by my actual reply in a real-life debate. From the contingent fact that I believe $\Diamond(\exists p)(\exists x)(\sim\!\Diamond p \ \& \ Bxp)$, the *possibility* of believing in impossibilities follows by the principle that whatever is actual is possible. Since whatever is possible is necessarily possible, my contingent belief constitutes decisive evidence for a necessary truth. Or to put the point cruelly, impossibilism is itself impossible. Belief in the thesis that impossibilities cannot be believed is a subtle instance of what it precludes!

The modal status of the commitment to believable impossibilities exposes a quasi-Gödelian tension between deductive closure and consistency. In addition to driving another nail into the coffin of doxastic logic, $\Box\Diamond(\exists p)(\exists x)(\sim\!\Diamond p \ \& \ Bxp)$, ruptures theories that link belief and necessity such as Brian Ellis's (1979) epistemic semantics and Robert Stalnaker's (1984) possible worlds analysis of propositions. This will be backed up at the end of the chapter.

Another welcome feature of my thesis is that its infallibility is dialectically robust; my adversaries cannot wriggle free by rejecting discretionary background assumptions. Some might think that the strength of this result is inversely proportional to its interest. If it is certain that impossibilities can be believed, then the impossibilists already have their trousers halfway down. Am I just pulling their trousers *all* the way down?

Only in the fashion praised through the ages. The skeptic, the egoist, and the hard determinist are partly refuted by obvious counterexamples —the sort volunteered by sophomores and refined by common-sense philosophers such as Thomas Reid and G. E. Moore. However, our teachers showed how these (usually authentic) counterexamples beg the question against subtle characters such as the skeptic, the egoist, and so on. Since question-begging is relative to an audience, the counterexamples may rightly shape the opinion of other people. Partial refutations are instructive. However, universal refutations have special value. These use premises that even one's adversary must grant.

Better yet would be an explanation of how one's adversary mis-reasoned. But all I have is my negative point. I have not found any master fallacy behind impossibilism. Indeed, their arguments strike me as careful deductions from attractive premises. The impossibilists certainly do not have their trousers half down in the sense of being slovenly dialecticians. Their premises are tenets from our most promising models of belief. Their logic is state of the art. I will survey the impossibilist's basic arguments and offer some criticisms. But I cannot specify where each argument goes wrong. Some have me stumped. Nevertheless, I know that all of the impossibilist's arguments are unsound. For I have an infallible belief in the negation of each argument's conclusion.

2. The Disappearance of Higher Order Appearances

Impossibilists grant that people often act *as if* they believe impossibilities. A shopper will heatedly assert that $4.39 + 9.84 = 13.23$. A chess novice who only has a king and a knight will attempt to checkmate his adversary's lone king. Experimenters report that some subjects judge town A as northeast of town B but B as not southwest of town A (Moar and Bower 1983). All philosophers have felt the pain of contradiction. Brother, I've had my share! Happily, *reductio ad absurdum* can't hurt me now. If an impossibilist were to extract an absurd consequence from my belief in believed impossibilities, then my belief would be self-exemplifying. If I'm wrong, I'm right, therefore, I'm right.

Impossibilists try to keep up appearances by distinguishing between what people really believe and what they believe they believe. For instance, the resemblance between a contradiction and a consistent statement may lead us to mistake the believer of the consistent statement as a believer in the contradiction. But given impossibilism, believing someone believes impossibilities should be a special case of believing an impossibility. Nor can they save appearances by scaling to the higher order hypothesis that we only look *as if* we seem to believe impossibilities. For higher order appearances would also be precluded by the impossibilist's shackle of impossibility results:

$$(p) \quad (\sim\Diamond p \supset \sim\Diamond Bp \sim\Diamond BBp \supset \sim\Diamond BBBp \supset \ldots \supset \sim\Diamond B^n p).$$

What goes for thought, goes for talk; the chain of impossibilities precludes (even insincere) assertion of impossibilities. One can only assert what one can give the appearance of believing. Nor can the appearance of appearances be reclaimed by distinguishing between senses of 'believe'. Any plausible reading of 'believe' must permit disagreement over the believability of impossibilities.

Of course, one can *stipulate* a sense of 'believe' that entails logical omniscience. It's a free country. But this liberty invites the charge of misleading advertising. For example, if the impossibilist has a technical sense of 'believe' in which it means 'consistently believe', then his audience will protest that they assumed he was using 'believe' in an ordinary sense.

Another stratagem is to abandon impossibilism about belief in favor of another propositional attitude that resembles belief (Marcus 1990). However, an attitude can resemble belief only if it allows for opposed attitudes to the same object. One can only countenance this dissonance by tolerating disharmony about the impossibility issue. The range of what is assumable or presumable is at least as wide as the range of what is believable. This difficulty will also haunt attempts to construct an interesting sort of impossibilism with respect to a technical term such as 'acceptance'.

One of the early impossibilists, George Berkeley (1710: 273), paraphrases apparent belief in terms of what we *imagine* we believe. However, like most impossibilists, Berkeley also denies that we can imagine impossibilities. After all, Berkeley subscribes to David Hume's (1739: 32) principle equating conceivability with possibility. Hume's principle generates its own nesting of impossibilities: if it is impossible to imagine an impossibility, then it is also impossible to imagine imagining an impossibility, and so on. Since imagination is the minimally encumbered propositional attitude, the progression of unimaginables is maximally constraining. Therefore, we cannot appeal to propositional attitudes to explicate the impossibilist's concession that we at least seem to believe impossibilities. But if this explication fails, all fail. Hence the impossibilist cannot afford to admit that we *seem* to believe impossibilities. Even the illusion of disagreement is lethal! Obviously, however, there is at least the appearance of disagreement. Therefore, we should infer that it is possible to believe impossibilities and should reject Hume's principle that conceivability implies possibility. This also scotches the logical positivist's claim that logical impossibilities can be sharply distinguished from empirical impossibilities by means of the unthinkability of contradictions (Schlick 1932/3: 42).

In one respect, the impossibilist is a lonelier debater than the solipsist. Sure, the solipsist has the same problem of self-defeating disputation; if the solipsist admits that someone else disagrees, the solipsist loses. However, the belief that only I exist is compatible with it *seeming* as if other people exist. So the solipsist can at least invent an imaginary friend and have pretend debates about solipsism. The impossibilist is also worse off than an eliminative materialist such as Paul Churchland (1979). Those who believe there are no beliefs can sustain debate by re-describing the controversy in a vocabulary free of 'folk psychology'. Or at least these eliminativists could issue the promissory note that future science will furnish this redescription. The same promissory note can be waved at the problem of higher order appearances. Just as one cannot prove *to the eliminativist* that there are beliefs by appealing to the infallibilty of belief in 'There are beliefs', one cannot prove to the eliminativist that some impossibilities can be believed by appealing to the infallibility of belief in 'Some impossibilities can be believed'. However, the *impossibilist* believes in belief; he restricts his skepticism to belief in impossibilities. He cannot emulate the eliminativist's *indiscriminate* rejection of belief in the impossible. Therefore, the anti-impossibilist argument is effective against its intended adversary.

3. Can Impossibilism be Restrained?

The impossibilist might try to salvage his thesis by restricting it to a special class of beliefs. Richard Purtill distinguishes between a strong and a weak sense of 'believe'. 'To believe in this weak sense is to do no more than to sincerely give it as one's opinion that p' (1970: 19). This sense is lenient enough to permit belief in impossibilities. The strong sense is intended to forbid belief in the impossible. An individual a 'believes p in the strong sense if and only if a understands p, and a has some reason (which seems to him to be a good reason) for thinking p to be true' (1970: 20).

The chapter you are now reading is jolly good evidence that I understand my thesis, $\Diamond(\exists p)(\exists x)(\sim\Diamond p\ \&\ Bxp)$, and have 'some reason' for thinking it true. So if Purtill applies his distinction to me in accordance with his stated criteria, he should count me as a believer in the *strong* sense. But then I will have achieved just what his distinction was intended to thwart. My second objection is to the whole idea of treating 'belief' as having disparate *senses*. If 'belief' is as ambiguous as 'bank', reflective equilibrium is impossible. To consider the case at hand, just how do my strong beliefs interact with my weak beliefs? A modest degree of epistemological holism will require that I draw inferences from mixtures of strong and weak beliefs. Yet applied logic demands an underlying unity in the attitude adopted towards the premises. The Bayesian meets this requirement by treating degrees of belief as commensurable units. But Purtill has made no gesture towards finding a common element between weak and strong belief. If he were to opt for a reductionist strategy, he would need to take strong belief as the fundamental attitude. Anything less renders the deduction of further strong beliefs intractable. But then the thinker will need to be able to identify which beliefs are strong beliefs. If these selectors must themselves be strong beliefs, there will be a vicious infinite regress because each strong belief must be backed with 'some reason' and this reason must be a strong belief.

The interaction problem does not arise if the impossibilist merely distinguishes between *species* of belief. (Then 'belief' is *general*, not ambiguous.) For example, Curtis Brown (1990: 283) maintains that one cannot *directly* believe an impossibility. A direct belief holds in virtue of intrinsic facts about the believer, not facts about his environment and society. So one test for directness is to imagine whether an exact replica of the believer must share the belief. Indirect beliefs can be analyzed as those that arise from the interaction of direct beliefs and extrinsic facts. Since the believer has limited knowledge of external conditions, he has an imperfect understanding of his indirect beliefs. For example, ignorance of the fact that the man called 'Samuel Clemens' is identical to the man called 'Mark Twain' might lead a student to (consistently) believe that the man called Twain is a better writer than the man called Clemens. Under actual conditions, a referential convergence generates the indirect belief in the impossibility that Mark Twain is a better writer than Samuel Clemens. Since direct beliefs are not vulnerable to these misfortunes, the object of direct beliefs must always be possible. A parallel line is pursued by Albert Casullo (1979). He defends Hume's principle that conceivability implies possibility by distinguishing between basic and derived conceivability.

Brown (1992) supplements the motivation for the direct/indirect distinction by applying it to the belief puzzles raised by Hilary Putnam, Tyler Burge, and Saul Kripke. The guiding precedent is perception. Analysis of illusion leads many to abandon naive realism in favor of representative realism. Brown's search for 'immediate objects of belief' is reminiscent of the perception theorist's rummagings for sense data (and the action theorist's quest for 'basic actions'). As J. L. Austin's

Sense and Sensibilia documented, the direct/indirect distinction is a slippery fish. So the historical record cannot be heartening to Professor Brown.

But in addition to these general worries, the direct/indirect distinction is particularly ill adapted to the specimen under scrutiny. My belief that impossibilities can be believed enjoys a Cartesian aloofness from the extrinsic factors cited by Brown. My Twin Earth doppelganger also believes that some impossibilities can be believed. The object of my belief is a necessary truth that only uses the concepts of belief and possibility.

Brown could reply that I only *indirectly* believe that impossibilities can be believed. After all, Tyler Burge (1986) has shown that factors outside the speaker's psychology affect the meanings of words such as 'arthritis', 'sofa', and 'contract'. Perhaps similar examples could be constructed for 'possible', 'belief', and 'there is'.

The first problem with this strategy is that Burgean cases always involve an omissive or commissive error about the term. It is implausible that *every* possible believer in 'It is possible to believe the impossible' has a misconception about one of the terms in the sentence. All I need to prove my thesis is the possible existence of a single conceptually well-adapted believer in believable impossibilities.

The second problem with the strategy of expanding the domain of indirect beliefs is that no direct beliefs would remain. Even Descartes's *cogito* uses 'I', 'think', and 'exists'. Notice that the Cartesian immediacy of my basic idea can be underscored by switching to a first person claim; 'I can believe an impossibility' is just as infallibly believed as the logically weaker 'Someone can believe an impossibility'. My thesis has as much independence from external conditions as the *cogito*.

4. Four Impossibilist Arguments

Precursors of the main arguments against relations with impossibilities can be found in Plato's dialogues. In the *Theaetetus* and *Sophist* it is argued that we cannot believe what is false because what is false is not the case and what is not the case does not exist. This is the absent relatum argument: to believe is to believe something, so where there can be no object of belief, there can be no belief. Subsequent philosophers flushed out plausible relata for *consistent* false beliefs. However, they still have the same problem with belief in the impossible. Causal theories of representation, for example, take the object of belief to be what causes it when the belief is formed under optimal conditions. But there are no optimal conditions under which an impossibility is true. Others take sets of possible worlds as the objects of belief. However, there is no possible world in which an impossibility holds. Sentences purporting to attribute belief in the impossible appear to be meaningless danglers.

Plato's discussion of false belief also touches upon the appeal to understanding. The human predilection for viewing words as names led Plato to view all errors as mis-identifications. For example, in a fog Socrates mistakes Theodorus as Theaetetus. However, Plato realized that this mental switch model is implausible because no one is irrational enough to judge that Theodorus is Theaetetus. As soon as the alleged object of belief becomes intelligible, it becomes unbelievable.

As philosophers gradually freed themselves from the assumption that all words are names, they were able to focus on more tractable cases of false beliefs. Most beliefs use the 'is' of predication rather than the 'is' of identity. Generalizations really use variables rather than names of abstract entities. Names were increasingly viewed as minority members of language. Bertrand Russell's theory of descriptions showed how ordinary names might be analyzed as definite descriptions. W. V. Quine modified this theory and recommended that scientific language avoid all names in favor of definite descriptions. However, Kripke's attack on the description theory of names has disinterred the Platonic problem of mis-identification.

Prominent philosophers of language in the twentieth century have equated understanding with knowledge of truth conditions (Heidelberger 1980). This link has strengthened the reasoning against the possibility of believing contradictions. Their opening premise is that one can only believe what one understands and regards as true. Understanding requires knowledge of truth conditions. A contradiction has no conditions under which it can be true, so understanding a contradiction precludes belief. (Indeed, understanding a contradiction automatically produces disbelief.) Therefore, belief in a contradiction is itself a contradiction (Foley 1986: 350). Although each of the three premises has been challenged, the argument has considerable influence.

To get the third argument against the possibility of believing the impossible, the appeal to charity, switch attention from the interpretee's need for understanding to the interpreter's need for understanding (Davidson 1967b: 605). The point of assigning beliefs and desires is to make sense of the agent's actions by setting up applications of belief-desire psychology. If we ascribe conflicting beliefs, then no predictive progress has been made. (So even instrumentalists are hostile to belief in contradiction (Dennett 1987, ch. 4).) Charity is forced upon the interpreter because his project requires selection of the most rational portrayal of the agent's attitudes. Therefore, the appearance of incoherence is just a projection of the *interpreter's* confusion. This confusion reflects a lack of ingenuity on the part of the listener rather than the presence of contradictory beliefs in the speaker. The interpreter is free to admit that he is stumped. He is also free to doubt whether the preconditions for interpretation obtain. (Perhaps some forms of insanity amount to resistance to belief attribution.) However, the interpreter is never free to infer that the speaker is irrational. More positively, 'In our need to make him make sense, we will try for a theory that finds him consistent, a believer of truths, and a lover of the good (all by our own lights, it goes without saying)' (Davidson 1970: 97).

Appeals to understanding frequently fuse with the *defeasibility* of belief. There is some temptation to think that we have immediate and infallible access to our own beliefs. However, defeasibilists note that we often describe ourselves as having been mistaken about our beliefs once an absurdity is exposed. Indeed, magnanimous practitioners of *reductio ad absurdum* describe themselves as showing that people do not really mean what they said. Patronizing? Not if thorough understanding is a precondition of belief. Just as knowledge must be a relation with actual states of affairs, belief must be a relation with possible states of affairs (Marcus 1983: 324). One can then go on to construe 'conceive' as a success verb, and dismiss the possibility of imagining an impossibility in the same way we dismiss the possibility of perceiving an impossible situation (Hart 1988: 28).

Defeasibilists admit that there are other defeaters of belief ascriptions. However, they under-represent the wide generality of the phenomenon. For the epicenter, go back to Plato's dialogues. In *Protagoras* 358 and *Meno* 77–8, Socrates contends that we cannot desire what is bad. If a man is unaware that something is evil, then he might say he wants it and act as if he wants it. But once he recognizes it as evil, he realizes that he really never wanted it. Socrates concludes that virtue is knowledge.

Defeasibility undergirds paternalism in medical ethics. A physician once illustrated how much baldness bothers men with an anecdote. A young patient kept insisting that there must be some cure for his baldness. The exasperated physician finally declared that the only way to stop baldness was castration. The young man thought a bit. And said 'Okay, whatever it takes'. But the story actually shows how little weight we assign baldness. For our reaction is that the young man hasn't thought the matter through; he doesn't understand what is entailed by castration. The paternalist insists that the patient should get the treatment he *really* wants—not the treatment he thinks he wants. What the patient *really* wants is determined by what he would want if he had rationally considered all the relevant information.

The political implications of defeasibility were taken up by some nineteenth-century idealists. They reasoned that real freedom lies in the satisfaction of our ideally rational and well-informed desires. Thus the state was duty bound to ignore the apparent wishes of its citizens in order to make them free. Totalitarian Marxists incorporated this theme and concluded that they were the real democrats.

Ruth Marcus (1983) bases her impossibilism on the principle that a belief attribution is defeated when it is discovered that no state of affairs could make the belief true. Just as knowledge requires truth, belief requires possibility. In addition to applying this defeasibilism to reductios and false identity statements, Marcus (1981) extends it to the Pierre puzzle. Pierre is a monolingual Frenchman who hears that 'Londres est jolie' and so believes it. He moves to a place he knows as London and begins to learn English by immersion. Since he does not realize that Londres is London and happens to be confined to its shabby parts, he sincerely says that London is not pretty. So it appears that Pierre has rationally acquired contradictory beliefs. For when we translate his sincere French utterance and conjoin it with his sincere English utterance, we obtain 'London is pretty and London is not pretty'. Marcus's solution is that the contradiction cancels the belief reports. Upon learning that London is Londres, Pierre would disavow his assertions about London.

Pierre may well recant after learning of the impossibility. But if defeasibilist intuitions sufficed, then a vitiatingly broader program of re-description would be in order. For people retract reports of beliefs and desires upon the discovery of almost any kind of unwelcome consequence. (They also frequently just admit error.) Some repudiations may be interpreted as a reaction to absent relata. A biology student may retract his claim to have believed that the largest single organism is a mushroom in Michigan after learning that 'the mushroom' is composed of clones and so is only a borderline case of a 'single organism'. Perhaps a statement is borderline when there is no truthmaker for it or its negation (as suggested in Ch. 11). This might explain why we are tempted to view vagueness as a kind of meaninglessness.

However, we also retract when the object of belief has defects other than non-existence. If a lecturer tells a student 'Although mental events have bodily effects, you are an epiphenomenalist', the student might believe it on authority. Once the student learns that epiphenomenalists deny that causes run from mind to body, he can recognize the resemblance between the teacher's remark and the Moorean variant 'It is raining but you do not believe it'. So the student denies that he ever really believed the lecturer's remark but not on the grounds that there is no state of affairs under which the remark could be true.

Many flaws provoke disavowals: triviality, empirical bizarreness, heresy, rudeness, and so on. When President Gerald Ford assured Americans in the midst of the cold war that Eastern Europe would never be dominated by the Soviet Union, his aides swiftly discounted the statement as a verbal slip. A central duty of Ronald Reagan's spokesman was to furnish reporters with official interpretations of presidential remarks. Unless we embrace the vintage real selves of the nineteenth-century idealists, we will need to rein in the implications of disavowals.

5. Propositional Guises of the Problem

Impossibilists are inconsistent about inconsistency. Plato depicts Socrates as embarrassing his interlocutors by exposing hidden inconsistencies and thereby compelling them to change their minds. But if Socrates' adversaries never really had the conflicting beliefs, what are they embarrassed about? How could Socrates be the gadfly of Athens?

In the *Meno*, Plato partly agrees that the Socratic method is uninformative. The concession is prompted by the paradox of inquiry: if Socrates really knows nothing, how can he hope to acquire knowledge by asking others? Recognition of the correct answer requires some background knowledge. Socrates responds by conceding that in one sense, learning is impossible. Not because we know nothing, but because we know everything! In particular, his doctrine of recollection credits us with atrophied omniscience. In a pre-existent state, we dwelt amongst the Forms and so knew all. The trauma of birth causes us to forget. The role of Socratic interrogation is to revive these heavenly memories.

The recollection model (minus the fairy tale about pre-existence) has some prospect of accounting for conflicting beliefs about contingent propositions. If I latently believe p but become persuaded that $\sim p$, then

I might seem to believe p & $\sim p$. The problem of finding an object for this apparent single belief can be resolved by analyzing it as *two* beliefs. However, this divide and conquer strategy fails for belief that there is a barber who shaves all and only those who do not shave themselves. This is a logical contradiction that is not a conjunction of opposed propositions. Thus the doctrine of recollection has no advantage in explaining how inquiry about necessities can be informative. This kind of cognitive advance cannot be reduced to the elimination of one member of a conflicting set of beliefs. The point generalizes to other distinctions used in the 'divide and conquer' strategy of understanding contradictory beliefs: implicit belief/explicit belief, conscious belief/unconscious belief, intuitive belief/theoretical belief, and so on.

Many logical contradictions at the level of sentence logic are divisible. Human beings are comfortable with conjunction and negation, and so tend to couch propositions in a form amenable to the divide and conquer strategy. Since all sentential truth functions can be expressed in terms of conjunction and negation, one might hope to reduce all sentential contradictions to divisible contradictions. This seems strained for contradictions such as $p \leftrightarrow \sim p$. The anthropocentrism of the reduction is also disturbing. Consider a Neanderthal who comfortably wields the Sheffer stroke function but can only fumble along with negation and conjunction. He can reduce all sentence contradictions to ones involving the stroke function. The Neanderthal's contradictions are not amenable to the divide and conquer strategy. Thus a human reduction of sentence contradictions to ones involving negation and conjunction would not show anything universal about the nature of contradictory belief.

The graver objection presented in Chapter 5 is that not all contradictions are divisible. (Recall the examples from Ch. 5). This infinite class of indivisible contradictions shows we cannot reduce human inconsistency to disagreement amongst self-consistent homunculi.

Some trace all inconsistency to a combinatorial explosion of individually self-consistent propositions. As more propositions enter the belief system, the number of conjunctions that can form grows exponentially. Recall Lewis Carroll's fondness for joint inconsistencies that involve 30, 40, or even 50 propositions. Consistency checking is an NP-complete problem. Thus a high speed computer would face the same limit. The combinatorial explosion is indeed a potent source of inconsistency (as emphasized by Christopher Cherniak in *Minimal Rationality*). But indivisible contradictions show that not all inconsistency arises from this quantitative phenomenon.

In one respect, belief in indivisible contradictions is easier to model than divisible contradictions. For in the case of divisible contradictions, there is a difficulty in distinguishing inconsistency about p from doubt whether p. The difficulty is prefigured in the etymology of 'doubt'. The Latin *'dubitare'* is the frequentative of *'dubare'*, which means to be of two minds. How is this kind of duality between p and $\sim p$ to be distinguished from inconsistency? Consider Spinoza's monistic theory of propositional attitudes in which only beliefs are allowed. According to Spinoza, there is a broad sense of 'believe' in which any proposition that comes to mind is believed. Spinoza denies that we can neutrally entertain a proposition. To think is to believe. So why do we seem fairly consistent? Well, beliefs vary in strength. Weak beliefs are suppressed by stronger beliefs. So I believe p in the discriminative sense just in case my belief that p is sufficiently stronger than my belief that not p. This precludes contradictory (discriminative) beliefs of the form Bp & $B\sim p$. Since Spinoza thinks that belief distributes over conjunction, this also rules out $B(p$ & $\sim p)$. Now the mystery is why there are any contradictory beliefs in the discriminative sense. It might be suggested that Spinoza accommodates contradictory discriminative beliefs by weakening the requirement to that of having an undominated belief. But now ties are an embarrassment. If I doubt whether the number of stars is even, then the criterion entails that I believe the number of stars is even and believe that it is not the case that the number of stars is even. This difficulty is inherited by psychological theories that emulate Spinoza's psychological monism (such as overwrite theories of memory).

David Hume also has the problem of distinguishing contradictory beliefs about p from doubting whether p. He says belief is lively entertainment of an idea. If the vivacity of p equals the vivacity of $\sim p$, do I doubt whether p or do I have inconsistent beliefs about p? Doubt does differ from inconsistency in its ability to survive exposure. I cannot wittingly believe p & $\sim p$. However, I can wittingly doubt whether p.

This suggests a strategy of distinguishing doubt from inconsistency by using a higher order level belief. Indeed, Alan Hart (1980) analyzes a doubts whether p as believing that one neither believes nor disbelieves p. One drawback is that this overly sophisticates doubt. A dog can doubt whether his mistress is in the bedroom without having any beliefs about his beliefs. So can her lover. The proper analysis of doubt puts doubt on all fours with other belief states: A entertains p without believing p and without disbelieving p.

Surprisingly, indivisible contradictions blindside many philo-sophers who are quite familiar with predicate logic. Echoing the later Wittgenstein, Peter Strawson (1952: 3 and 21) contends that con-tradictory beliefs cancel each other out. The analogy is with a man who walks 6 feet to the left and then 6 feet to the right. By vector addition, there is no net movement. Similarly, says Strawson, nothing is really said when one says p and not p. This analogy presupposes that there are two distinct propositions. The idea is that the assertion of one pro-position cancels the assertion of the other. But when an indivisible contradiction is involved, there are not two propositions to assert. Furthermore, contradictory beliefs are sometimes presupposed rather than asserted. Russell's riddle of the barber is posed as a question that makes the audience presuppose that there could be a barber who shaves all and only those who do not shave themselves.

The contemporary paradox of analysis and the problem of modeling belief in impossibilities are two sides of the same coin. This paradox focuses on belief in analytical truths instead of analytical falsehoods. If a conceptual analysis states exactly what the original statement says, then the analysis is trivial. If it says something different from the ori-ginal, then the analysis is mistaken. Hence, all analyses are either trivial or false. The case for 'Sameness of meaning = triviality' meshes with the case against believing contradictions: since disbelieving p is just believing $\sim p$, the incredibility of contradictions precludes disbelief in tautologies. Could one be an agnostic about a tautology? If one under-stands a proposition, one understands the conditions under which it is true and false. But in the case of a tautology, this entails recognition that the proposition is true under all circumstances—and hence is actually true. Therefore, understanding a tautology entails knowledge that it is true. Knowledge implies belief. Consequently, to understand a tautology is to believe it. In addition to precluding agnosticism about tautologies, the connection between understanding an analytic truth and believing it 'demonstrates' that conceptual analysis is never informative.

The self-intimating nature of tautologies would also preclude un-witting belief in them, that is, belief unaccompanied by the recogni-tion of their tautologous nature. For example, some philosophers believe that 'All causes precede their effects' but are not sure whether the proposition is a tautology. That would be impossible if belief requires understanding of the nature of the proposition. Moreover, belief in a tautology would always have proper grounds. Fallacious proofs of mathematical theorems would be impossible because anyone who understood the tautology would automatically have cogent proof of it.

Contingencies would be partially self-intimating; although their truth-values could still be hidden, their modal status would always make itself known. For understanding a contingent proposition means understanding some conditions under which it is true and some conditions under which it is false. Moreover, contingencies would always *look* like contingencies. No one could believe they believe of a contingency that it is non-contingent.

Propositions bear necessary relations with other propositions, so understanding a proposition would mean understanding what entails it and what it entails. But the entailers and entailees must themselves be understood. This holistic slippery slope is reminiscent of the idealist's arguments that to know anything one must know everything. But it is even more overbearing. At least the idealists could concede that we appear to know some things without knowing everything. The purveyor of logical omniscience cannot admit that we seem to understand some propositions without understanding their logical relations with all others.

Some philosophers accept this dismal conclusion and cite the failure of reductive programs as vindication. But most philosophers view the paradox of analysis as unsound or misleading. For example, my impression had been that the paradox goes through if one decides to set the high standard for 'belief' implicit in the principle that belief requires understanding. The background idea is that 'understand' is an absolute term like 'flat'. Just as a flat surface cannot be flatter than another flat surface, someone who understands a proposition cannot understand it better than another person who understands it. This follows from an absolutist definition of 'understand': A understands p iff A can discriminate p from all other propositions. This definition quantifies over propositions, thus a person who can discriminate p from foils drawn from one domain of propositions might not be able to discriminate p from the alternatives drawn from another set. When our quantifiers are 'wide open', there are so many look-alikes that one understands very few propositions. As with 'flat', I concluded that although one can consistently relativize 'understand' to high standards, it is impractical to do so. Thus I agreed that the paradox of analysis is correct for the limit case in which we quantify over all propositions but not for the ordinary cases. The philosopher's preoccupation with the paradox could then be explained as an artifact of idealization. Usually, we simplify a problem by considering extreme cases. But when it comes to understanding the informativeness of analysis, the strategy eliminates the resources needed for the solution.

Although I still think that the paradox of analysis is partly due to context-shifting shenanigans, I now think that there are *semantic* restrictions on how high one can set the standards. To put the matter another way, the paradox of analysis rests on two premises that are open to a context-independent refutation. Recall that the paradox proceeds by eliminating the two ways in which an analysis might enlighten a thinker. The first path is by revealing that a belief is actually contradictory. The anti-analyst blocks this possibility by appealing to the principle that belief requires understanding. However, my belief that 'Belief does *not* require understanding' is infallible. I could only be wrong if belief requires understanding. But then I would understand 'Belief does not require understanding' and so know that there are no conditions under which it could be true. This knowledge that the proposition is false would prevent me from believing it— contradicting the original assumption that I believed it. The proponent of 'Belief requires understanding' faces the same dialectical trap as his impossibilist ancestors. If he concedes that I believe 'Belief does not require understanding', then he loses. Nor can he admit that I believe that I believe my thesis, because my belief that I believe 'Belief does not require understanding' would itself be a belief in a contradiction. Like the impossibilist, he must deny even the appearance of disagreement. He must insist that the infallibility claim, 'If someone believes that belief does not require understanding, then he must be right', is only *vacuously* true. The proponent of 'Belief requires understanding' must say the antecedent of the conditional expresses a logical impossibility— and he must say the same for all the higher order infallibility theses. And he must say it for all contexts.

The paradox of analysis also attacks the second way analysis can be informative—revealing tautologies to those who had not previously believed them. The anti-analyst attacks the possibility of being agnostic about tautologies by arguing that understanding a tautology entails believing it. However, 'Understanding a tautology entails believing it' would then itself be a tautology. So if I understand the principle, then I must believe it. However, I understand the principle and do not believe it. Therefore, some tautologies can be understood without being believed.

This proof that one can understand a tautology without believing it might be challenged on the grounds that I only appear to understand 'Understanding a tautology entails believing it'. The idea would be that I mistakenly believe that I understand the principle. But this is impossible given the anti-analyst's other principle that belief requires understanding and his allegiance to the principle that understanding is divisional (one can understand a complex proposition only if one understands its component propositions). For then my belief that I understand the proposition that p would be infallible. For 'I believe that I understand p' would entail 'I understand I understand p'. But I can only understand 'I understand p' by understanding all of the components of the complex proposition—which includes the p component.

6. Deductive Guises of the Problem

The puzzles of deduction distend in similar fashion. If we cannot believe impossibilities, we cannot mistake valid arguments as invalid. To believe that an argument is invalid is to believe it is possible for the premises to be true while the conclusion is false. But if the argument is valid after all, this would be a belief in an impossibility. The possibility of error in the opposite direction can be 'refuted' by adapting the argument against agnosticism about tautologies. For uncertainty about the validity of an argument requires uncertainty about the status of the corresponding tautology. This challenge to the informativeness of deduction is best known in the form of John Stuart Mill's (1843: 120) thesis that all valid arguments are circular. As with tautologies, the informativeness of a deduction seems to evaporate under the light of reason. The more one can be said to *understand*, the more trivial the deduction appears.

Let's sharpen the deductive dilemma with a slippery-slope argument. For openers, nothing can be learned from an invalid deduction. And even some sound deductions are epistemically impotent. To argue 'I jog on a treadmill, therefore I jog on a treadmill' is just to run in place. Ditto for *any* argument of the form 'p therefore p'. Conjoining p with another proposition brings no improvement: 'p and q, therefore, p' is just as question-begging. Separate assertion of the premises does not matter ('p, q, therefore, p'), so an argument with truth functionally equivalent premises only *looks* more persuasive: $q \supset p$, q, therefore, p. The *apparent* persuasiveness can be increased by further tactics of obfuscation such as rewording. But rearrangements of the same information don't increase knowledge. Repackaging a circular argument leaves it circular. However, a combination of these camouflage techniques can take us from '*p* therefore *p*' to *any* valid argument form. Therefore, all deductive reasoning is impotent. Or so runs this self-defeatingly interesting deduction.

Notice now that these implications can be expanded by ascent to higher order appearances: people cannot commit fallacies *and* cannot even appear to. People cannot be informed by deduction *and* cannot even appear to. This extra layer of commitment topples extremists into an abyss of absurdity.

7. Closure Conflicts with Universal Consistency

In 1968, Leonard Linsky pointed out that Jaakko Hintikka's (1962) model-theoretic account of belief condemns as indefensible the belief that someone else is inconsistent. Roughly, a proposition is doxastically indefensible if one cannot consistently believe it even though it might be true. For example, Moore's sentence 'It is raining but I do not believe it' is logically consistent but believing it commits the speaker to conflicting beliefs. Thus Hintikka's system generates a weak analogue of impossibilism. Instead of dismissing 'Someone believes an impossibility' as a contradiction, it condemns *belief* in that proposition as indefensible.

This implication might be viewed as an awkward side-effect of using model theory. A model set cannot contain an inconsistency because it represents a (partial) description of a *possible* set of affairs. So a believer in 'Someone else believes an inconsistency' cannot embed the object of belief in a model set. This inability of the belief to come out true is not the same thing as logical inconsistency. There is no way to make *belief* in 'No one has a belief' come out true but that does not show that 'Someone has a belief' is a necessary truth.

Not all view the result as a technical embarrassment. Some make a virtue out of necessity and defend the result as a bold discovery: although 'Someone else believes an inconsistency' does not sound odd, it is a subtle Moorean sentence. Bolder still are the impossibilists who think that Hintikka's result is an understatement; instead of being merely indefensible, 'Someone else believes an inconsistency' is a contradiction (Purtill 1970).

However, the infallibility of belief in 'Some impossibilities are believable' suggests that it is Linsky's result that is understated. Linsky's complaint is that Hintikka's system cannot *permit* belief that someone else is inconsistent. The real problem is that a model-theoretic approach cannot *require* belief in the believability of impossibilities. Hintikka's believers are supposed to have deductively closed beliefs. Hence, every necessary truth should appear within every belief system. But given the necessary truth that 'It is possible to believe an impossibility', each believer must then think that a belief system can be inconsistent. However, a model set is *inherently* consistent. Thus all of Hintikka's ideal believers reject Hintikka's theory of belief.

The ingratitude generalizes. Any theory that correlates belief and necessity will create Frankensteins who repudiate the theorems of their creators. In Brian Ellis's epistemic semantics, necessity is defined in terms of belief. In particular, a proposition is possible if, and only if, it is believed in at least one rational belief system. A proposition is necessary only when believed in every rational belief system. So the necessary truth of 'Some impossibilities can be believed' demands its presence in every system. Consequently, each system is committed to the possibility of a rational belief system containing an impossibility. But this is possible only if there is at least one rational belief system containing an impossibility. Such a rational belief system is inconsistent. Thus the attempt to reflect all necessities by means of ideal beliefs comes into conflict with the requirement that all ideal belief systems be consistent.

The same conflict between closure and universal consistency arises with the converse attempt to analyze belief in terms of necessity. For example, Robert Stalnaker (1984) takes the object of belief to be a subset of possible worlds. When I believe my cat or my dog tipped a vase, I believe I am in a possible world in which my cat or my dog tipped a vase. After learning that the dog was outdoors when the vase broke, I narrow down the range of possible worlds to those in which the cat is the culprit. The possible worlds account neatly models contingent beliefs by providing a clear contrast between the worlds I may occupy and those I exclude. However, this contrast is not to be found for necessary truths. Necessary truths hold in all possible worlds, so they all have the same content, namely, the set of all possible worlds. Since necessary truths appear in every possible world, everybody believes all of them. Stalnaker deftly defends deductive closure and the second consequence of consistency. However, the details of this defense do not protect his account from the objection used against epistemic semantics. As a necessary truth, 'Some impossibilities can be believed' must appear in every possible world and hence every belief state. But for an impossibility to be believed is to appear in a belief state, that is, a possible world. But no possible world contains an impossibility. Hence closure conflicts with universal consistency.

Stalnaker does have a resource for accommodating the appearance of inconsistent beliefs. He allows a single agent to be in more than one belief state. That is, in one complete belief state p holds and in another complete belief state $\sim p$ holds. Each belief state is 'a separate center of rationality'. Deduction is 'the integration of the separate belief states of a single agent' (Stalnaker 1984: 87). However, this maneuver does not apply when the object of belief is a single necessary truth. For 'Some impossibilities are believable' must be reflected within each and every belief state. There is no variation in belief to integrate, so belief in the believability of impossibilities does not stimulate the search for deductive relief of internal dissonance.

Neighborly conflict between closure and consistency should be distinguished from the self-referential sort associated with Kurt Gödel's incompleteness theorem. Roughly, Gödel showed that one can express 'This statement cannot be proved in this system' in a language strong enough to do arithmetic. This creates an *internal* conflict between consistency and completeness. The conflict precipitated by 'Some impossibilities are believable' is between systems. For a belief system need not attribute belief in an impossibility to itself. It can say that some other belief systems contain impossibilities. The attribution pattern for inconsistency could resemble one that some anthropologists allege for cannibalism; all groups abominate some groups as cannibals but no group admits to being cannibals. This self-serving finger-pointing carries a price. An anti-cannibal group cannot say that its forbearance is guaranteed by human nature. Likewise, a belief system that abominates inconsistency cannot claim that its own consistency is guaranteed by the nature of belief systems.

Belief in cannibalism could be a cultural universal without there being any cannibals. Perhaps each group accuses other groups to increase local solidarity. However, those who link belief and necessity cannot hope that the believability of impossibilities is a universal myth. For they take the presence of a belief in every system to be sufficient for its truth; indeed, it must count as a necessary truth.

8. The Limits of Illusion

I have purposely reviewed the impossibilists' arguments in broad historical strokes. The modern refinements surpass Plato's first efforts.

Nevertheless, they inherit a rare disorder. Philosophers can typically help themselves to an appearance/reality distinction. A Francis Herbert Bradley or a George Berkeley or a Zeno can admit that their thesis appears false and then triumphantly argue that it is, against all odds, really true. Indeed, much of the value of speculative reasoning lies in the prospect of dispelling an illusion. The preconditions for illusion are so modest that they are commonly ignored. However, impossibilism is an unprecedented case in which this minimal condition of speculative debate is violated. Consequently, students of belief are in a unique position to lay down an adequacy condition with instructive connections to puzzles about reasoning, representation, and analysis: all discriminative accounts of belief must permit belief in impossibilities.

This completes my defense of the presupposition that it is possible to believe the impossible. But the reader is apt to be struck by how much further I must travel. My diagnosis of the sorites entails that all competent speakers of the language *actually* believe *infinitely* many contradictions. Where is the independent justification for this more sweeping proposition?

As my adversary in this chapter might sourly concur, there is actually little distance between

Point A: It is possible to believe an impossibility, and
Point B: Everybody actually believes infinitely many contradictions.

The distance can be covered in three steps. First, one must show that a rational person ought to believe a contradiction. Secondly, one shows how the principle of charity pressures us to interpret all people as actually believing contradictions. Thirdly and finally, one exploits the relational aspect of belief to show that infinitely many contradictions are believed.

On to the first step.

9 Reason Demands Belief in Infinitely Many Contradictions

I believe that I believe an inconsistent proposition (i.e. one that entails its own negation—as demonstrable by *reductio ad absurdum*). This meta-belief about the set of propositions I actually now hold is infallible.

Proof by *reductio ad absurdum*: assume each proposition I now believe is consistent—including the proposition that I believe an inconsistency. If p is consistent, then ⌜p is inconsistent⌝ is itself inconsistent. For if p is consistent, it is logically impossible for p to entail its own negation. Yet if ⌜p is inconsistent⌝ is consistent, then it is possible for p to entail its own negation. Just as it is inconsistent to call a consistent proposition inconsistent, it is inconsistent to say of two consistent propositions that either the first one is inconsistent or the second one is inconsistent. In general, it is inconsistent to say of a set of consistent propositions that at least one member of that set is inconsistent. Therefore, if each proposition that I now believe is consistent, then my meta-belief that at least one of my beliefs is inconsistent is itself inconsistent. That is, if all of my beliefs are consistent, then at least one of my beliefs is inconsistent. Contradiction. Therefore, necessarily, if I believe that I believe at least one inconsistent proposition, then I indeed believe at least one inconsistent proposition.

'The set of propositions I actually now hold' is a *rigid* definite description (like 'the *actual* inventor of bifocals' which picks out Benjamin Franklin even in those worlds in which Franklin is not the inventor of bifocals). I need a rigid designator because my thesis is *de re*: Of the set of propositions that I actually believe, at least one of them is inconsistent.

'The set of propositions I actually now hold' is also an indexical expression. Its reference shifts with the circumstances of utterance. However, the phrase picks out the same *kind* of thing and there is much overlap between what I believed at past stages and what I currently believe (especially with respect to logical truths). Therefore, fruitful generalizations can be made about these belief sets. These generalizations are not merely autobiographical. Nothing special turns on who 'I' refers to or which period is designated by 'now' or which possible world gets selected by 'actual'. I am using 'I' representatively like René Descartes uses 'I' in his *Meditations*. The reader is intended to follow along with his own parallel thoughts about his own current set of beliefs and see his thoughts as representative of human beings in general.

1. Beyond the Preface Paradox

If I merely believe that at least one of my beliefs is *false*, then it is impossible for that belief to be true along with all of my other beliefs. Ironically, this rationally mandatory meta-belief stops my beliefs from collectively constituting a coherent picture of reality (Makinson 1965). I used to take solace in the distinction between believing an inconsistency and merely having jointly inconsistent beliefs. A necessary condition of retaining this comfort is rejection of the agglomeration principle which alleges that (Bp & Bq) entails B(p & q).

The surprise is that the denial of agglomeration is not a sufficient condition. My opening reductio secures an inconsistent belief independently of the agglomeration principle.

I must still deny agglomeration because it would saddle me with *identifiable* inconsistencies. In particular, I would believe the conjunction of my beliefs and the negation of that conjunction. To believe that a proposition is a contradiction is to believe it is false—and hence to not believe it. Lesson: the identities of my logical lapses are personal blindspots; though consistent, ' "p is inconsistent" but I believe it' is just one deduction away from G. E. Moore's ' "p is false" but I believe p'. Only others can single out the inconsistencies that I presently believe.

Graham Priest (1987: 120) professes to believe the contradiction that Russell's set is and is not a member of itself. Perhaps he does. But not simply in virtue of having thoughtfully and sincerely asserted it. Priest uses 'contradiction' in a deviant way—he thinks a few contradictions are *both* true and false! This deprives contradiction of its constitutive role in *reductio ad absurdum*. Instead of being the point of closure in a premise-less refutation, the 'contradiction' becomes a deniable assumption in a *modus tollens* argument. Consequently, Priest seems as much a skeptic about the existence of contradictions as he seems a daringly open-minded believer in contradictions.

Am I being paternalistic? No more than Professor Priest is when he interprets self-attributions of *massive* inconsistency by Heraclitus,

Laotse, and Engels (Priest and Routley 1989). To avoid triviality (by counting all propositions as true), Priest accepts the principle that the number of contradictions be minimized. Priest must wield the same principle against self-attributions of triviality. Anyone who accepts all propositions is in total (degenerate) agreement with any other acceptor of triviality. Hence they can only be interpreted as having *distinct* positions by overriding their thoughtful, sincere self-attributions of maximal inconsistency.

Some may feel that I have none the less accompanied Priest too far down the path to contradiction. They will insist 'I believe an inconsistency' is less reasonable than 'I believe a falsehood'. However, the evidence for my logical fallibility has same pattern as my generic fallibility. The preface paradox uses my past errors and the errors of people similar to me. A subset of these errors, logical errors, provides ample inductive justification for my logical fallibility. Logicians are just as apt as physicists to apologize for the errors that are sure to exist in their books. Psychological studies of deduction provide ample experimental corroboration of the commonplace observation that human beings are prone to logical errors.

My belief in inconsistencies can also be established as an inference to the best explanation. The hypothesis that some of the propositions I believe are inconsistent simply accounts for how *reductio ad absurdum* can teach me a lesson. This method of proof derives a contradiction from the proposition under attack. So it can refute me only if I believe some inconsistent propositions. The efficacy of *reductio ad absurdum* cannot be better explained by the hypothesis that I *merely* believe that I believe some inconsistencies. For that meta-belief entails that I would really believe an inconsistent proposition.

Many eminent philosophers have maintained that we can only believe what is possible. But, as was demonstrated in the previous chapter, their position has an unusual dialectical vulnerability. The mere belief that it is possible to believe the impossible ensures that it is possible to believe the impossible. For if the belief is mistaken, then it is necessarily mistaken. Hence, the belief would itself be a belief in the impossible. Consequently, we need only disagree with the eminent philosophers to prove them wrong. Philosophy never gets easier than this.

The belief that I believe an inconsistency is a consistent report of the bad news that I believe an inconsistency. The meta-belief does not *cause* me to become inconsistent. It is overwhelmingly probable that the reductio scenario in which the meta-belief forces me into an inconsistency is a logically impossible scenario. Rather than being a spoiler, the meta-belief is almost certainly a non-intrusive observer, a truth that is logically but not causally self-supportive. And it is helpful. Adding 'I have inconsistent beliefs' to my stock of beliefs makes it more complete and offers the best explanation of my logical curiosity.

I have considerable non-deductive evidence for believing it anyway. The surprise is that once I make the 'inductive leap' to the meta-belief, there is no longer any chance of it being false. There is sugar in this humble pie! This multiplier effect has precedents. A non-introspective empiricist might infer that he has beliefs only on the basis of his behavioral or neural similarity with believers. His inductive argument yields a conclusion that is then infallibly believed.

2. The Resemblance to the Liar is a False Alarm

If I say 'The next thing you say is true', you might enmesh us in a liar paradox by saying 'What was just said is false'. In addition to risky definite descriptions, there are risky existential generalizations:

List A:
1. There is an inconsistent proposition on list A.
2. Some people have blue eyes.

Since 2 is consistent, 1 is true only if it is inconsistent. If 1 is inconsistent, 1 is false. But then there would be an inconsistent proposition on the list and thus 1 would be true after all. How do I know that my meta-belief is not mired in a liar paradox like the existential generalization in List A?

The quick answer sounds circular: I know because I know my list of beliefs contains some inconsistencies. That is, I know my meta-belief has the same character as

List B:
1. There is an inconsistent proposition on list B.
2. Some people have blue eyes.
3. It is raining and it is not raining.

The existential generalization in B is risky in the sense that it would have been semantically defective (i.e. liar paradoxical) if the other items on the list had all been consistent. This risk is only an epistemic possibility given that the existential generalization is read *de re*. That is, if we take 'List B' to *name* the set of propositions composed of the items actually on that list, then in every possible world (B1) is free of semantic defect. For names are rigid designators.

Since my set of actual beliefs contains some inconsistencies, my meta-belief 'I believe some inconsistencies' is also *necessarily* unparadoxical. Notice that this metaphysical assertion differs from the epistemological claim that 'I believe some inconsistencies' is *certainly* unparadoxical. Many necessities are not certainties. After all, many mathematical truths will never even seem probable to us. The point is that my strong inductive evidence puts me in a position to assert that the meta-belief is not a risky sentence. Just as a look at my hand-held calculator puts me in position to assert that there is no possible world in which $823 + 483 = 1307$, reflection on my fallibility puts me a position to assert that there is no possible world in which my *de re* meta-belief gives rise to a paradox.

Still, one may insist that epistemic possibility is relevant in argumentative contexts. My *reductio ad absurdum* may be necessarily free of any liar-paradoxical element. But to know that it is a good argument, it seems I must have independent knowledge that I believe some inconsistent propositions. Therefore, my critic could concede that induction gives me this independent knowledge but still complain that the induction renders my original argument superfluous.

However, not all of the preconditions of a successful argument are premises. Whenever I argue, I assume my rule of inference is valid. But as illustrated by Lewis Carroll's (1895) dialogue between Achilles and the Tortoise, categorizing this assumption as a premise generates an infinite regress. A similar infinite regress follows if we categorize as a premise my assumption that I am not equivocating, or my assumption that my premises are jointly consistent, or my assumption that my argumentative discourse is composed of meaningful sentences. People can learn by argument even when they lack proof for the various propositions that constitute the infrastructure of argument. My inability to prove that I did not equivocate does not always stop me from acquiring knowledge by means of the argument in question. A proof that I did not equivocate might merely play the role of confirming that my knowledge of the conclusion was not defeated by an equivocation. In my opening reductio, I did assume that my reasoning is not liar paradoxical. This assumption is a precondition of expressing a premise. Therefore, when I provide inductive evidence that this precondition is satisfied, I am only showing that the argument is not a pseudo-reductio. The project of showing that someone learned a conclusion from an argument is more onerous than simply learning the conclusion from the ostensible argument. Non-logicians learn much from their deductions without understanding how they do it. So do logicians!

3. Self-Reference is Better than Hierarchy

Wise men have advised me to avoid even the appearance of paradox by casting my thesis hierarchically. Instead of (self-referentially) saying that my entire corpus of beliefs contains some inconsistencies, their counsel is to narrow my thesis to the claim that some of my first order beliefs are inconsistent. If all of these first order beliefs are consistent, then I can report (at the third order) that this second-order belief is inconsistent.

All of this is true and compatible with my original argument. I prefer my original self-referential argument because it is less artificial and complicated, and hence a better candidate for the aesthetically sensitive status of 'inference to the best explanation'. My grounds for believing that I believe inconsistencies are generic ones about the nature of belief. I have no special reason to think that my *first* order beliefs are inconsistent. I form inconsistent beliefs because consistency competes with other desiderata such as simplicity and completeness. Induction confirms the hypothesis that the trade-offs occur at all levels of beliefs: my beliefs about my beliefs are just as frequently inconsistent as my first order beliefs. For instance, many of my past beliefs about principles of 'doxastic logic' were refuted by *reductio ad absurdum*. So my only motive to shepherd my beliefs into separate orders is the 'risk' of the liar paradox. This danger has already proven to be objectively baseless.

Therefore, my fear should cease. An argument cannot be refuted by its mere *resemblance* to a paradoxical form of reasoning. Refutation by logical analogy is a danger only to the extent that the resemblance is a *sign* that there is something wrong with the argument itself. One should relax after one finds that the argument is free of the flaw suggested by the resemblance. Those who treat resemblance as a cause fall into the pseudo-scientific thinking that lies behind the voodoo practice of sticking pins in dolls. It is pseudo-scientific to doubt Cantor's diagonal argument or Gödel's incompleteness theorem or Turing's result for the halting problem merely because of their historic connection and similarity to the liar paradox. To reconfigure my argument in terms of hierarchy would just pander to a logical superstition.

4. Counter-Logicals and Reductio Illusions

When I assert 'If the egg falls, it will crack', I conversationally implicate that the egg could fall. This implicature leads us to misinterpret counter-logical conditionals in general and *reductio ad absurdum* reasoning in particular.

Conditionals with impossible antecedents are standard in *reductio ad absurdum* proofs. Indeed, such conditionals are indispensable because the reductio fails unless the supposition is inconsistent. Thus in my opening proof, I did not suggest that the antecedent of the following conditional is possible.

(i) If I mistakenly believe that I believe at least one inconsistency, then this meta-belief is itself inconsistent.

Granted, the antecedent is 'epistemically possible'. But an epistemic possibility need be no more a possibility than a suspected murderer need be a murderer. The conditional must be understood in the same stern way as other contrary to necessity conditionals such as Euclid's 'If there is a largest prime number, then there is a larger prime number less than or equal to the successor of the product of all the prime numbers'. If Euclid were to allow that the antecedent is possible, he would be committed to agreeing that it is necessary. The whole proof method of *reductio ad absurdum* would backfire.

There is *irony* in the assertion 'My belief that I believe an inconsistency is infallible in virtue of its possible inconsistency'. The irony would be outright absurdity if 'possible' here meant more than epistemic 'possibility'. Nothing is both possible and possibly impossible. Every possibly inconsistent belief is necessarily inconsistent, so every possibly inconsistent belief is necessarily false—the reverse of infallible.

5. *Contingent Membership lets you Keep Essential Properties*

The Barcan formula, $(x)\Box Fx \supset \Box(x)Fx$, licenses the inference from a *de re* necessity to its *de dicto* counterpart. An apparent counterexample is a world that happens to be filled with immaterial things (numbers, God, sets). Each member of this domain possesses its immateriality necessarily. Yet there could have been some material beings in this world.

Now consider a blackboard that happens to hold only consistent propositions. Each proposition is necessarily consistent: (p) $\Box^\ulcorner p$ is consistent$^\urcorner$. However, it is not a necessary truth that the blackboard comprises only consistent sentences. There could have been some inconsistent sentences. (Although the blackboard scenario involves an unrestricted modality, logical possibility, the domain of discourse is restricted to the sentences on the blackboard. Even friends of the Barcan formula say that the formula only holds when *both* the modality and the quantification are unrestricted (Parsons 1995).) Distinguish the true $(p) \Box \ulcorner p$ is consistent$\urcorner$ from the false $\Box(p) \ulcorner p$ is consistent$\urcorner$.

The point can be put unequivocally by fixing the domain of discourse with a rigid designator. Name the set of propositions expressed on the blackboard 'B'. Notice that I do not need to know which propositions are on the board. I can use the reference-fixing description 'the propositions expressed on that blackboard' to fix the membership of B without knowing which propositions are. The blackboard could be covered with a curtain. My christening of the set ensures that B picks out the same propositions in every possible world. Then from $(p) \Box \ulcorner p$ is consistent$\urcorner$ we can conclude $\Box((p)(p$ is a member of B$) \supset \Box \ulcorner p$ is consistent$\urcorner)$. Or to put the same conclusion negatively, it is necessarily false that some proposition in B is inconsistent: $\Box \sim (\exists p)(p$ is a member of B & $\ulcorner p$ is inconsistent$\urcorner$. More generally, it is inconsistent to say of a set of consistent propositions that at least one of them is inconsistent or even that one of them is possibly inconsistent (or even possibly possibly inconsistent, and so on.) Thus the opening reductio can be easily changed into a proof of the following thesis: if I believe that one of my beliefs is *possibly* inconsistent, then one of my beliefs is *actually* inconsistent.

I am like the blackboard. I do not need any introspective power to specify the set of propositions I believe. And the propositions I hold are only contingently held. But their contingent membership in my belief system is compatible with each of them being necessarily consistent. Likewise, the fact that I only contingently believe a particular inconsistency is compatible with it being necessarily inconsistent. My belief that I believe at least one inconsistent proposition is a belief about the nature of the beliefs I actually hold. Whichever beliefs I happen to hold, there will be an inconsistent belief—given that I also hold, as I ought, that at least one of my beliefs is inconsistent.

10 The Viral Theory of Inconsistency

In 1964, J. R. Lucas published a Gödelian argument to prove that he is not a thinking machine: computers physically instantiate formal systems. A consistent formal system that is powerful enough to prove the theorems of arithmetic is also powerful enough to construct a sentence to the same effect as 'This sentence is not a theorem of the system'. The sentence could only be a theorem if its negation was also a theorem. So given that the system is consistent, the sentence is a truth that is missed by the system. Therefore, the system is incomplete. Lucas contends that he is not limited by this incompleteness result.

> We have adequate, more than adequate, reason for affirming our own consistency and the truth, and hence also the consistency, of informal arithmetic, and so can properly say that we know, and that any machine representation of the mind must manifest an output expressed by a formal (since it is a machine) system which is consistent and includes Elementary Number Theory (since it is supposed to represent the mind). (Lucas 1996: 121)

I regard total consistency as an unattainable ideal. To maximize consistency, we must adopt policies that precipitate some inconsistency as a side-effect. Just as each immune system is constantly combating incipient infections, each belief system constantly struggles to detect and eliminate contradictions. Both systems operate under the assumption that the enemy already lurks within the gates. This assumption is probably hard-wired, making the meta-belief in my own inconsistency innate. Since this *de re* meta-belief in my own inconsistency is infallible, it would follow that I am an *innately* inconsistent being.

Lucas pictures contradictions as occasional intruders—like squirrels in your attic. The squirrels can be detected with reasonable vigilance and then promptly expelled:

> The fact that we are all sometimes inconsistent cannot be gainsaid, but from this it does not follow that we are tantamount to inconsistent systems. Our inconsistencies are mistakes rather than set policies. They correspond to the occasional malfunctioning of a machine, not its normal scheme of operations.

Witness to this that we eschew inconsistencies when we recognize them for what they are. If we really were inconsistent machines, we should remain content with our inconsistencies, and would happily affirm both halves of a contradiction. Moreover, we would be prepared to say absolutely anything—which we are not. (Lucas 1964: 53)

I agree that *detected* contradictions are instantly abandoned. (We cannot believe what we regard as false.) But this very process of elimination creates a selective advantage for hidden contradictions. Contradictions rarely parade as p & $\sim p$. Most are small, quiet, and color-less. Like biological parasites, contradictory beliefs jeopardize their own survival if they invite their hosts to make reckless deductions. A contradictory belief that did little harm (or which even benefited its host) would have better long-term prospects.

Each belief is formed under pressure for completeness. Con-sequently, beliefs crowd each other in logical space. Any combination of beliefs might be jointly inconsistent. Given a set of n propositions, there are $2^n - 1$ combinations of propositions. Therefore, the search space for a check of consistency grows exponentially. Since this version of the satisfiability problem is NP-complete, it is intractable even for future super-computers. (For a popular discussion of NP-completeness, see Poundstone (1988, ch. 9). The classic presentation is that of Garey and Jonson (1979).)

Inconsistencies come in quantity. Each belief system is under relent-less, massive assault. Contradictions are not like squirrels; they are like viruses. By strength of numbers, some contradictions inevitably slip through.

The only feasible way to cope with contradictions is with fallible heuristics rather than algorithms. Recognition of this necessity forces a policy that guarantees, as a foreseeable side-effect, that one will have some contradictions. For instance, instead of devoting all resources to preventing entry, we devote substantial resources to the pursuit and elimination of the contradictions that do slip through. We deliberately sacrifice opportunities to be contradiction-free for the certainty of hav-ing a tolerable frequency of contradiction. An analogy: after disease-fighters learned that cowpox immunized milkmaids from smallpox, they deliberately infected all of their patients with the cowpox disease. The physicians realized that most unvaccinated people end up in the ideal position of contracting neither smallpox nor cowpox. But physicians reckoned that it was better to accept the certainty of a small loss rather than risk a catastrophic loss.

The most lucrative investment I could make with the dollar in my pocket is to buy the winning ticket in the state lottery. But prudence dictates that I should act in a way that would preclude this optimal outcome—by investing in something with better odds. The good should not be sacrificed in pursuit of the perfect. Well let's not understate: the perfect *should* be sacrificed in pursuit of the good. Instead of maximizing my chance at achieving a maximal outcome, I should maximize my expected utility—even at the cost of rendering a maximal outcome impossible. I should burn my bridges to perfection—for the right price.

This point also holds for epistemic value. If I believe that I have at least one false belief, then I preclude the optimal outcome of having entirely true beliefs. But it is a good bargain. The probability of having entirely true beliefs is so low that I lose little by further reducing the probability to zero. In exchange, I acquire an interesting, true belief. The same holds for more humbling self-attributions—the belief that some of my beliefs are inconsistent, ill-founded, and so forth. These contribute to a useful self-profile that helps me to tailor cognitive practices to my strengths and weaknesses. The meta-beliefs put me out of contention for the title of 'ideal believer' but it would be irrational for me not to take myself out of the running. It is rationally mandatory to acknowledge cognitive imperfections even when this acknowledgment is logically self-fulfilling.

Epistemologists have naturally simplified the agents with an assumption of perfect rationality. Of course, they have been aware that ordinary agents are imperfect: human beings are not logically omniscient, consistent, and so forth. Yet the commentators have still forbidden the agent from forming beliefs that would foreclose the attainment of perfectionist ideals. For instance, Keith Lehrer says that I ought not to believe 'At least one of my beliefs is false' because that would doom me to having jointly inconsistent beliefs (1974: 203). Such counsel against self-injury may seem even more compelling when it comes to contradictions rather than mere falsehoods. But this is a perfectionist illusion.

1. *Unreflective Inconsistency*

In the previous chapter, I used an argument based on a global, self-referential meta-belief that employs *reductio ad absurdum*. However, the basic case for believing contradictions can be made without any of these anxiety-provoking features.

Consider a student (much like the one mentioned in Chapter 3) who is given a test in propositional logic. He is required to pick as many truths as he can from a list. The list is composed solely of logical truths and logical falsehoods but the student has not been told this. The student believes each of his answers, $p_1, p_2, \ldots, p_n$. However, he also believes that at least of one these answers is false, that is, he believes $\sim(p_1 \,\&\, p_2 \,\&\, \ldots \,\&\, p_n)$.

Here is a direct proof (by constructive dilemma) that the student believes a logical falsehood. If any of his answers $p_1, p_2, \ldots, p_n$ are false, then the student believes a logical falsehood (because the only falsehoods on the question list are logical falsehoods). If all of his test answers are true, then the student believes the following logical falsehood: $\sim(p_1 \,\&\, p_2 \,\&\, \ldots \,\&\, p_n)$. For if $p_1, p_2, \ldots, p_n$ are true, they are all logical truths. A conjunction of logical truths is itself a logical truth. And the negation of any logical truth is a logical falsehood. Hence, if all the student's test answers are true, then his belief that $\sim(p_1 \,\&\, p_2 \,\&\, \ldots \,\&\, p_n)$ is itself a belief in a logical falsehood.

With minimal modal logic (such as the system T), this proof generalizes to a broader reading of 'non-contingent'. Just substitute 'necessary' for 'logical' in the above two paragraphs. The result is a sound proof about necessary falsehoods (since necessity collects over conjunction). For instance, an essentialist could have the student pick from metaphysical necessities and impossibilities such as 'Water is H_2O', 'Bo Derek is the number 10', etc. If this metaphysics student disbelieved the conjunction of his sincere answers, then he would thereby believe at least one necessary falsehood.

If the disbelieved necessary truth is a posteriori, then the student's disbelief does not raise issues about his rationality. In contrast, disbelief in an a priori truth betokens carelessness. Investigation of this asymmetry threatens to lead us into the labyrinth of modal epistemology. Happily, I can afford a retreat from the metaphysics student to the logic student. For the argument featuring the logic student involves only sentence logic and yet takes us a long way to showing that rational agents believe contradictions.

My assumptions about the logic student are minimal. I do not assume that he is applying the concept of a logical truth. His task is only to identify truths. Nor do I require that the student apply the concept of belief. Some introverted students believe that $\sim(p_1 \,\&\, p_2 \,\&\, \ldots \,\&\, p_n)$

on the strength of reflections on their personal fallibility. But such meta-beliefs are not essential to the anti-agglomerative belief pattern: $(Bp_1 \& Bp_2 \& \ldots \& Bp_n) \& B\sim(p_1 \& p_2 \& \ldots \& p_n)$. An unreflective student may base his belief that $\sim(p_1 \& p_2 \& \ldots \& p_n)$ directly on the improbability of such a long list containing only truths.

The student could shed his belief in a contradiction by gaining new evidence. For instance, if the teacher showed the student the answer key, the student might learn on authority that p_1 is false and so stop believing the contradiction that p_1.

However, other contradictions are likely to remain after a genuine contradiction is uprooted. For instance, the student might have a belief in a contradiction that arose from an earlier tautology test. The student answered that $q_1, q_2, \ldots, q_m$ are each true but the student also believed $\sim(q_1 \& q_2 \& \ldots, \& q_m)$.

A second answer key could eliminate the contradiction dwelling within this anti-agglomerative constellation. However, purging contradictions by appealing to authority becomes less feasible as the number and complexity of the statements increase. Instructors are themselves fallible. True, there are algorithms for deciding whether a given formula is a tautology in sentence logic. But they are too time consuming to be a complete, practical remedy. For instance, the truth table for a sentence that is composed of n sub-sentences has 2^n lines. This is an exponential function that grows unmanageably complex as n increases. In any case, there is no such algorithm once we turn to predicate logic.

2. Awareness that One Believes a Contradiction

It might be thought that the contradiction will go away if the student becomes aware of his situation. Very well, let the instructor carefully explain the meaning of 'contradiction' and 'tautology'. Have the student master the above proof that he believes a contradiction.

This tutorial might have the byproduct of improving the student's ability to discriminate between the truths and falsehoods on the question list. It might also intensify the student's desire to eliminate the false belief. Many people feel that belief in a logical falsehood indicts their rationality in a way that belief in a false contingency does not. After all, if one unwittingly believes a contradiction, C, then one is disposed to reject valid inferences such as $\ulcorner C$, therefore, $A \urcorner$ (where A is an arbitrary proposition). One will also be disposed to accept invalid inferences such as ⌜A, therefore, ~C is consistent⌝ (because one will view ⌜~C is consistent⌝ as a tautology). Hence, concern about one's rationality may stimulate further inquiry or prompt heightened standards of evidence.

However, even authors of logic textbooks make mistakes. The logician's belief that his solutions manual has errors is sometimes volunteered explicitly in the preface. Hence, the student's anti-agglomerativity can continue even after he has mastered logical theory and emulated his instructor's scholarly virtues. The student can have a stable, rational belief in a contradiction.

3. Meta-beliefs and Anti-agglomerativity

Even more stable would be the belief that one believes a contradiction. This meta-belief is apt to arise from the very process of purging a contradictory belief.

A person who discovers that one of his beliefs is a contradiction is like a man who discovers a louse on his head. The detection leads to a response that decreases the amount of harm—immediate termination of the louse. But the detection also constitutes evidence that there are further lice. The man who eliminates a contradiction benefits himself by causing himself to become more consistent and hence rational. However, the process is humbling because it turns up evidence that he has further irrationalities.

This modesty becomes a further basis for believing that one believes an inconsistency. It is logically independent of anti-agglomerativity:

Modesty: $B[\sim(p_1 \& p_2 \& \ldots \& p_n) \& (Bp_1 \& Bp_2 \& \ldots \& Bp_n)]$
Anti-agglomerativity: $(Bp_1 \& Bp_2 \& \ldots \& Bp_n) \& B\sim(p_1 \& p_2 \& \ldots \& p_n)$.

Since belief distributes over conjunction, both principles entail disbelief in the conjunction: $B\sim(p_1 \& p_2 \& \ldots \& p_n)$. However, anti-agglomerativity fails to entail what modesty explicitly asserts; the meta-belief that some of one's beliefs are false. And only the anti-agglomerative proposition implies that one really has the individual beliefs, $(Bp_1 \& Bp_2 \& \ldots \& Bp_n)$.

Anti-agglomerativity would be equivalent to modesty if each individual were omniscient about his own beliefs. A strong logic of belief could approximate this inner omniscience by combining the principle that we are infallible about our beliefs (if BBp then Bp) with the principle that beliefs are self-intimating (if Bp, then BBp). Since both of these principles are implausible, no logic of belief challenges the independence of modesty and anti-agglomerativity.

Only anti-agglomerativity implies that the agent believes a proposition that is jointly inconsistent with other propositions that the agent believes. Modesty does entail that the agent has a false belief. But this kind of inevitable falsehood need not be in virtue of the propositions believed. Consider a deluded 'author' who falsely believes he has written a book. He composes a preface in which he apologizes for the mistakes in the text. Since there is no text, the pseudo-author's preface belief 'There is a false belief in the text' is false. The pseudo-author's meta-belief guarantees that he has at least one false belief. However, the pseudo-author's meta-belief does not guarantee that the propositions he believes are jointly inconsistent. For the pseudo-author only has one relevant belief and the proposition he believes is consistent.

Unlike *de dicto* modesty, *de re* modesty implies the existence of other beliefs. If the author believes of the beliefs expressed in the text, that one of them is false, then the propositions he believes are jointly inconsistent. For if all of his text beliefs are true, then his preface belief is false.

De re modesty implies anti-agglomerativity but not vice versa. The student who disbelieves the conjunction of his test answers need not realize that those are *his* answers. He might have just picked up a test at random and predicted, on actuarial grounds, that not all the answers are correct. In summary, *de dicto* modesty is not enough to entail joint inconsistency while *de re* modesty is more than enough. Anti-agglomerativity has the distinction of being exactly enough.

The deluded author shows how the *absence* of beliefs can force a distinction between the inevitability of a false belief and a joint inconsistency. However, the distinction is also prompted by the *presence* of beliefs that a meta-belief excludes:

1. I have no disjunctive beliefs.
2. Either Europa has life or it is not the case that Europa has life.

Although 1 and 2 are jointly consistent, my belief in both of them would imply that I have a false belief (in particular, the meta-belief is false).

We know that $\Diamond p$ does not entail $\Diamond(p \ \& \ Bp)$ because p could be a proposition about belief such as 'No one has a belief'. This helps to explain relative blindspots in which each conjunct of a consistent conjunction is consistently believable but the consistent conjunction as a whole is not consistently believable.

4. Meta-statements

Meta-beliefs are beliefs about beliefs. Meta-statements are statements about other statements such as ' "Some sentences are long" is a short sentence'.

A meta-statement can be jointly inconsistent with its object statement:

(a) 'Snow is white' is false.
(b) Snow is white.

Similarly (b) is jointly inconsistent with

(c) 'Snow is white' is inconsistent.

Indeed, since (b) is consistent, it is actually (c) that is inconsistent. For if (b) is consistent, then it is not a logical truth that a contradiction can be derived from (b). But if (c) were true, then it would be a logical truth that a contradiction can be derived from (b). Since a logical falsehood is derivable from (c) (namely, that a logical falsehood is derivable from (b)), (c) must itself be a logical falsehood.

In general, false accusations of inconsistency are themselves inconsistent:

(I) If $\ulcorner p$ is consistent$\urcorner$, then $\ulcorner p$ is inconsistent$\urcorner$ is inconsistent.

The principle bears a likeness to the characteristic formula of the modal system S5, $\Diamond p \supset \Box \Diamond p$, which states that whatever is possible is necessarily possible. The analogy invites the inference to

(II) If $\ulcorner p$ is inconsistent$\urcorner$, then $\ulcorner p$ is consistent$\urcorner$ is inconsistent.

The reasoning for (II) echoes that of (I). If p entails a contradiction, then $\ulcorner p$ is consistent$\urcorner$ entails that p does not entail a contradiction. But $\ulcorner p$ does not entail a contradiction$\urcorner$ entails that $\ulcorner p$ does not entail a contradiction$\urcorner$ is a contradiction (by principle I).

Combining (I) and (II) yields the moral that statements bear their consistency status in a logically mandatory fashion just as modal statements bear their modal status necessarily. All errors about whether a statement is consistent are inconsistencies.

It follows that a policy of refusing to form opinions about non-contingencies is self-defeating. If I resolve to form beliefs only about contingencies, then I must form beliefs about whether candidates for beliefs are contingent. The problem is that this higher order belief is never itself a belief in a contingent proposition. If I am right about whether p is contingent, then I am necessarily right, and if wrong, then necessarily wrong.

Principle (II) suggests that there is also a danger in avoiding the incoherence of agnosticism by positively believing that one's beliefs are jointly consistent (like Professor Lucas). For if they are not jointly consistent, then one's meta-belief is a logical falsehood. Those who argue that we should believe our beliefs to be jointly consistent are likely to be promoting a belief in an inconsistency. Ironically, their effort to prevent jointly inconsistent beliefs leads to the more severe sort of inconsistency—believing an inconsistency. The inconsistency would be the very assertion of joint consistency!

5. The Scale of the Inconsistency

The logic student illustrates the anti-agglomerative path to contradiction. His beliefs just naturally fail to collect over conjunction. This leads him to a rational belief in contradictions even if he does not engage in reflections about his fallibility. However, if he does engage in those reflections, he acquires another basis for believing that he believes an inconsistency. The path of modesty turns on the self-fulfilling nature of the meta-belief. Believing so, makes it so.

The modest meta-belief bears a risk of liar paradoxicality that is inversely proportional to the size of the belief system. If there are few beliefs, then the meta-belief has a significant chance of *causing* me to become inconsistent. But in the global variation, it is far more likely that the belief that I believe an inconsistency is a consistent report of the bad news that I believe an inconsistency. The meta-belief in the high strength version covers a much larger number of beliefs. There is safety in numbers. The more comprehensive the meta-belief, the more likely that some *other* belief is the inconsistency. And in that case, the reductio scenario in which the meta-belief forces me into an inconsistency is logically impossible.

Just how many contradictions do I believe? Anti-agglomerativity is a general *pattern* of belief, so I should expect to believe many contradictions in the same manner as the logic student.

Belief holism ensures that anyone who believes one inconsistency, will believe many inconsistencies. As illustrated by the impact of Duhem's thesis on the verification principle, beliefs operate within collectives. I cannot have exactly one false belief. Any error infects some ancillary beliefs. Since the ancillary beliefs of a logical belief are themselves logical, holism makes any logical imperfection a corporate set-back.

Indeed, any logical error precipitates infinitely many logical errors. Those who believe an inconsistency, X, at least tacitly believe the conjunction of X and T where T is a perceived tautology. For the conjunction has the same probability as X. (Agglomeration only fails when the additional conjunct *lowers* the probability.) Everyone believes $\ulcorner n = n \urcorner$ is a tautology, for each n. Hence everyone believes infinitely many tautologies. Obviously, these beliefs cannot all be occurrent. They are dispositions. A finite object can have infinitely many relational dispositions when there are infinitely many relata. I have the ability to lift a 1 kilogram weight, a 1.1 kilogram weight, a 1.11 kilogram weight, and so on. Similarly, I am disposed to affirm $1 = 1$, $2 = 2$, and so on. Therefore, I have infinitely many inconsistent beliefs of the form $\ulcorner X \ \& \ n = n \urcorner$.

Logic equips us with many ways of showing how error multiplies. Instead of conjoining X with other propositions, one could simply consider successive double negations. If X is inconsistent, so is $\sim \sim X$, $\sim \sim \sim \sim X$, and so on. Modal error can also issue from non-logical error. Correctly informed that $Y \vee \sim Z$, the believer in Z will infer Y. When Y turns out to be an inconsistency, a new inconsistency has come home to roost. (Notice this pattern simply trades on mistaken belief in Z—it works even if Z is meaningless.)

Incompleteness has the same infectious character. Gödel's incompleteness theorem does not merely entail that a consistent, arithmetically competent system must have at least one unprovable truth. It entails that such a system must have infinitely many. For instance, the conjunction of an unprovable truth with a theorem is an unprovable truth. Since there are infinitely many theorems of a system strong enough to express arithmetic, there are infinitely many unprovable truths.

A corollary of Gödel's theorem is that there are as many unprovable truths as provable truths. If there is any incompleteness, there is infinite incompleteness. Therefore, it is impossible to minimize the incompleteness in the sense of reducing the total number of unproved truths.

Similarly, if there is some inconsistency, there is infinite inconsistency. Since reason demands belief in at least one contradiction, I cannot minimize inconsistencies in the sense of reducing their total number. The only numeric goal is to minimize the frequency of inconsistencies in small subsets of my beliefs. If every hundredth belief of mine is a contradiction, then I would be increasing my rate of consistency by changing to a belief system in which only every thousandth belief was a contradiction. One sign of this higher consistency is a reduced vulnerability to deductive refutation. A belief can only be deductively refuted by exploiting inconsistencies. A deductive argument must exploit inconsistencies that can arise from finitely many premises. Human limits on working memory and attention radically reduce the size of psychologically effective premise sets to about seven chunks of information (Miller 1956). Therefore, if my inconsistencies are spread thinly, others will rarely be able to show that my belief in the premises conflicts with my lack of belief in the conclusion. I can become more and more logical in the sense of having a lower probability of being actually refuted by someone. But all along, I will believe infinitely many contradictions—just as reason demands.

11 Truthmaker Gaps

An inflationary correspondence theory of truth appears to be inhospitable terrain for the epistemicist. Such a theory legitimates the plea for a substantial fact that would make, say, 15 minutes after noon the last noonish minute.

In contrast, a deflationary theory of truth forms a congenial setting by quietly smothering the primal plea. If 'true' does little more than remove quotation marks and serve as a sentence variable, then talk of 'facts' is similarly thin and linguistic. What makes a borderline tall man actually tall? Well, the *fact* that he is tall. What is the nature of that fact? Well it just consists in 'He is tall' being true. Facts and truths are just two sides of the same slim coin.

If deflationism is correct, then epistemicism is hard to avoid. Witness Paul Horwich's spiral into epistemicism in the first edition of *Truth*. But what if the recent revival of the correspondence theory succeeded? Would the epistemicist need to hunker down? Or could he adapt and draw sustenance from this initially unpromising landscape?

My answer is that an epistemicist could do surprisingly well. Resources of a truthmaking theory can be commandeered to generate absolute borderline cases. The enterprise connects the sorites paradox with a neglected cousin of the liar paradox.

1. The No-No Paradox

While reading Paul Hoffman's delightful biography of Paul Erdos, *The Man Who Loved Only Numbers*, Cliff Landesman noticed that Hoffman quoted a near miss of Philip Jourdain's card paradox from Bertrand Russell's autobiography:

A contradiction essentially similar to that of Epimenides can be created by giving a person a piece of paper on which is written: 'The statement on the other side of this paper is false.' The person turns the paper over, and finds on the other side: 'The statement on the other side of this paper is false.' (Russell 1951/67: 222)

As Landesman observed, the quoted version permits us to consistently assign a T to the first sentence and an F to the second sentence. Russell intended a standard 'looped liar'—the kind that appears on the official T-shirt of the American Philosophical Association. The second printing of the 1967 edition corrects the slip by substituting 'true' for the last word in the quotation.

This unintended pair of sentences manages to be logically interesting. Let us call it 'the no-no paradox'. Formally, one can assign a T to the first sentence and an F to the second. However, symmetry considerations militate against assigning different truth-values to tokens of the same sentence type in the absence of a contextual difference between the sentences. There is a prospect for a contextual difference between the liar sentence, 1, and a distinct sentence, 2, that comments on 1:

1. 1 is not true.
2. 1 is not true.

For instance, Charles Parsons (1974) has argued that 'true' is indexical. He contends the first utterance of 'true' in sentence 1 alters the context for the 'true' used in sentence 2. However, the sentences in the no-no paradox are uttered in parallel (at least in the card version). They share a single context.

Nor is there a hidden structural difference between the sentences. The early Jean Buridan thought that every sentence is tacitly self-referential: each declarative sentence affirms its own truth. Consequently 1 says of itself that it is true and that it is not true. Therefore, 1 is a contradiction. In contrast, 2 correctly records the falsehood of 1 and so is true. Neither no-no sentence denies its own truth. They only differ with respect to which sentence they refer. And since they refer to each other, there is no difference in the *kind* of sentence to which they are referring. Their symmetry is perfect. Unlike the liar paradox, the no-no paradox is driven by a principle of indifference—like Buridan's ass (Makin 1993).

In one respect, the no-no paradox resembles the truth-teller paradox. 'This sentence is true' can be consistently assigned T and can be consistently assigned F. Some regard the question of *which* truth-value to assign as a 'don't care'. However, most commentators believe the existence of two consistent assignments is an embarrassment of riches (Mortensen and Priest 1981). They want a principled reason for assigning the truth-value to the truth-teller sentence. This demand should equally apply to the assignment of truth-values in the no-no paradox. However, satisfaction of this demand would not completely solve the no-no paradox. There would still be the matter of how to justify assigning different truth-values to qualitatively identical sentences. Notice that the mutual truth-teller does not pose this problem. If I write 'The sentence on the other side is true' on each side of a paper slip, then I can consistently assign T to both or F to both.

In the standard liar paradox, the problem is that there is no consistent assignment of truth-values. In the truth-teller paradox, the problem is that there are too many consistent assignments. An assignment must involve an arbitrary choice as to which truth-value should be assigned. The no-no paradox shares this feature but poses the further problem of assigning asymmetrical truth-values to symmetrical sentences. The no-no paradox has *two* dimensions of arbitrariness.

In the case of the no-no paradox, formal considerations rule out some combinations of truth-values but fail to narrow the field of contenders to a unique solution. There are other sentence pairs in which formal considerations *do* suffice for a unique solution. Consider list A which is composed of these two sentences:

The sentences on list A have the same truth-value.
The sentences on list A have the same truth-value.

The following assignments of truth-values lead to an inconsistency: T-F, F-T, F-F. The only remaining possibility is T-T. So if the sentences have any truth-value, T-T must be the correct assignment.

Formal considerations can also ensure a unique truth-value in a positive way. Assume there is a truth-value for 'If the antecedent of this conditional is true, then the antecedent of this conditional is true'. It then follows that the statement is a tautology because it is an instance of the valid form 'If A then A'.

Some people reject assignments of truth-values that only have a formal justification. They maintain that a sentence must be made true by something substantive. Hans Herzberger (1970) spells out this demand with the concept of groundedness. Roughly, the truth of a sentence needs to be grounded within the real world. If sentence A attributes truth to sentence B, then the truth-value of A depends on the truth-value of B. The truth-value of sentence B may depend on a third sentence C. This is permitted as long as the chain ends in a finite number of steps and does not loop back on itself. If the chain is infinite or circular, then none of the sentences has a truth-value.

A simple ban on ungrounded sentences would be too broad: 'in semantics it wreaks havoc, banishing the laws of logic on their naive construal (as statements about all statements including themselves) along with the general principles of semantic theory including the grounding condition itself' (Herzberger 1970: 151). Meta-statements describing the ungroundedness of other statements are themselves ungrounded. Thus Herzberger engineers a gentler, more complicated grounding condition. Saul Kripke (1975) elaborates the grounding architecture with his characteristic blend of technical prowess and vision.

The ban on ungroundedness is reminiscent of the earlier ban on self-reference. In both cases, the strategy is to fashion a semantic sieve that will filter out paradoxical sentences. The self-referential sieve is generally conceded to be inadequate. The old objection to the ban on self-reference is that it is too broad; it bans innocent sentences such as 'This very sentence is in English'. The more recent objection is that the ban is also too narrow (Yablo 1993). For the liar paradox can be generated without self-reference:

Descending liar: (1) All of the subsequent sentences are false;
    (2) All of the subsequent sentences are false;
    (3) All of the subsequent sentences are false; and so on.

Just as in the self-referential liar, there is no consistent assignment of truth-values to the sentences in this sequence. If sentence 1 is true, then sentence 2 correctly describes all of its successors as being false. So 2 would be both true and false. If sentence 1 is false, then there must be a true successor, sentence n. But if sentence n is true, then sentence $n + 1$ correctly describes all of its successors as being false. So $n + 1$ would be both true and false. The basic technique of substituting infinity for self-reference generalizes to all 'self-referential' paradoxes (Sorensen 1998).

A ban on ungroundedness would successfully rule out the descending liars. The ban is also better motivated. Think of how we would explain 'true' to someone who did not understand the word (Kripke 1975: 701). We can helpfully point out the redundancy feature of 'true': we are entitled to assert S is true whenever we are entitled to assert S itself. We are entitled to deny S is true just when we are entitled to deny S. This accounts for most ordinary sentences but we still need to explain sentences that themselves contain the word 'true'. We can explain some of these by noting that inference rules such as existential generalization can be applied to attributions of truth. Since the redundancy rule entitles us to move from 'Snow is white' to ' "Snow is white" is true', we can also apply existential generalization and assert 'Something is true'. The redundancy rule can then be applied again to yield ' "Something is true" is true'. By recursion, all grounded sentences can be explained in this fashion. Ungrounded sentences such as the truth-teller sentence, 'This is true', cannot be explained by this process. The grounder is tempted to infer ' "This is true" is not true'. But he refrains because of the rule that we should deny that S is true exactly when we would deny S itself. One of the problems for grounders is to furnish rules for resolving this dilemma. At this juncture, deviant logics strike Kripke as a resource. Kripke entertains Kleene's three-valued logic and Bas van Fraassen's supervaluationism as possible solutions.

The ban on ungrounded sentences is better than a ban on self-referential sentences. Nevertheless, it shares the self-referentialist's problem of ruling out too many sentences. The ungrounded 'This statement is either true or not' is true by virtue of being an instance of the law of excluded middle. If we say it is not true, we run into a contradiction. For if it is not true, then one of its disjuncts is true, so 'This statement is either true or not' would be true after all.

Groundedness is surprisingly tricky. As Mortensen and Priest (1981: 384) note, we are humbled by 'This sentence is provable in Peano arithmetic'. This sentence appears to be as unsubstantive as the truth-teller sentence 'This is true'. However, it is actually a theorem of Peano arithmetic (Boolos and Jeffrey 1974: 188–9).

As Herzberger noted, the laws of logic are ungrounded because they include themselves in their own domains of discourse. To abide by a grounding restriction, one must reject these self-referential laws and substitute an infinite hierarchy of laws. Thus the grounder's theory has the same skyline as Alfred Tarski's metropolis of levels and meta-levels.

A truth-value could be assigned to the truth-teller if there were some asymmetry between the truth-values of true and false. For example, some view truth as achievement and so regard falsehood as the default state. Advocates of the principle of charity may find reason to regard truth as the preferred state. Melvin Fitting (1997) explores the consequences of taking one truth-value as a default truth-value in his study of fixed points and the liar paradox.

The no-no paradox can be strengthened to survive any asymmetry between true and false:

The neighboring italicized sentence is not true.
The neighboring italicized sentence is not true.

If each lack a truth-value, they are true. Therefore, they cannot both be without a truth-value. If exactly one of them has a truth-value, then there is no explanation of why it has that truth-value (whatever that truth-value might be). If both of them have a truth-value, then one is true and the other is false. But then there is no basis for the difference in truth-value. Consequently, in all cases, there is an ungrounded possession of a truth-value.

There are infinitely many ungrounded truths because there are infinitely many enlarged no-no paradoxes of the following form:

1. Statement 2 is not true.
2. Statement 3 is not true.

.
.
.

$n-1$. Statement n is not true.
n. Statement 1 is not true.

When n is an odd number, the result is a liar paradox. When n is an even number, the result is a no-no paradox.

Unexplained truths are familiar from foundationalism. But foundational truths are only relationally brute. A proposition which serves as an axiom in one system can serve as a proper theorem of another. In contrast, the inexplicability of ungrounded truths is not system relative.

An ungrounded truth can be an element of an orderly assignment of truth-values to infinitely many sentences. Hans Herzberger (1970: 150) taught us how to free the truth-teller from self-reference by using an infinite descending sequence:

Descending truth-teller: (1): (2) is true; (2): (3) is true; (4) is true; . . .

Here the choice is between an assignment of infinitely many Ts and an assignment of infinitely many Fs. The infinite version of the no-no has a similar pattern:

Descending no-no: (1): (2) is false; (2): (3) is false; (4) is false; . . .

There are two consistent assignments of truth-values to the descending no-no. The first assignment makes the odd numbered sentences true and the even numbered sentences false. The second makes the odd numbered sentences false and the even numbered sentences true. Replacing the particular falsehood attributions with universal generalizations yields the descending liar paradox (stated above).

2. Underspecific Truthmakers

The truthmaker principle says that for each contingent truth there must be something in the world that makes it true (Armstrong 1989: 88). David Armstrong has objected to a number of philosophical positions (analytical behaviorism, phenomenalism, presentism, and nominalism) on the grounds that they violate the truthmaker principle. Proponents of these positions are typically motivated by parsimony. They subsist on thin wafers of reality. To save appearances, these metaphysicians paraphrase otherwise fattening truths. For instance, the phenomenalist says that chairs continue to exist when unperceived because it is true that if someone were to have looked, the looker would have perceived the chair. Armstrong asks the phenomenalist what makes this conditional true. The phenomenalist cannot answer 'The truth of each conditional is guaranteed by the enduring material object'. Nor can he say that the conditional is made true by *actual* experiences. Consequently, the phenomenalist cannot moor these conditionals to what is really real.

A violation of the truthmaker principle is serious business. In addition to grating against metaphysical principles, the violations are epistemologically grave. The phenomenalist claims to *know* that a chair continues to exist while unobserved. If there is no truthmaker for the proposition, how can the knower discriminate between the proposition being true and it being false? As Albert Einstein said 'I am a little piece of nature'. I know contingent truths in virtue of connections between me and the bits of reality that make those statements true. Absolute skepticism follows when there is no connection between a contingent statement and a state affairs upon which it is contingent. Armstrong's other targets are equally affected by this epistemological point about truthmakers. The analytical behaviorist wants to concede that I love my wife and further concede that I know I love her. But if my love is a disposition unconnected with any categorical property, then my love is unknowable.

Nevertheless, the force of the truthmaker principle is easily over-estimated. 'Reality' and 'depends on' are slippery fish. The cool-headed phenomenalist agrees 'There are unobserved chairs' is true and there-fore trivially accepts 'Unobserved chairs are part of reality'. To reach a point of disagreement, the truthmaker theorist must trade loose talk of 'reality' for more precise metaphysical terminology. When truthmaker theorists make this exchange, the truthmaker principle no longer looks like simple common sense.

Donald Davidson (1967*a*) says that the world is a truthmaker for all contingent truths. But is there anything more specific that necessitates 'This needle is threaded'? Only a small part of the world seems relevant to that statement. Indeed, one might hope to find a smallest part of reality that makes the statement true—a minimal truthmaker. The logical atomists also hoped that there would be a unique minimal truthmaker for each fact. Then there would be an isomorphism between the sentences of an ideal language and the facts. Rather grandly, an ideal language would reflect the structure of reality.

Thomas Huxley remarked on 'The great tragedy of science—the slaying of a beautiful hypothesis by an ugly fact'. Greater yet is the tragedy of logical atomism—slayed by the ugly *absence* of facts. This beautiful theory requires facts corresponding to negative predications, generalizations, and other important classes of truths. But there is a hole in reality where these facts ought to be.

The contemporary revival of truthmakers is built on many compromises. Nowadays, everybody concedes there is no one to one correspondence between truths and truthmakers. A complex disjunction can be made true by a simple fact and a simple proposition can be made true by a complex fact. The structure of reality cannot be read off the structure of language. Some are reluctant to even demand a unified truthmaker for each truth. 'There are at least twelve condors' may have twelve separate condors as truthmakers.

Is there always a smallest truthmaker that makes a statement true? Combinatorialism encourages belief in these minimal truthmakers. But friends of gunk will deny truthmaker minimalism. Gunk is infinitely divisible matter. In a gunky world, 'There is gunk' is made true by a portion of reality but there is no smallest portion of reality that makes the proposition true. If a world is composed solely of gunk without that gunk composing anything else, then there would be no minimal truthmakers at all.

Barry Smith (1999: 288) has a non-gunky argument against truthmaker minimalism. It is reminiscent of Peter Unger's (1980) problem of the many. There is no way to tell exactly which water molecules are part of a cloud and which are part of its environment. The many ways of drawing the line between cloud and non-cloud present us with an embarrassment of riches. If we are to avoid arbitrariness, we must either say that there are many clouds or none. Smith's concern is the absence of a smallest candidate rather than the sheer plurality of candidates. There is a portion of reality that makes 'There is a cloud' true but no smallest portion. Just as there is no shortest tall man, there is no smallest truthmaker. Microphysicists teach us that tables and trees and frogs are surprisingly like clouds. Thus Smith's argument against minimal truthmakers seems to apply to everything except simples and 'precise' complex objects.

Barry Smith is also prepared to surrender some of the objectivity of truthmakers. He believes that truthmakers must be *relevant* to their truths. Smith supplies the relevance through the psychology of judgment. Just as Thomas Jefferson's presidential declaration brought Indiana into existence, ordinary speakers bring truthmakers into existence through their delineations. Of course, these gerrymanderings do not create entities from nothing. There is an underlying substrate for the fiats. Indiana is mind-dependent but you can still grow corn in it.

These compromises are not enough for some critics of the truthmaker principle. David Lewis (1999a: 204) concedes that many truths have truthmakers. But he argues for exceptions. 'There are no arctic penguins' is true in virtue of an absence of falsemakers (arctic penguins) rather than the presence of a truthmaker. Also, many predications owe their truth to how things are rather than to the existence of certain kinds of entities (truthmakers). And aren't we foreclosing the possibility of an empty world (Lewis 1999b)? If nothing exists, then there are no truthmakers that could make 'Nothing exists' true.

In addition to this problem about nothing, there is a problem about everything (Rowe 1975, ch. 2). Call the conjunction of all contingent propositions C. The only thing that could explain C would be a necessary truth. But necessary truths only explain by entailing their explanandum. If C were entailed by a necessary truth, C would be a necessary truth rather than a contingent truth. Therefore, there can be no explanation for C. This point about explanation suggests that there can be no truthmaker for C understood as a comprehensive statement of what is contingently true. Sure, there may be truthmakers for each conjunct of C. But the mere fusion of these truthmakers would not explain the totality of C. For C has the extra clause 'and that is all there is'.

Armstrong has thoughtful rejoinders. But Lewis is content to characterize Armstrong's demand for truthmakers as an overreaction to an insight captured by John Bigelow's slogan 'Truth supervenes on being'. Lewis articulates Bigelow's slogan:

. . . no two possibilities can differ about what's true unless they also differ in what things there are, or in how they are. In saying just this much, we do not join Armstrong in demanding truth-makers for negative existentials, or for all predications. Yet I think we do justice to the insight behind his demand: truths are about things, they don't float in a void. (Lewis 1999a: 206)

I think the no-no paradox is a counterexample to even this dilution of the truthmaker principle. A truthmaker must have a consistent direction of support. It must point to a statement rather than an incompatible statement. The symmetry of the no-no sentences frustrates this directionality.

Granted, a single truthmaker can support distinct statements. My umbrella being black supports both 'There is an umbrella' and 'There is something black'. But if a truthmaker supported *incompatible* statements, there would be a contradiction.

Truthmakers can also support general statements. My placement of three dollars in my two pockets is a truthmaker for 'At least two dollars were put in the same pocket'. But truthmaker theorists generally require that there also be a specific truthmaker accounting for which dollars ended up where. The problem is that the mereological sum of the no-no sentences is only a truthmaker for 'Exactly one of the statements is true'. There is not a more specific truthmaker. Therefore, the truthmaker is vague in the sense of being underspecific.

Underspecific truthmakers are excluded by Gregory Restall's (1996: 334) disjunction thesis that any truthmaker for a disjunction must be a truthmaker for one of the disjuncts. These vague truthmakers are also excluded by Stephen Read's (2000: 74) weaker principle that every true disjunction has a truthmaker for one of its disjuncts. Read's principle can be deduced from the truthmaker principle and the addition principle that any truthmaker for a disjunct is a truthmaker for the disjunction. (Addition is the converse of Restall's disjunction thesis). Since the addition principle is compelling, rejecting Read's principle requires rejecting the truthmaker principle itself. Very well then, I reject it.

Underspecific truthmakers disappoint the curious in much the same way as objectively random events. The principle of sufficient reason assures us that there is some explanation for each event even if that explanation is beyond our ken. Objective randomness introduces explanatory dead ends.

However, there are other explanatory benefits. Thanks to objective randomness, there are good statistical explanations of the decay of radioactive piles. We can also explain certain limits to physical knowledge.

Ironically, explanatory dead ends can themselves be the explanans of a good explanation. As we shall see, underspecific truthmakers offer similar compensation.

3. Epistemic Islands

If 'This is true' is true, then it is an epistemic island. There is no access to its truth via a truthmaker to the truth of the truth-teller. One could not have an objective reason for believing that the truth-teller is true, so one cannot have objectively justified true belief that the truth-teller is true. If an eminent logician told a student that the truth-teller is true, then the student would justifiably believe it by authority. So if the truth-teller is indeed true, the student would have justified true belief that the truth-teller is true. But the student's justification would have a defective lineage.

The pair of sentences in the no-no paradox constitutes a more complex epistemic island. If someone knew the truth of one member of the no-no pair, he could deduce the falsehood of the other. Even so, both members are absolutely unknowable because there is no way to learn the truth-value of any particular member.

The situation may not seem so hopeless with big epistemic islands such as:

1. Some other sentence on this list is false.
2. Some other sentence on this list is false.
3. Some other sentence on this list is false.

     .

     .

     .

100. Some other sentence on this list is false.

There are exactly 100 consistent interpretations corresponding to the 100 ways of assigning a single falsehood. Thus the probability that any given member is true is 0.99. Normally, probabilities are dynamic, changing in light of new evidence. The probabilities of propositions belonging to an epistemic island are static. They are impervious to news. The ancient Egyptians would have admired such epistemological aloofness and stability. Epistemic islands should be engraved in hieroglyphics.

Epistemologists deny that probable true belief suffices for knowledge. According to them, there is no way on to the island.

4. Truthmaker Gaps and the Sorites Paradox

The truthmaker gap solution to the no-no paradox is a precedent for an epistemic solution to the sorites paradox. The epistemic solution is to accept standard logic and reject the induction step of arguments such as:

1. Base step: 1 second after noon is noonish.
2. Induction step: for each n, if n seconds after noon is noonish, then $n + 1$ seconds after noon is noonish.
3. Conclusion: 10,000 seconds after noon is noonish.

The believer in the truthmaker gap solution to the no-no paradox is poised, on independent grounds, to join the epistemicist in rejecting the second premise. The negation of the second premise implies that there is a value for n at which 'n seconds after noon is noonish' is true and '$n + 1$ seconds after noon is noonish' is false. Most people find this assignment implausible because of the nearly perfect symmetry between the sentences. They see that the sorites monger can increase this symmetry asymptotically by choosing smaller and smaller increments. Instead of moving in 1 second increments, the monger can use tenths of a second, or hundredths of a second, and so on. At the limit, there cannot be a difference in truth-value between neighboring pairs of sentences.

No sorites argument is valid at the limit because the induction step requires some change even if there is no minimum amount of change. However, a close approximation to perfect symmetry is enough to prompt many people to behave as if the principle of sufficient reason precluded equal treatment. Actually, the principle does not mention any minimum difference. Some applications of the principle ignore tiny differences just as we ignore tiny bumps when describing a surface as flat. In particular, many people believe the same truth-value must be assigned to sentence pairs of the form 'n nanoseconds after noon is noonish' and '$n + 1$ nanoseconds after noon is noonish'. They dismiss the suggestion that there could be a value for n at which the first is true and the second is false: 'What could *make* the first true and second false?'.

The believer in the truthmaker gap solution to the no-no paradox has already accepted a T-F assignment for a perfectly symmetrical pair of sentences. Hence he will not oppose the possibility that a particular threshold for 'noonish' groundlessly exists. Just as there is absolutely no way to know which no-no sentence is true, the threshold for 'noonish' is absolutely unknowable.

'Tolerance conditionals' located near the threshold constitute an epistemic island. Each has the form 'If n seconds after noon is noonish, then $n + 1$ seconds after noon is noonish'. When n is distant from the threshold, the conditional can be known with certainty. But when n is near the threshold noonish, the conditional is only highly probable. Unlike the previously mentioned islands, the borders of this epistemic island are vague. The epistemic island is surrounded by accessible propositions and there is no way to tell where they stop and the island begins.

Epistemicism is natural given truthmaker gaps. The reverse does not hold because some epistemicists accept the use theory of meaning. For instance, Timothy Williamson (1994) maintains that the truth-values of all utterances depend solely on facts about speakers and their environment. There are no free-floating assignments of truth-values. He accounts for our ignorance of certain statements by an appeal to chaos. The facts about usage and the environment are so complex that it is impossible to ascertain the truth-values of many utterances.

Williamson's chaos hypothesis only delivers relative ignorance. What counts as an unknowable threshold for a human being does not count as one for a creature with a greater power of discrimination. In contrast, supervaluationists deliver absolute ignorance—albeit of a degenerate sort. They say that the threshold is unknowable because there is nothing to know. Statements of the form 'n minutes after noon is noonish but $n + 1$ minutes after noon is not noonish' lack a truth-value. (Notoriously, however, supervaluationists say the statement is true when prefixed with an existential quantifier.)

Like the supervaluationist, the truthmaker-gap epistemicist proposes a cognitively universal explanation of the ignorance. But instead of invoking truth-value gaps, he invokes truthmaker gaps. A contingent statement that does not owe its truth-value to anything else is epistemically isolated. When the truth of a statement rests on further facts, then I can gain evidence by examining those further facts. But when the truth-value is possessed autonomously, then there is no trail of truthmakers. The truthmaker-gap epistemicist preserves the supervaluationist's intuition that there is no truthmaker for borderline propositions such as 'Pudding is a solid'. He just rejects the supervaluationist's assumption that every truth rests on a truthmaker. Truthmakers are a sufficient condition for truth, not a necessary condition.

The unity of truth is menaced by truthmakerless truths only in the way that chemosynthetic life-forms threaten the unity of life.

Gas-eating worms at the edge of deep-sea thermal vents are not part of the photosynthetic chain of being. But these isolated creatures do not force a distinction between two senses of 'organism'. 'Organism' is just more disparate than we thought. Ditto for 'true statement'.

The peculiar isolation of truthmakerless truths explains why they look like something less than full-fledged truths. Characterizations of truth-value gaps can be viewed as confused descriptions of truthmaker gaps. Complaints about the inconceivability of epistemicism can be viewed as correct but misguided reactions to these truthmakerless truths. Terry Horgan stresses that while he can imagine the conditions that would create a threshold for a chaotic phenomenon such as an avalanche, he cannot imagine a condition that would create a threshold of 'heap':

We cannot imagine *why* it should be the case that any particular candidate for precise boundaries for the term 'heap', as opposed to numerous other candidates, would be the unique boundaries that actually supervene on the total use-pattern governing this term. That is, we cannot imagine what could possibly constitute the explanatory basis for the putative fact (call it a 'precise supervenience fact') that such-and-such specific precise boundaries supervene on so-and-so overall pattern of usage. In the case of an avalanche, we know what constitutes an explanatory basis of avalanche-onset—viz., the relevant laws of physics. But in the case of vague terms like 'heap', we cannot even conceive what kinds of facts, principles, or laws could possibly play an analogous explanatory role *vis-à-vis* putative precise supervenience facts. Even *given* some specific overall use-pattern as the total supervenience base for the meaning of 'heap', it seems there still would be numerous equally good candidates for precise boundaries, and there would be no reason whatever why one of these candidates should win out over the others. (Horgan 1997: 231–2)

The truthmaker-gap epistemicist can agree on the inconceivability and impossibility of an explanatory basis for a threshold of 'heap'. He can agree that it follows that there is no supervenience fact for 'heap'. He can instead deny the validity of the inference Professor Horgan finds most compelling, viz. from the absence of supervenience facts to the absence of a boundary for vague terms and concepts.

The truthmaker-gap epistemicist is well positioned to handle attempts to stipulate truth-value gaps. In Williamson's (1990: 138) pre-epistemicist days, he tried to refute epistemicism by stipulation. He invented a predicate, 'dommal', that applies to all dogs and never applies to a non-mammal. That is the explicit end of Williamson's definition.

His goal was to ensure that cats would be borderline cases of dommals. The truthmaker-gap epistemicist may grant the premise that the only truthmakers issue exclusively from either linguistic decisions or the world. He will just insist that the truth-value can be acquired without the help of a truthmaker. Thus the truthmaker-gap epistemicist takes himself to be continuing the historical debate about the principle of sufficient reason.

Williamson's own solution to the problem of incomplete stipulations consists of a bold attempt to break the apparent symmetry between ruling 'Cats are dommals' as true and ruling it as false. He proposes a default principle that the meanings of atomic predicates must be as specific as possible. So cats are non-dommals. Michael Tye (1997: 250) objects that this proposal fails to respect the borderline status of 'Cats are dommals'. Tye's objection can be amplified. 'No cats are dommals' is *analytically* true on Williamson's account. Whereas 'No cats are dommals' struck the pre-epistemicist Williamson as obviously unde-cidable, his new position makes the statement an a priori truth.

Williamson could regain borderline status for 'No cats are dommals' if he repudiated the knowability of the specification principle. He could instead present the specification principle merely as an illustration of how default principles could fill in meaning without the active involve-ment of speakers. This humbler position is available to a generic epi-stemicist. However, the retreat will not be attractive to Williamson if it involves the postulation of a new kind of unknowable. Williamson's project in *Vagueness* is to explain the ignorance with the margin for error principle. Roughly, this principle says that case n can be known to be an F only if its neighboring case $n + 1$ is an F. The unknowability of the specification principle does not seem related to this principle.

Williamson concedes that the specification principle does not handle all symmetry cases. Consider a disjunctive stipulation: Either 'edd' applies to all and only even numbers, or 'edd' applies to all and only odd numbers. 'Edd' has two possible application cases of equal specificity. Since the specification principle cannot break the tie, Williamson concludes that the disjunctive stipulation fails to establish any meaning at all. So, strangely, an inequality in the specificity of alternatives becomes critical for a successful stipulation.

Williamson's 'edd' inadvertently raises a further problem of measur-ing specificity. Consider the following disjunctive stipulation: either 'primposite' applies to all and only prime numbers or it applies to all and only composite numbers. On one hand, we feel that 'primposite' would be more specific if it covered the primes rather than the composites. Primes become rarer and rarer down the number line, so finite subsequences of the integers will normally have more composites than primes. On the hand, there is a one to one correspondence between primes and composites. This equality implies that the stipulation failed. Almost all predicates have intensions that cover infinitely many cases. So the problem of measuring specificity is highly general. Indeed, the problem arises for 'dommal' itself. The number of possible dogs equals the number of possible dogs plus the number of possible cats. So one may doubt that the exclusion of possible cats makes 'dommal' more specific.

The postulation of truthmaker gaps provides a simpler, comprehensive solution to the problem of incomplete stipulation. 'Cats are dommals' has a truth-value even though it lacks a truthmaker. Ditto for 'All even numbers are edd' and 'All prime numbers are primposite'. The borderline status of each is preserved. Their unknowability is uniformly explained.

5. An Historical Twist

Andrew Irvine cautioned me against attributing the no-no paradox to Russell. He notes that the slip reappears on page 147 of volume 1 of the George Allen and Unwin 1971 paperback edition of Russell's autobiography. By that time Russell had died. Irvine noted the no-no paradox also appears in the first edition of R. M. Sainsbury's *Paradoxes*. Jean Buridan's Eighth Sophism is reported as follows: 'Socrates in Troy says, "What Plato is now saying in Athens is false." At the same time, Plato in Athens says, "What Socrates is now saying in Troy is false." ' (1988: 145). In Sainsbury's second edition (1995: 145), the last occurrence of 'false' is changed to 'true'.

But this is a mis-correction! Jean Buridan's Eighth Sophism is just as Sainsbury's first edition states. The second edition corresponds to Buridan's Ninth Sophism. The first edition accurately cites the relevant pages of G. E. Hughes's translation of the eighth chapter of Buridan's *Sophismata*.

Buridan's original Eighth Sophism is not as lean as the version found in Russell's autobiography (or in Sainsbury's first edition of *Paradoxes*), for it does not use tokens of the same sentence type or a parallel presentation. Nevertheless, Buridan immediately emphasizes the logical similarity between the sentences in his less streamlined version. He quickly lays down an adequacy condition: the sentences must be assigned the same truth-values. Buridan then argues that both the sentences are false. His analysis involves a more cautious version of his early principle that all propositions are self-referential. Buridan concedes that most propositions are not self-referential. However, he insists that each proposition implies its own truth (when combined with the premise that the proposition exists). Since the liar sentence says that it is false, the liar sentence implies it is both true and not true. Thus it is false.

Yablo's liar paradox side-steps Buridan's analysis. Although each member of the Yablo sequence implies its own truth, none of them affirms its own falsehood. This vicious incompleteness is also inherited by recent revivals of Buridan's approach (Mills 1998).

The incompleteness extends to the descending no-no paradox. For none of the sentences describes itself. Nor does any sentence indirectly refer to itself via another sentence.

6. Goldstein's Proliferation of Truth-Bearer Illusions

Other philosophers have come across the no-no paradox since Buridan. Laurence Goldstein (1992) presents Buridan's Eighth Sophism as evidence for a truth-value gap solution to the liar. He agrees with Buridan that the symmetry of the sentences shows that the pair cannot have different truth-values. But unlike Buridan, he thinks both the T-T assignment and the F-F assignment are untenable. Goldstein concludes that no truth-value should be assigned to either.

Goldstein deals with the strengthened version of the paradox by maintaining that some sentences cannot bear truth-values. He proves, to my satisfaction, that the assumption that the liar sentence bears a truth-value leads to a contradiction. This forces us to say that there is a dramatic logical difference between the following two sentences:

1: Sentence 1 is not true.
2: Sentence 1 is not true.

Whereas 1 has no truth-value, 2 is true. 2 is a sentence in the sense of sentence logic. 1 is not an item for logical evaluation. If it were, then it could be inserted into the Tarski truth schema. But that effort yields the contradiction 'Sentence 1 is not true' is true iff sentence 1 is not true.

Sentence 1 is not a legitimate input. Consequently, it is no more a counterexample to Tarski's schema than other pseudo truth-bearers such as open sentences and sentence schemas.

Epistemicists are particularly motivated to preserve Tarski's schema and standard logic because the simplest arguments for their position involve an unwavering application of both. If epistemicists permitted exceptions to logic or to the truth schema, their solution to the sorites would be an ad hoc insistence on applying independently counterexampled principles. If they stand firm, their method of avoiding the counterexample is no more arbitrary than the biologist's method of defending 'All fish have gills' from the 'counterexample' of whales. Common sense assures us that the whale is just as much a fish as a tuna. With comparable force, common sense assures us that 1 is just as much a proposition as 2. The epistemicist can plausibly challenge common sense on this fine point.

There are a priori resources for always avoiding an inappropriate application of logic to open sentences and schemas. But indirect variations of the liar paradox, such as Jourdain's card paradox, show that the intrinsic properties of a sentence do not always suffice to make it a truth-bearer. Consequently, we sometimes must take a risk in applying logic to an apparent proposition.

Notice that Goldstein is not advocating supervaluationism. The supervaluationist says that logic can evaluate sentences that do not have truth-values. Goldstein accepts bivalence. He is saying the liar sentence is not a proposition. The supervaluationist says the liar sentence is a proposition that lacks a truth-value. I side with Goldstein.

Logic can locate some truth-bearer illusions. Can semantics do so as well? Goldstein thinks symmetry considerations suffice. In particular, he takes the sentences in the strengthened no-no paradox to show that this pair of sentences fails to bear truth-values. I disagree. Symmetry principles have been empirically fruitful but they have no standing in analytic contexts.

Goldstein also employs a third basis for postulating truth-bearer illusions: groundlessness. All known variations of the liar paradox involve ungrounded sentences. Hence, he argues that ungrounded utterances are not genuine statements. Goldstein buttresses this claim with other ungrounded speech acts. For instance, there is a Frank and Ernest cartoon set in a restaurant. Frank and Ernest each point to each other and tell the waiter 'I will have what he's having'. According to Goldstein, they each fail to order.

Actually, the Frank and Ernest sentences make no use of the truth predicate and so are not ruled as ungrounded by Kripke's sieve. Even so, Goldstein is tracking the property that motivated Kripke to construct the sieve.

I am inclined to say Frank and Ernest ordered but their order has a defect. The underspecificity of each order prevents their utterances from having the perlocutionary effect Frank and Ernest desired— getting fed. Logical underspecificity is not always an obstacle. Suppose the waiter asks Frank and Ernest if they will share a pizza. Frank turns to Ernest and says 'I will, if you will'. Ernest replies 'And I will, if you will'. The conjunction of their answers does not entail that they will share a pizza. For both of the conditionals can be satisfied by each refusing to share a pizza. However, the conditionals have the pragmatic force of an agreement (Radford 1984). Their dinner order is thereby consummated.

Truthmaker gaps provide a perspective on other mysteries of commerce. I bought a package containing two toothbrushes. I was enticed by the offer printed on the package 'Buy one, get one free'. But I now puzzle over the asymmetry: which toothbrush did I buy and which one did I get free? The symmetry could be broken by the merchant's stipulation that 'This one is being bought and that one is free'. But merchants do not actually bother to distinguish. Offers of 'Two for the price one' maintain symmetry and so do not pose the enigma. As a practical matter, the two styles of offer are treated as financially equivalent. But they differ metaphysically, not just psychologically. When I purchase two for the price of one, I do not get anything for free. Those who believe that each contingent truth has a truthmaker are forced to conclude that the typical 'Buy one, get one free' offer is false. The believer in truthmaker gaps has the option of concluding that one was bought and one was free even though there is no telling which was which.

A good theory saves appearances. Hence, we should minimize attributions of truth-bearer illusions—especially when they weaken our ability to apply logic. An illusion must be postulated in the case of liar sentences. But we have freedom in the case of the other ungrounded sentences.

Of course, if one is satisfied with a minimal theory of truth, this kind of freedom is superfluous. Minimalism drives one relentlessly toward epistemicism. The point of the exploration is to show how epistemicism can take root in a metaphysically rich conception of truth.

The hardiness of epistemicism is guaranteed by its excellent a priori credentials. Getting the details correct involves the usual back and forth adjustment between principles and intuitions. But the framework is as certain as logic itself. A few trivial inference rules can derive the heart of epistemicism from the empty set of premises. Consequently, the right attitude to epistemicism is to presuppose it. The philosophical problem is to explain why the previous assertion seems so dogmatic and question-begging.

References

ALTRICHTER, FERENC (1985). 'Belief and Possibility'. *Journal of Philosophy*, 82: 363–82.

AMBROSE, ALICE, and LAZEROWITZ, MORRIS (1984). 'Assuming the Logically Impossible'. *Metaphilosophy*, 15/2: 91–9.

ARMSTRONG, DAVID (1989). *Universals: An Opinionated Introduction*. Bolder, Colo.: Westview Press.

—— (1996). *A World of States of Affairs*. Cambridge: Cambridge University Press.

AUSTIN, J. L. (1962). *Sense and Sensibilia*. Oxford: Oxford University Press.

BERKELEY, GEORGE (1710). *A Treatise Concerning the Principles of Human Knowledge*. Dublin.

BIGELOW, JOHN (1988). *The Reality of Numbers*. Oxford: Oxford University Press.

—— (1992). 'The Doubtful A Priori'. *Canadian Journal of Philosophy*, suppl. vol. 18, *Return of the A Priori*, ed. Philip Hanson and Bruce Hunter: 151–66.

BONJOUR, LAURENCE (1998). *In Defense of Pure Reason*. Cambridge: Cambridge University Press.

BOOLOS, GEORGE (1991). 'Zooming Down the Slippery Slope'. *Nous*, 25: 695–706.

—— and JEFFREY, RICHARD (1974). *Computability and Logic*. Cambridge: Cambridge University Press.

BROWN, CURTIS (1990). 'How to Believe the Impossible'. *Philosophical Studies*, 58: 275–85.

—— (1991). 'Believing the Impossible'. *Synthese*, 89: 353–64.

—— (1992). 'Direct and Indirect Belief'. *Philosophy and Phenomenological Research*, 52/2: 289–316.

BURGE, TYLER (1979). 'Individualism and the Mental'. *Midwest Studies in Philosophy*, 4: 73–121.

—— (1986). 'Intellectual Norms and Foundations of Mind'. *The Journal of Philosophy*, 83/12: 697–719.

—— (1988). 'Individualism and Self Knowledge'. *Journal of Philosophy*, 85: 649–63.

—— (1993). 'Content Preservation'. *Philosophical Review*, 102/4: 457–88.

—— (1998). 'Computer Proof, Apriori Knowledge, and Other Minds'. *Philosophical Perspectives*, 12: 1–37.

BURIDAN, JOHN (1966). *Sophisms on Meaning and Truth*, trans. Theodore Kermit Scott. New York: Appleton-Century-Crofts.

CAMPBELL, RICHMOND (1974). 'The Sorites Paradox'. *Philosophical Studies*, 26: 175–91.

CARGILE, JAMES (1969). 'The Sorites Paradox'. *British Journal for the Philosophy of Science*, 20/3: 550–63.

CARNAP, RUDOLPH (1947). *Meaning and Necessity*. Chicago: University of Chicago Press.

—— (1950). *Logical Foundations of Probability*. Chicago: University of Chicago Press.

CARROLL, LEWIS (1895). 'What the Tortoise Said To Achilles'. *Mind*, 4: 278–80.

CASULLO, ALBERT (1979). 'Reid and Mill on Hume's Maxim of Conceivability'. *Analysis*, 39/4: 212–19.

CHAITIN, GREGORY (1970). 'On the Difficulty of Computations'. *IEEE Transactions on Information Theory*, 16: 5–9.

—— (1986). 'Information-Theoretic Computational Complexity and Godel's Theorem and Information', in *New Directions in the Philosophy of Mathematics*, ed. Thomas Tymoczko. Boston: Birkhauser.

CHERNIAK, CHRISTOPHER (1986). *Minimal Rationality*. Cambridge, Mass.: MIT Press.

CHIHARA, CHARLES (1979). 'The Semantic Paradoxes: A Diagnostic Investigation'. *The Philosophical Review*, 88: 590–618.

CHISHOLM, RODERICK (1942). 'The Problem of the Speckled Hen'. *Mind*, 51/204: 349–52.

—— (1973). 'The Truths of Reason', in *Theory of Knowledge*, 2nd edn. Englewood Cliffs, NJ: Prentice Hall.

CHOMSKY, NOAM (1965). *Aspects of the Theory of Syntax*. Cambridge, Mass.: MIT Press.

—— (1971). *Problems of Knowledge and Freedom*. New York: Pantheon Books.

—— (1986). *Knowledge of Language*. New York: Praeger Publishers.

CHURCHLAND, PAUL (1979). *Scientific Realism and Plasticity of Mind*. New York: Cambridge University Press.

CUMMINS, ROBERT (1996). *Representation, Targets, and Attitudes*. Cambridge, Mass.: MIT Press.

DAVIDSON, DONALD (1967a). 'Causal Relations'. *The Journal of Philosophy*, 64: 691–703.

—— (1967b). 'Meaning and Truth'. *Basic Topics in the Philosophy of Language*, ed. Robert M. Harnish. Englewood Cliffs, NJ: Prentice Hall, 1994: 598–614.

—— (1970). 'Mental Events', in L. Foster and J. Swanson, eds., *Experience and Theory*. London: Duckworth.

DEHAENE, STANISLAS (1997). *The Number Sense*. New York: Oxford University Press.

DENNETT, DANIEL (1987). *The Intentional Stance*. Cambridge, Mass.: MIT Press.

—— (1995). *Darwin's Dangerous Idea: Evolution and the Meanings of Life*. New York: Simon and Schuster.

DENTON, G. G. (1973). 'The Influence of Visual Pattern on Perceived Speed at Newbridge M8, Midlothian'. *Report LR531*, Crowthorne, Berks: Department of the Environment, TRRK.

DRIVER, JULIA (1992). 'Caesar's Wife: On the Moral Significance of Appearing Good'. *Journal of Philosophy*, 99/7: 331–43.

DUMMETT, MICHAEL (1991). *The Logical Basis of Metaphysics*. London: Duckworth.

ELLIS, BRIAN (1979). *Rational Belief Systems*. Totawa, NJ: Rowman and Littlefield.

ERNST, BRUNO (1986). *Optical Illusions*. New York: Taschen.

EVANS-PRITCHARD, E. E. (1937). *Witchcraft, Oracles and Magic among the Azande*. Oxford: Clarenden Press.

FINE, KIT (1975). 'Vagueness, Truth and Logic'. *Synthese*, 54: 235–59. Reprinted in *Vagueness: A Reader*, ed. Rosanna Keefe and Peter Smith. Cambridge, Mass.: MIT Press, 1996: 119–50.

—— (1985). *Reasoning with Arbitrary Objects*. Oxford: Basil Blackwell.

FITTING, MELVIN (1997). 'A Theory of Truth that Prefers Falsehoods'. *Journal of Philosophical Logic*. 26/5: 477–500.

FLANDERS, HARLEY, and PRICE, JUSTIN J. (1981). *Precalculus Mathematics*, 2nd edn. Philadelphia: Saunders College Publishing.

FODOR, JERRY (1983). *The Modularity of Mind*. Cambridge, Mass.: MIT Press.

FOLEY, RICHARD (1986). 'Is it Possible to have Contradictory Beliefs?' *Midwest Studies in Philosophy*, 10, Minneapolis: University of Minnesota Press: 327–55.

FRIEDMAN, MILTON (1953). 'The Case for Flexible Exchange Rates', in his *Essays in Positive Economics*. Chicago: University of Chicago Press: 157–203.

GALLIE, W. B. (1955–6). 'Essentially Contested Concepts'. *Proceedings of the Aristotelian Society*, 56.

GAREY, MICHAEL R., and JONSON, DAVID S. (1979). *Computers and Intractibility: A Guide to the Theory of NP-Completeness*. New York: W. H. Freeman and Company.

GETTIER, EDMUND (1963). 'Is Justified True Belief Knowledge?' *Analysis*, 23: 121–3.

GOGUEN, J. (1969). 'The Logic of Inexact Concepts'. *Synthese*, 19: 325–73.

GOLDMAN, ALAN (1975). 'A Note on the Conjunctivity of Knowledge'. *Analysis*, 36/1: 5–9.

GOLDMAN, ALAN (1989). 'Psychology and Philosophical Analysis'. *Proceedings of the Aristotelian Society*, 89: 195–209. Reprinted in his *Liaisons: Philosophy Meets the Cognitive and Social Sciences*. Cambridge, Mass: MIT Press, 1992: 143–53.

—— (1999). 'A Priori Warrant and Naturalistic Epistemology'. *Philosophical Perspectives: Epistemology*, ed. James Tomberlin, Cambridge: Blackwell.

GOLDSTEIN, LAURENCE (1985). 'The Paradox of the Liar—A Case of Mistaken Identity'. *Analysis*, 45: 9–13.

—— (1992). ' "This Statement is Not True" is Not True'. *Analysis*, 52/1: 1–5.

—— (1999). 'Circular Queue Paradoxes—The Missing Link'. *Analysis*, 59/4: 284–90.

GOLDSTICK, D. (1989). 'When Inconsistency is Logically Impossible'. *Logique et Analyse*, 125–6: 139–42.

GOODMAN, NELSON (1954). *Fact, Fiction and Forecast*. Cambridge, Mass.: Harvard University Press.

HARE, R. M. (1981). *Moral Thinking*. New York: Oxford University Press.

HART, ALAN M. (1980). 'Toward a Logic of Doubt', *International Logic Review*, 11: 31–45.

HART, W. D. (1988). *The Engines of the Soul*. Cambridge: Cambridge University Press.

—— (1991–2). 'Hat-Tricks and Heaps'. *Philosophical Studies* (Dublin), 33: 1–24.

HEIDELBERGER, HERBERT (1980). 'Understanding and Truth Conditions'. *Midwest Studies in Philosophy*, 5, Minneapolis: University of Minnesota Press: 401–10.

HELLER, MARK (1990). *The Ontology of Physical Objects*. New York: Cambridge University Press.

HERZBERGER, HANS A. (1970). 'Paradoxes of Grounding in Semantics'. *Journal of Philosophy*, 67: 145–67.

HICK, JOHN (1957). *Faith and Knowledge*. Ithaca, NY: Cornell University Press.

HINTIKKA, JAAKKO (1962). *Knowledge and Belief*. Ithaca, NY: Cornell University Press.

HOFFMAN, PAUL (1998). *The Man Who Loved Only Numbers*. New York: Hyperion.

HORGAN, TERRY (1995). 'Transvaluationism: A Dionysian Approach to Vagueness'. *The Southern Journal of Philosophy*, 33: 97–126.

—— (1997). 'Deep Ignorance, Brute Supervenience and the Problem of the Many'. *Philosophical Issues*, 8: 229–36.

HUGHES, G. E. (1982). *John Buridan on Self-Reference*. Cambridge: Cambridge University Press.

HUME, DAVID (1739). *A Treatise of Human Nature*, ed. L. A. Selby-Bigge, Oxford: Clarendon Press, 1978.

HUNTER, GEOFFREY (1996). *Metalogic*. Berkeley and Los Angeles: University of California Press.

HURVICH, L. M. (1981). *Color Vision*. Sunderland, Mass.: Sinauer.

IRVINE, ANDREW (1992). 'Gaps, Gluts, and Paradox'. *Canadian Journal of Philosophy*, suppl. vol. 18, *Return of the A Priori*, ed. Philip Hanson and Bruce Hunter: 273–99.

JENNINGS, R. E. (1994). *The Genealogy of Disjunction*. New York: Oxford University Press.

KITCHER, PHILIP (1983). *Mathematical Knowledge*. New York: Oxford University Press.

KRIPKE, SAUL (1972). *Naming and Necessity*. Cambridge, Mass.: Harvard University Press, 1980.

—— (1975). 'Outline of a Theory of Truth'. *Journal of Philosophy*, 72.

—— (1976). 'A Puzzle about Belief', in *Meaning and Use*, ed. Avishi Margalit. Dordrecht: D. Reidel.

—— (1977). 'Speaker's Reference and Semantic Reference', in *Midwest Studies in Philosophy*, ii. Morris, Minn.: University of Minnesota Press: 255–76.

KYBURG, H. E. (1970). 'Conjunctivitis', in *Induction, Acceptance, and Rational Belief*, ed. M. Swain. Dordrecht, Holland: D. Reidel.

KYLE, J. G., and WOLL, B. (1985). *Sign Language: The Study of Deaf People and Their Language*. Cambridge: Cambridge University Press.

LEHRER, KEITH (1974). *Knowledge*. Oxford: Clarendon Press.

LEWIS, DAVID (1999a). 'Armstrong on Combinatorial Possibility', in his *Papers in Metaphysics and Epistemology*. Cambridge: Cambridge University Press: 196–214.

—— (1999b). 'A World of Truthmakers?' in his *Papers in Metaphysics and Epistemology*. Cambridge: Cambridge University Press: 215–20.

LINSKY, LEONARD (1968). 'On Interpreting Doxastic Logic'. *Journal of Philosophy*, 65: 500–2.

LOCKE, JOHN (1690). *An Essay Concerning Human Understanding*. New York: Dover.

LUCAS, J. R. (1964). 'Minds, Machines and Godel', in *Minds and Machines*, ed. Alan Ross Anderson. Englewood Cliffs, NJ: Prentice Hall.

—— (1996). 'Minds, Machines, and Godel: A Retrospect', in *Machines and Thought*, i. Oxford: Clarendon Press, 1996.

LYCAN, WILLIAM (1994). *Modality and Meaning*. Dordrecht: Kluwer Academic Publishers.

LYONS, D. (1965). *Forms and Limits of Utilitarianism*. Oxford: Clarendon Press.

McCARTHY, T. (1981). 'The Idea of a Logical Constant'. *Journal of Philosophy*, 78: 499–523.

McGEE, VANN, and McLAUGHLIN, BRIAN (1995). 'Distinctions Without a Difference'. *The Southern Journal of Philosophy*, 33: 204–51.

McGinn, Colin (1993). *Problems in Philosophy: The Limits of Inquiry.* Cambridge, Mass.: Blackwell.

Makin, Stephen (1993). *Indifference Arguments.* Oxford: Blackwell.

Makinson, D. C. (1965). 'The Paradox of the Preface'. *Analysis,* 25: 205–7.

Marcus, Ruth Barcan (1981). 'A Proposed Solution to a Puzzle about Belief'. *Midwest Studies in Philosophy,* 6: 501–10.

—— (1983). 'Rationality and Believing the Impossible'. *The Journal of Philosophy,* 80: 321–38.

—— (1990). 'Some Revisionary Proposals about Belief and Believing'. *Philosophy and Phenomenological Research,* 1 (suppl.): 133–53.

Margalit, Avishai (1983). 'What the Tortoise Told Tertullian'. *How Many Questions? Essays in Honor of Sidney Morgenbesser,* ed. Leigh S. Cauman, Isaac Levi, Charles Parsons, and Robert Schwartz. Indianapolis: Hackett: 195–207.

Mates, Benson (1965). *Elementary Logic.* New York: Oxford University Press.

Mill, John Stuart (1843). *A System of Logic.* London: Longmans, Green, and Co., 1919.

Miller, George (1956). 'The Magical Number Seven Plus or Minus Two: Some Limits of Our Capacity for Processing Information'. *Psychological Review,* 63: 81–97.

Mills, Eugene (1998). 'A Simple Solution to the Liar'. *Philosophical Studies,* 197–211.

Minsky, Marvin (1967). *Computation: Finite and Infinite Machines.* Englewood Cliffs, NJ: Prentice Hall.

Moar, I., and Bower, G. H. (1983). 'Inconsistency in Spatial Knowledge'. *Memory and Cognition,* 11: 107–13.

Mortensen, Chris, and Priest, Graham (1981). 'The Truth Teller Paradox'. *Logique et Analyse,* 95–6: 381–8.

Moser, Paul (1987). *A Priori Knowledge.* Oxford: Oxford University Press.

Nolan, Daniel (1997). 'Quantitative Parsimony'. *British Journal for the Philosophy of Science,* 48/3: 329–43.

Parfit, D. (1984). *Reasons and Persons.* Oxford: Oxford University Press.

Parsons, Charles (1974). 'The Liar Paradox'. *Journal of Philosophical Logic,* 3: 381–412.

Parsons, Terence (1995). 'Ruth Barcan Marcus and the Barcan Formula', in *Modality, Morality, and Belief,* ed. Walter Sinnot-Armstrong. Cambridge: Cambridge University Press.

Peacocke, Christopher (1976). 'What is a Logical Constant?' *Journal of Philosophy,* 73: 221–40.

Peirce, C. S. (1902). 'Vague', in *Dictionary of Philosophy and Psychology,* ed. J. M. Baldwin, New York: Macmillan: 748.

Penrose, Lionel S., and Penrose, Roger (1958). 'Impossible Objects: A Special Type of Illusion'. *British Journal of Psychology,* 49: 31–3.

PETTIT, PHILIP (1984). 'Dissolving Kripke's Puzzle about Belief'. *Ratio*, 26/2: 181–93.

PINKER, STEVEN (1994). *The Language Instinct.* New York: W. Morrow and Co.

—— (1997). *How the Mind Works.* New York: W. W. Norton.

PLANTINGA, ALVIN (1993). *Warrant and Proper Function.* New York: Oxford University Press.

POUNDSTONE, WILLIAM (1988). *Labyrinths of Reason.* New York: Doubleday.

PRIEST, GRAHAM (1987). *In Contradiction.* Dordrecht: Martinus Nijhoff.

—— (1998). 'What Is So Bad about Contradictions?' *Journal of Philosophy*, 95/8: 410–26.

—— and ROUTLEY, RICHARD (1989). 'First Historical Introduction: A Preliminary History of Paraconsistent and Dialethic Approaches', in *Paraconsistent Logic: Essays on the Inconsistent*, ed. Graham Priest, Richard Routley, and Jean Norman. Munich: Philosophica Verlag.

PRIOR, ARTHUR (1978). 'The Runabout Inference Ticket', repr. in Irving M. Copi and James A. Gould, *Contemporary Philosophical Logic.* New York: St Martin's Press: 37–8.

PURTILL, RICHARD L. (1970). 'Believing the Impossible'. *Ajatus*, 32: 18–24.

PUTNAM, HILARY (1975). 'The Meaning of "Meaning" '. *Language, Mind and Knowledge.* Minneapolis: University of Minnesota Press: 131–93.

QUINE, W. V. (1951a). 'Two Dogmas of Empiricism'. *Philosophical Review*, 60: 20–43.

—— (1951b). 'On Carnap's Views on Ontology'. *Philosophical Studies*, 2; repr. in W. V. Quine, *The Ways of Paradox.* New York: Random House.

—— (1953). 'Mr Strawson on Logical Theory'. *Mind*, 62.

—— (1970). *Philosophy of Logic*, Englewood Cliffs, NJ: Prentice Hall.

RADFORD, COLIN (1975). 'How Can We be Moved by the Fate of Anna Karenina?' *The Aristotelian Society Proceedings*, suppl. vol. 49. Methuen & Co.

—— (1984). 'I Will, If You Will'. *Mind*, 93: 577–83.

RAFFMAN, DIANA (1994). 'Vagueness without Paradox'. *Philosophical Review*, 103: 41–74.

RAMACHANDRAN, V. S. (1992). 'Blind Spots'. *Scientific American*, 266: 86–91.

READ, STEPHEN (2000). 'Truthmakers and the Disjunction Thesis'. *Mind*, 109: 67–79.

RESTALL, GREG (1996). 'Truthmakers, Entailment, and Necessity'. *Australasian Journal of Philosophy*, 74/2: 331–40.

ROWE, WILLIAM (1975). *The Cosmological Argument.* Princeton: Princeton University Press.

RUBEN, DAVID-HILLEL (1992). 'Simple Attentive Miscalculation'. *Analysis*, 52/3: 184–90.

RUSSELL, BERTRAND (1903). *The Principles of Mathematics.* Cambridge: Cambridge University Press.

RUSSELL, BERTRAND (1948). *Human Knowledge: Its Scope and Limits.* New York: Allen and Unwin.

—— (1951/1967). *The Autobiography of Bertrand Russell: 1872–1914,* 1st pub., 1951. Boston: Little, Brown and Company in association with the Atlantic Monthly Press, 1967, 1st American edn.

SAINSBURY, R. M. (1991). 'Concepts without Boundaries'. King's College London Department of Philosophy. Repr. in *Vagueness: A Reader,* ed. Rosanna Keefe and Peter Smith. Cambridge, Mass.: MIT Press, 1996: 251–64.

—— (1995). *Paradoxes,* 2nd edn. New York: Cambridge University Press, 1st pub. 1988.

SCHEFFLER, ISRAEL (1979). *Beyond the Letter.* London: Routledge & Kegan Paul.

SCHIFFER, STEPHEN (1995/6). 'Contextualist Solutions to Scepticism'. *Proceedings of the Aristotelian Society for 1995/6:* 317–33.

—— (1998). 'Two Issues of Vagueness'. *Monist,* 81/2: 193–214.

SCHLICK, MORITZ (1932/3). 'Positivism and Realism'. Repr. in *The Philosophy of Science,* ed. Richard Boyd, Philip Gasper, and J. D. Trout. Cambridge, Mass.: MIT Press, 1991: 37–55.

SINNOTT-ARMSTRONG, WALTER (1988). *Moral Dilemmas.* Oxford: Basil Blackwell.

SHOTCH, PETER K., and JENNINGS, RAYMOND E. (1981). 'Non-Kripkean Deontic Logic', in *New Studies in Deontic Logic.* Dordrecht: D. Reidel: 149–62.

SMITH, BARRY (1999). 'Truthmaker Realism'. *Australasian Journal of Philosophy,* 77/3: 274–91.

SOBER, ELLIOTT (1981). 'Revisability, A Priori Truth, and Evolution'. *Australasian Journal of Philosophy,* 59/1: 68–85.

SORENSEN, ROY (1986). 'Nozick, Justice, and the Sorites'. *Analysis,* 46/2: 102–6.

—— (1988) *Blindspots.* Oxford: Clarendon Press.

—— (1990). 'Process Vagueness'. *Linguistics and Philosophy,* 13/5: 591–622.

—— (1993). *Pseudo-Problems.* London: Routledge.

—— (1996). 'Modal Bloopers: Why Believable Impossibilities are Necessary'. *American Philosophical Quarterly,* 33/1 (July): 247–61. Repr. in *The Philosopher's Annual 1996,* xix, ed. Patrick Grim, Kenneth Baynes, and Gary Mar. Atascardero, Calif.: Ridgeview Publishing, 1998.

—— (1998). 'Yablo's Paradox and Kindred Infinite Liars'. *Mind,* 107/425 (Jan.): 137–55.

STALNAKER, ROBERT (1984). *Inquiry.* Cambridge, Mass.: MIT Press.

—— (1991). 'The Problem of Logical Omniscience, I'. *Synthese,* 89: 425–40.

STRAWSON, PETER F. (1952). *Introduction to Logical Theory.* New York: John Wiley & Sons.

—— (1959). *Individuals: An Essay in Descriptive Metaphysics*. London: Methuen.

TARSKI, ALFRED (1929). 'The Concept of Truth in Formalized Languages', in his *Logic, Semantics, Metamathematics*. Indianapolis: Hacket, 1983, 2nd edn., trans. J. H. Woodger, ed. John Concoran.

TATTERSALL, IAN (2000). 'Once We were Not Alone'. *Scientific American*, 282/1: 56–62.

THOMSON, J. F. (1962). 'On Some Paradoxes', in *Analytical Philosophy*, ed. R. J. Butler. New York: Barnes & Noble: 104–19.

TYE, MICHAEL (1989). 'Supervaluationism and the Law of Excluded Middle'. *Analysis*, 49/3: 141–3.

—— (1994). 'Sorites Paradoxes and the Semantics of Vagueness'. *Philosophical Perspectives*, 8: 189–206.

—— (1997). 'On the Epistemic View of Vagueness'. *Philosophical Issues*, 8: 247–54.

UNGER, PETER (1979). 'There are No Ordinary Things'. *Synthese*, 4: 117–54.

—— (1980). 'The Problem of the Many'. *Midwest Studies in Philosophy*, 6: 411–67.

—— (1982). 'Toward a Psychology of Common Sense'. *American Philosophical Quarterly*, 19: 117–29.

WERTHEIMER, ROGER (1972). *The Significance of Sense*. Ithaca, NY: Cornell University Press.

WHEELER, SAMUEL C. (1967). 'Reference and Vagueness'. *Synthese*, 30/3–4: 367–79.

WILLIAMS, BERNARD (1976). 'Moral Luck'. *Aristotelian Society Supplement*, 50: 115–36.

WILLIAMS, JOHN (1982). 'Believing the Self-Contradictory'. *American Philosophical Quarterly*, 19: 279–85.

WILLIAMSON, TIMOTHY (1984). 'The Infinite Commitment of Finite Minds'. *Canadian Journal of Philosophy*, 14/2: 235–55.

—— (1990). *Identity and Discrimination*. Oxford: Blackwell.

—— (1994). *Vagueness*. London: Routlege.

—— (1996). 'Wright on the Epistemic Theory of Vagueness'. *Analysis*, 56/1: 39–45.

—— (1999). 'On the Structure of Higher-Order Vagueness'. *Mind*, 108: 127–43.

—— (1997). 'Imagination, Stipulation and Vagueness'. *Philosophical Issues*, 8: 215–28.

WRIGHT, CRISPIN (1975). 'On the Coherence of Vague Predicates'. *Synthese*, 30: 325–65.

—— (1995). 'The Epistemic Conception of Vagueness'. *Southern Journal of Philosophy*, 33 (suppl.): 133–59.

—— 'On Being in a Quandary'. *Mind*, 110/437: 45–98.

YABLO, STEPHEN (1993). 'Paradox without Self-reference'. *Analysis*, 53: 251–2.

ZAMAN, ASAD (1987). 'On the Impossibility of Events of Zero Probability'. *Theory and Decision*, 23: 157–9.

ZIFF, PAUL (1960). *Semantic Analysis*. Ithaca, NY: Cornell University Press.

—— (1974). 'The Number of English Sentences'. *Foundations of Language*, 11: 519–32.

Index